THE FOURTH PARADIGM

The

FOURTH
PARADIGM

DATA-INTENSIVE SCIENTIFIC DISCOVERY

EDITED BY
**TONY HEY, STEWART TANSLEY,
AND KRISTIN TOLLE**

MICROSOFT RESEARCH
REDMOND, WASHINGTON

ISBN 978-0-9825442-0-4

Printed in the United States of America.

Microsoft, Amalga, Bing, Excel, HealthVault, Microsoft Surface, SQL Server,
Virtual Earth, and Windows are trademarks of the Microsoft group of companies. All other trademarks are property of their respective owners.

The information, findings, views, and opinions contained in this publication
are those of the authors and do not necessarily reflect the views of Microsoft
Corporation or Microsoft Research. Microsoft Corporation does not guaran-
tee the accuracy of any information provided herein.

Microsoft Research
http://research.microsoft.com

For Jim

CONTENTS

Foreword

GORDON BELL | Microsoft Research

T HIS BOOK IS ABOUT A NEW, FOURTH PARADIGM FOR SCIENCE based on data-intensive computing. In such scientific research, we are at a stage of development that is analogous to when the printing press was invented. Printing took a thousand years to develop and evolve into the many forms it takes today. Using computers to gain understanding from data created and stored in our electronic data stores will likely take decades—or less. The contributing authors in this volume have done an extraordinary job of helping to refine an understanding of this new paradigm from a variety of disciplinary perspectives.

In many instances, science is lagging behind the commercial world in the ability to infer meaning from data and take action based on that meaning. However, commerce is comparatively simple: things that can be described by a few numbers or a name are manufactured and then bought and sold. Scientific disciplines cannot easily be encapsulated in a few understandable numbers and names, and most scientific data does not have a high enough economic value to fuel more rapid development of scientific discovery.

It was Tycho Brahe's assistant Johannes Kepler who took Brahe's catalog of systematic astronomical observations and discovered the laws of planetary motion. This established the division between the mining and analysis of captured and carefully archived experimental data and the creation of theories. This division is one aspect of the Fourth Paradigm.

In the 20th century, the data on which scientific theories were based was often buried in individual scientific notebooks or, for some aspects of "big science," stored on magnetic media that eventually become unreadable. Such data, especially from individuals or small labs, is largely inaccessible. It is likely to be thrown out when a scientist retires, or at best it will be held in an institutional library until it is discarded. Long-term data provenance as well as community access to distributed data are just some of the challenges.

Fortunately, some "data places," such as the National Center for Atmospheric Research[1] (NCAR), have been willing to host Earth scientists who conduct experiments by analyzing the curated data collected from measurements and computational models. Thus, at one institution we have the capture, curation, and analysis chain for a whole discipline.

In the 21st century, much of the vast volume of scientific data captured by new instruments on a 24/7 basis, along with information generated in the artificial worlds of computer models, is likely to reside forever in a live, substantially publicly accessible, curated state for the purposes of continued analysis. This analysis will result in the development of many new theories! I believe that we will soon see a time when data will live forever as archival media—just like paper-based storage—and be publicly accessible in the "cloud" to humans and machines. Only recently have we dared to consider such permanence for data, in the same way we think of "stuff" held in our national libraries and museums! Such permanence still seems far-fetched until you realize that capturing data provenance, including individual researchers' records and sometimes everything about the researchers themselves, is what libraries insist on and have always tried to do. The "cloud" of magnetic polarizations encoding data and documents in the digital library will become the modern equivalent of the miles of library shelves holding paper and embedded ink particles.

In 2005, the National Science Board of the National Science Foundation published "Long-Lived Digital Data Collections: Enabling Research and Education in the 21st Century," which began a dialogue about the importance of data preservation and introduced the issue of the care and feeding of an emerging group they identified as "data scientists":

> The interests of data scientists—the information and computer scientists, database and software engineers and programmers, disciplinary experts, curators and expert annotators, librarians, archivists, and others, who are crucial to the successful management of a digital data collection—lie in having their creativity and intellectual contributions fully recognized." [1]

[1] www.ncar.ucar.edu

THE FOURTH PARADIGM: A FOCUS ON DATA-INTENSIVE SYSTEMS AND SCIENTIFIC COMMUNICATION

In Jim Gray's last talk to the Computer Science and Telecommunications Board on January 11, 2007 [2], he described his vision of the fourth paradigm of scientific research. He outlined a two-part plea for the funding of tools for data capture, curation, and analysis, and for a communication and publication infrastructure. He argued for the establishment of modern stores for data and documents that are on par with traditional libraries. The edited version of Jim's talk that appears in this book, which was produced from the transcript and Jim's slides, sets the scene for the articles that follow.

Data-intensive science consists of three basic activities: capture, curation, and analysis. Data comes in all scales and shapes, covering large international experiments; cross-laboratory, single-laboratory, and individual observations; and *potentially individuals' lives.*[2] The discipline and scale of individual experiments and especially their data rates make the issue of tools a formidable problem. The Australian Square Kilometre Array of radio telescopes project,[3] CERN's Large Hadron Collider,[4] and astronomy's Pan-STARRS[5] array of celestial telescopes are capable of generating several petabytes (PB) of data per day, but present plans limit them to more manageable data collection rates. Gene sequencing machines are currently more modest in their output due to the expense, so only certain coding regions of the genome are sequenced (25 KB for a few hundred thousand base pairs) for each individual. But this situation is temporary at best, until the US$10 million X PRIZE for Genomics[6] is won—100 people fully sequenced, in 10 days, for under US$10,000 each, at 3 billion base pairs for each human genome.

Funding is needed to create a generic set of tools that covers the full range of activities—from capture and data validation through curation, analysis, and ultimately permanent archiving. Curation covers a wide range of activities, starting with finding the right data structures to map into various stores. It includes the schema and the necessary metadata for longevity and for integration across instruments, experiments, and laboratories. Without such explicit schema and metadata, the interpretation is only implicit and depends strongly on the particular programs used to analyze it. Ultimately, such uncurated data is guaranteed to be lost. We

---

[2] http://research.microsoft.com/en-us/projects/mylifebits
[3] www.ska.gov.au
[4] http://public.web.cern.ch/public/en/LHC/LHC-en.html
[5] http://pan-starrs.ifa.hawaii.edu/public
[6] http://genomics.xprize.org

must think carefully about which data should be able to live forever and what additional metadata should be captured to make this feasible.

Data analysis covers a whole range of activities throughout the workflow pipeline, including the use of databases (versus a collection of flat files that a database can access), analysis and modeling, and then data visualization. Jim Gray's recipe for designing a database for a given discipline is that it must be able to answer the key 20 questions that the scientist wants to ask of it. Much of science now uses databases only to hold various aspects of the data rather than as the location of the data itself. This is because the time needed to scan all the data makes analysis infeasible. A decade ago, rereading the data was just barely feasible. In 2010, disks are 1,000 times larger, yet disc record access time has improved by only a factor of two.

DIGITAL LIBRARIES FOR DATA AND DOCUMENTS: JUST LIKE MODERN DOCUMENT LIBRARIES

Scientific communication, including peer review, is also undergoing fundamental changes. Public digital libraries are taking over the role of holding publications from conventional libraries—because of the expense, the need for timeliness, and the need to keep experimental data and documents about the data together.

At the time of writing, digital data libraries are still in a formative stage, with various sizes, shapes, and charters. Of course, NCAR is one of the oldest sites for the modeling, collection, and curation of Earth science data. The San Diego Supercomputer Center (SDSC) at the University of California, San Diego, which is normally associated with supplying computational power to the scientific community, was one of the earliest organizations to recognize the need to add data to its mission. SDSC established its Data Central site,[7] which holds 27 PB of data in more than 100 specific databases (e.g., for bioinformatics and water resources). In 2009, it set aside 400 terabytes (TB) of disk space for both public and private databases and data collections that serve a wide range of scientific institutions, including laboratories, libraries, and museums.

The Australian National Data Service[8] (ANDS) has begun offering services starting with the Register My Data service, a "card catalog" that registers the identity, structure, name, and location (IP address) of all the various databases, including those coming from individuals. The mere act of registering goes a long way toward organizing long-term storage. The purpose of ANDS is to influence national policy on data management and to inform best practices for the curation

[7] http://datacentral.sdsc.edu/index.html
[8] www.ands.org.au

of data, thereby transforming the disparate collections of research data into a cohesive collection of research resources. In the UK, the Joint Information Systems Committee (JISC) has funded the establishment of a Digital Curation Centre[9] to explore these issues. Over time, one might expect that many such datacenters will emerge. The National Science Foundation's Directorate for Computer and Information Science and Engineering recently issued a call for proposals for long-term grants to researchers in data-intensive computing and long-term archiving.

In the articles in this book, the reader is invited to consider the many opportunities and challenges for data-intensive science, including interdisciplinary cooperation and training, interorganizational data sharing for "scientific data mashups," the establishment of new processes and pipelines, and a research agenda to exploit the opportunities as well as stay ahead of the data deluge. These challenges will require major capital and operational expenditure. The dream of establishing a "sensors everywhere" data infrastructure to support new modes of scientific research will require massive cooperation among funding agencies, scientists, and engineers. This dream must be actively encouraged and funded.

REFERENCES

[1] National Science Board, "Long-Lived Digital Data Collections: Enabling Research and Education in the 21st Century," Technical Report NSB-05-40, National Science Foundation, September 2005, http://www.nsf.gov/pubs/2005/nsb0540/nsb0540.pdf.
[2] Talk given by Jim Gray to the NRC-CSTB in Mountain View, CA, on January 11, 2007, http://research.microsoft.com/en-us/um/people/gray/JimGrayTalks.htm. (Edited transcript also in this volume.)

[9] www.dcc.ac.uk

Jim Gray on eScience:
A Transformed Scientific Method

Based on the transcript of a talk given by Jim Gray
to the NRC-CSTB[1] in Mountain View, CA, on January 11, 2007[2]

EDITED BY **TONY HEY, STEWART TANSLEY, AND KRISTIN TOLLE** | Microsoft Research

W E HAVE TO DO BETTER AT PRODUCING TOOLS to support the whole research cycle—from data capture and data curation to data analysis and data visualization. Today, the tools for capturing data both at the mega-scale and at the milli-scale are just dreadful. After you have captured the data, you need to curate it before you can start doing any kind of data analysis, and we lack good tools for both data curation and data analysis. Then comes the publication of the results of your research, and the published literature is just the tip of the data iceberg. By this I mean that people collect a lot of data and then reduce this down to some number of column inches in *Science* or *Nature*—or 10 pages if it is a computer science person writing. So what I mean by data iceberg is that there is a lot of data that is collected but not curated or published in any systematic way. There are some exceptions, and I think that these cases are a good place for us to look for best practices. I will talk about how the whole process of peer review has got to change and the way in which I think it is changing and what CSTB can do to help all of us get access to our research.

[1] National Research Council, http://sites.nationalacademies.org/NRC/index.htm; Computer Science and Telecommunications Board, http://sites.nationalacademies.org/cstb/index.htm.

[2] This presentation is, poignantly, the last one posted to Jim's Web page at Microsoft Research before he went missing at sea on January 28, 2007—http://research.microsoft.com/en-us/um/people/gray/talks/NRC-CSTB_eScience.ppt.

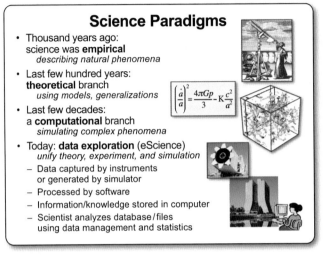

Science Paradigms

- Thousand years ago:
  science was **empirical**
  describing natural phenomena
- Last few hundred years:
  theoretical branch
  using models, generalizations
- Last few decades:
  a **computational** branch
  simulating complex phenomena
- Today: **data exploration** (eScience)
  unify theory, experiment, and simulation
  - Data captured by instruments
    or generated by simulator
  - Processed by software
  - Information/knowledge stored in computer
  - Scientist analyzes database/files
    using data management and statistics

$$\left(\frac{\dot{a}}{a}\right)^2 = \frac{4\pi Gp}{3} - K\frac{c^2}{a^2}$$

FIGURE 1

eSCIENCE: WHAT IS IT?

eScience is where "IT meets scientists." Researchers are using many different methods to collect or generate data—from sensors and CCDs to supercomputers and particle colliders. When the data finally shows up in your computer, what do you do with all this information that is now in your digital shoebox? People are continually seeking me out and saying, "Help! I've got all this data. What am I supposed to do with it? My Excel spreadsheets are getting out of hand!" So what comes next? What happens when you have 10,000 Excel spreadsheets, each with 50 workbooks in them? Okay, so I have been systematically naming them, but now what do I do?

SCIENCE PARADIGMS

I show this slide [Figure 1] every time I talk. I think it is fair to say that this insight dawned on me in a CSTB study of computing futures. We said, "Look, computational science is a third leg." Originally, there was just experimental science, and then there was theoretical science, with Kepler's Laws, Newton's Laws of Motion, Maxwell's equations, and so on. Then, for many problems, the theoretical models grew too complicated to solve analytically, and people had to start simulating. These simulations have carried us through much of the last half of the last millennium. At this point, these simulations are generating a whole lot of data, along with

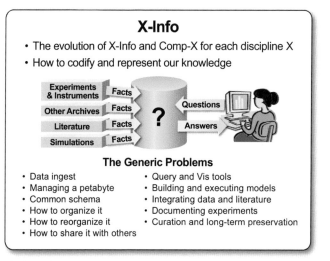

X-Info

- The evolution of X-Info and Comp-X for each discipline X
- How to codify and represent our knowledge

Experiments & Instruments → Facts

Other Archives → Facts

Literature → Facts

Simulations → Facts

? Questions

Answers

The Generic Problems

- Data ingest
- Managing a petabyte
- Common schema
- How to organize it
- How to reorganize it
- How to share it with others

- Query and Vis tools
- Building and executing models
- Integrating data and literature
- Documenting experiments
- Curation and long-term preservation

FIGURE 2

a huge increase in data from the experimental sciences. People now do not actually look through telescopes. Instead, they are "looking" through large-scale, complex instruments which relay data to datacenters, and only then do they look at the information on their computers.

The world of science has changed, and there is no question about this. The new model is for the data to be captured by instruments or generated by simulations before being processed by software and for the resulting information or knowledge to be stored in computers. Scientists only get to look at their data fairly late in this pipeline. The techniques and technologies for such data-intensive science are so different that it is worth distinguishing data-intensive science from computational science as a new, *fourth paradigm* for scientific exploration [1].

X-INFO AND COMP-X

We are seeing the evolution of two branches of every discipline, as shown in the next slide [Figure 2]. If you look at ecology, there is now both computational ecology, which is to do with simulating ecologies, and eco-informatics, which is to do with collecting and analyzing ecological information. Similarly, there is bioinformatics, which collects and analyzes information from many different experiments, and there is computational biology, which simulates how biological systems work and the metabolic pathways or the behavior of a cell or the way a protein is built.

This is similar to Jeannette Wing's idea of "computational thinking," in which computer science techniques and technologies are applied to different disciplines [2].

The goal for many scientists is to codify their information so that they can exchange it with other scientists. Why do they need to codify their information? Because if I put some information in my computer, the only way you are going to be able to understand that information is if your program can understand the information. This means that the information has to be represented in an algorithmic way. In order to do this, you need a standard representation for what a gene is or what a galaxy is or what a temperature measurement is.

EXPERIMENTAL BUDGETS ARE ¼ TO ½ SOFTWARE

I have been hanging out with astronomers for about the last 10 years, and I get to go to some of their base stations. One of the stunning things for me is that I look at their telescopes and it is just incredible. It is basically 15 to 20 million dollars worth of capital equipment, with about 20 to 50 people operating the instrument. But then you get to appreciate that there are literally thousands of people writing code to deal with the information generated by this instrument and that millions of lines of code are needed to analyze all this information. In fact, the software cost dominates the capital expenditure! This is true at the Sloan Digital Sky Survey (SDSS), and it is going to continue to be true for larger-scale sky surveys, and in fact for many large-scale experiments. I am not sure that this dominant software cost is true for the particle physics community and their Large Hadron Collider (LHC) machine, but it is certainly true for the LHC experiments.

Even in the "small data" sciences, you see people collecting information and then having to put a lot more energy into the analysis of the information than they have done in getting the information in the first place. The software is typically very idiosyncratic since there are very few generic tools that the bench scientist has for collecting and analyzing and processing the data. This is something that we computer scientists could help fix by building generic tools for the scientists.

I have a list of items for policymakers like CSTB. The first one is basically to foster both building tools and supporting them. NSF now has a cyberinfrastructure organization, and I do not want to say anything bad about them, but there needs to be more than just support for the TeraGrid and high-performance computing. We now know how to build Beowulf clusters for cheap high-performance computing. But we do not know how to build a true data grid or to build data stores made out of cheap "data bricks" to be a place for you to put all your data and then analyze the information. We have actually made fair progress on simulation tools, but not very much on data analysis tools.

PROJECT PYRAMIDS AND PYRAMID FUNDING

This section is just an observation about the way most science projects seem to work. There are a few international projects, then there are more multi-campus projects, and then there are lots and lots of single-lab projects. So we basically have this Tier 1, Tier 2, Tier 3 facility pyramid, which you see over and over again in many different fields. The Tier 1 and Tier 2 projects are generally fairly systematically organized and managed, but there are only relatively few such projects. These large projects can afford to have both a software and hardware budget, and they allocate teams of scientists to write custom software for the experiment. As an example, I have been watching the U.S.-Canadian ocean observatory—Project Neptune—allocate some 30 percent of its budget for cyberinfrastructure [3]. In round numbers, that's 30 percent of 350 million dollars or something like 100 million dollars! Similarly, the LHC experiments have a very large software budget, and this trend towards large software budgets is also evident from the earlier BaBar experiment [4, 5]. But if you are a bench scientist at the bottom of the pyramid, what are you going to do for a software budget? You are basically going to buy MATLAB[3] and Excel[4] or some similar software and make do with such off-the-shelf tools. There is not much else you can do.

So the giga- and mega-projects are largely driven by the need for some large-scale resources like supercomputers, telescopes, or other large-scale experimental facilities. These facilities are typically used by a significant community of scientists and need to be fully funded by agencies such as the National Science Foundation or the Department of Energy. Smaller-scale projects can typically get funding from a more diverse set of sources, with funding agency support often matched by some other organization—which could be the university itself. In the paper that Gordon Bell, Alex Szalay, and I wrote for *IEEE Computer* [6], we observed that Tier 1 facilities like the LHC get funded by an international consortium of agencies but the Tier 2 LHC experiments and Tier 3 facilities get funded by researchers who bring with them their own sources of funding. So funding agencies need to fully fund the Tier 1 giga-projects but then allocate the other half of their funding for cyberinfrastructure for smaller projects.

---

[3] www.mathworks.com
[4] http://office.microsoft.com/en-us/excel/default.aspx

LABORATORY INFORMATION MANAGEMENT SYSTEMS

To summarize what I have been saying about software, what we need are effectively "Laboratory Information Management Systems." Such software systems provide a pipeline from the instrument or simulation data into a data archive, and we are close to achieving this in a number of example cases I have been working on. Basically, we get data from a bunch of instruments into a pipeline which calibrates and "cleans" the data, including filling in gaps as necessary. Then we "re-grid"[5] the information and eventually put it into a database, which you would like to "publish" on the Internet to let people access your information.

The whole business of going from an instrument to a Web browser involves a vast number of skills. Yet what's going on is actually very simple. We ought to be able to create a Beowulf-like package and some templates that would allow people who are doing wet-lab experiments to be able to just collect their data, put it into a database, and publish it. This could be done by building a few prototypes and documenting them. It will take several years to do this, but it will have a big impact on the way science is done.

As I have said, such software pipelines are called Laboratory Information Management Systems, or LIMS. Parenthetically, commercial systems exist, and you can buy a LIMS system off the shelf. The problem is that they are really geared towards people who are fairly rich and are in an industrial setting. They are often also fairly specific to one or another task for a particular community—such as taking data from a sequencing machine or mass spectrometer, running it through the system, and getting results out the other side.

INFORMATION MANAGEMENT AND DATA ANALYSIS

So here is a typical situation. People are collecting data either from instruments or sensors, or from running simulations. Pretty soon they end up with millions of files, and there is no easy way to manage or analyze their data. I have been going door to door and watching what the scientists are doing. Generally, they are doing one of two things—they are either looking for needles in haystacks or looking for the haystacks themselves. The needle-in-the-haystack queries are actually very easy—you are looking for specific anomalies in the data, and you usually have some idea of what type of signal you are looking for. The particle physicists are looking

---

[5] This means to "regularize" the organization of the data to one data variable per row, analogous to relational database normalization.

for the Higgs particle at the LHC, and they have a good idea of how the decay of such a heavy particle will look like in their detectors. Grids of shared clusters of computers are great for such needle-in-a-haystack queries, but such grid computers are lousy at trend analysis, statistical clustering, and discovering global patterns in the data.

We actually need much better algorithms for clustering and for what is essentially data mining. Unfortunately, clustering algorithms are not order N or N log N but are typically cubic in N, so that when N grows too large, this method does not work. So we are being forced to invent new algorithms, and you have to live with only approximate answers. For example, using the approximate median turns out to be amazingly good. And who would have guessed? Not me!

Much of the statistical analysis deals with creating uniform samples, performing some data filtering, incorporating or comparing some Monte Carlo simulations, and so on, which all generates a large bunch of files. And the situation with these files is that each file just contains a bundle of bytes. If I give you this file, you have to work hard to figure out what the data in this file means. It is therefore really important that the files be self-describing. When people use the word *database,* fundamentally what they are saying is that the data should be self-describing and it should have a schema. That's really all the word *database* means. So if I give you a particular collection of information, you can look at this information and say, "I want all the genes that have this property" or "I want all of the stars that have this property" or "I want all of the galaxies that have this property." But if I give you just a bunch of files, you can't even use the concept of a galaxy and you have to hunt around and figure out for yourself what is the effective schema for the data in that file. If you have a schema for things, you can index the data, you can aggregate the data, you can use parallel search on the data, you can have ad hoc queries on the data, and it is much easier to build some generic visualization tools.

In fairness, I should say that the science community has invented a bunch of formats that qualify in my mind as database formats. HDF[6] (Hierarchical Data Format) is one such format, and NetCDF[7] (Network Common Data Form) is another. These formats are used for data interchange and carry the data schema with them as they go. But the whole discipline of science needs much better tools than HDF and NetCDF for making data self-defining.

[6] www.hdfgroup.org
[7] www.unidata.ucar.edu/software/netcdf

The other key issue is that as the datasets get larger, it is no longer possible to just FTP or grep them. A petabyte of data is very hard to FTP! So at some point, you need indices and you need parallel data access, and this is where databases can help you. For data analysis, one possibility is to move the data to you, but the other possibility is to move your query to the data. You can either move your questions or the data. Often it turns out to be more efficient to move the questions than to move the data.

THE NEED FOR DATA TOOLS: LET 100 FLOWERS BLOOM

The suggestion that I have been making is that we now have terrible data management tools for most of the science disciplines. Commercial organizations like Walmart can afford to build their own data management software, but in science we do not have that luxury. At present, we have hardly any data visualization and analysis tools. Some research communities use MATLAB, for example, but the funding agencies in the U.S. and elsewhere need to do a lot more to foster the building of tools to make scientists more productive. When you go and look at what scientists are doing, day in and day out, in terms of data analysis, it is truly dreadful. And I suspect that many of you are in the same state that I am in where essentially the only tools I have at my disposal are MATLAB and Excel!

We do have some nice tools like Beowulf[8] clusters, which allow us to get cost-effective high-performance computing by combining lots of inexpensive computers. We have some software called Condor[9] that allows you to harvest processing cycles from departmental machines. Similarly, we have the BOINC[10] (Berkeley Open Infrastructure for Network Computing) software that enables the harvesting of PC cycles as in the SETI@Home project. And we have a few commercial products like MATLAB. All these tools grew out of the research community, and I cannot figure out why these particular tools were successful.

We also have Linux and FreeBSD Unix. FreeBSD predated Linux, but somehow Linux took off and FreeBSD did not. I think that these things have a lot to do with the community, the personalities, and the timing. So my suggestion is that we should just have lots of things. We have commercial tools like LabVIEW,[11]

[8] www.beowulf.org
[9] www.cs.wisc.edu/condor
[10] http://boinc.berkeley.edu
[11] www.ni.com/labview

for example, but we should create several other such systems. And we just need to hope that some of these take off. It should not be very expensive to seed a large number of projects.

THE COMING REVOLUTION IN SCHOLARLY COMMUNICATION

I have reached the end of the first part of my talk: it was about the need for tools to help scientists capture their data, curate it, analyze it, and then visualize it. The second part of the talk is about scholarly communication. About three years ago, Congress passed a law that recommended that if you take NIH (National Institutes of Health) funding for your research, you should deposit your research reports with the National Library of Medicine (NLM) so that the full text of your papers should be in the public domain. Voluntary compliance with this law has been only 3 percent, so things are about to change. We are now likely to see all of the publicly funded science literature forced online by the funding agencies. There is currently a bill sponsored by Senators Cornyn and Lieberman that will make it compulsory for NIH grant recipients to put their research papers into the NLM PubMed Central repository.[12] In the UK, the Wellcome Trust has implemented a similar mandate for recipients of its research funding and has created a mirror of the NLM PubMed Central repository.

But the Internet can do more than just make available the full text of research papers. In principle, it can unify all the scientific data with all the literature to create a world in which the data and the literature interoperate with each other [Figure 3 on the next page]. You can be reading a paper by someone and then go off and look at their original data. You can even redo their analysis. Or you can be looking at some data and then go off and find out all the literature about this data. Such a capability will increase the "information velocity" of the sciences and will improve the scientific productivity of researchers. And I believe that this would be a very good development!

Take the example of somebody who is working for the National Institutes of Health—which is the case being discussed here—who produces a report. Suppose he discovers something about disease X. You go to your doctor and you say, "Doc, I'm not feeling very well." And he says, "Andy, we're going to give you a bunch of tests." And they give you a bunch of tests. He calls you the next day and says,

---

[12] See Peter Suber's Open Access newsletter for a summary of the current situation: www.earlham.edu/~peters/fos/newsletter/01-02-08.htm.

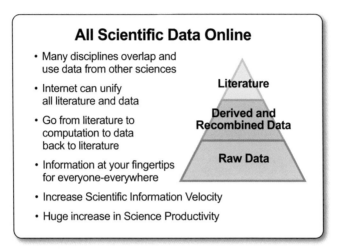

All Scientific Data Online

- Many disciplines overlap and use data from other sciences
- Internet can unify all literature and data
- Go from literature to computation to data back to literature
- Information at your fingertips for everyone-everywhere
- Increase Scientific Information Velocity
- Huge increase in Science Productivity

Literature

Derived and Recombined Data

Raw Data

FIGURE 3

"There's nothing wrong with you. Take two aspirins, and take some vacation." You go back a year later and do the same thing. Three years later, he calls you up and says, "Andy, you have X! We figured it out!" You say, "What's X?" He says, "I have no idea, it's a rare disease, but there's this guy in New York who knows all about it." So you go to Google[13] and type in all your symptoms. Page 1 of the results, up comes X. You click on it and it takes you to PubMed Central and to the abstract "All About X." You click on that, and it takes you to the *New England Journal of Medicine,* which says, "Please give us $100 and we'll let you read about X." You look at it and see that the guy works for the National Institutes of Health. Your tax dollars at work. So Lieberman[14] and others have said, "This sucks. Scientific information is now peer reviewed and put into the public domain—but only in the sense that anybody can read it if they'll pay. What's that about? We've already paid for it."

The scholarly publishers offer a service of organizing the peer review, printing the journal, and distributing the information to libraries. But the Internet is our distributor now and is more or less free. This is all linked to the thought process that society is going through about where intellectual property begins and ends. The scientific literature, and peer reviewed literature in particular, is probably one of the places where it ends. If you want to find out about X, you will probably be

---

[13] Or, as Jim might have suggested today, Bing.
[14] The Federal Research Public Access Act of 2006 (Cornyn-Lieberman).

able to find out that peach pits are a great treatment for X. But this is not from the peer reviewed literature and is there just because there's a guy out there who wants to sell peach pits to you to cure X. So the people who have been pioneering this movement towards open access are primarily the folks in healthcare because the good healthcare information is locked up and the bad healthcare information is on the Internet.

THE NEW DIGITAL LIBRARY

How does the new library work? Well, it's free because it's pretty easy to put a page or an article on the Internet. Each of you could afford to publish in PubMed Central. It would just cost you a few thousand dollars for the computer—but how much traffic you would have I don't know! But curation is not cheap. Getting the stuff into the computer, getting it cross-indexed, all that sort of stuff, is costing the National Library of Medicine about $100 to curate each article that shows up. If it takes in a million articles a year, which is approximately what it expects to get, it's going to be $100 million a year just to curate the stuff. This is why we need to automate the whole curation process.

What is now going on is that PubMed Central, which is the digital part of the National Library of Medicine, has made itself portable. There are versions of PubMed Central running in the UK, in Italy, in South Africa, in Japan, and in China. The one in the UK just came online last week. I guess you can appreciate, for example, that the French don't want their National Library of Medicine to be in Bethesda, Maryland, or in English. And the English don't want the text to be in American, so the UK version will probably use UK spellings for things in its Web interface. But fundamentally, you can stick a document in any of these archives and it will get replicated to all the other archives. It's fairly cheap to run one of these archives, but the big challenges are how you do curation and peer review.

OVERLAY JOURNALS

Here's how I think it might work. This is based on the concept of overlay journals. The idea is that you have data archives and you have literature archives. The articles get deposited in the literature archives, and the data goes into the data archives. Then there is a journal management system that somebody builds that allows us, as a group, to form a journal on X. We let people submit articles to our journal by depositing them in the archive. We do peer review on them and for the ones we like, we make a title page and say, "These are the articles we like" and put it into the archive as well. Now, a search engine comes along and cranks up the page rank on all of those articles as being good because they are now referenced by this very significant front page. These articles, of course, can also point back to the data. Then there will be a collaboration system that comes along that allows people to annotate and comment on the journal articles. The comments are not stored in the peer reviewed archive but on the side because they have not been peer reviewed—though they might be moderated.

The National Library of Medicine is going to do all this for the biomedical community, but it's not happening in other scientific communities. For you as members of the CSTB, the CS community could help make this happen by providing appropriate tools for the other scientific disciplines.

There is some software we have created at Microsoft Research called Conference Management Tool (CMT). We have run about 300 conferences with this, and the CMT service makes it trivial for you to create a conference. The tool supports the whole workflow of forming a program committee, publishing a Web site, accepting manuscripts, declaring conflicts of interest and recusing yourself, doing the reviews, deciding which papers to accept, forming the conference program, notifying the authors, doing the revisions, and so on. We are now working on providing a button to deposit the articles into arXiv.org or PubMed Central and pushing in the title page as well. This now allows us to capture workshops and conferences very easily. But it will also allow you to run an online journal. This mechanism would make it very easy to create overlay journals.

Somebody asked earlier if this would be hard on scholarly publishers. And the answer is yes. But isn't this also going to be hard for the IEEE and the ACM? The answer is that the professional societies are terrified that if they don't have any paper to send you, you won't join them. I think that they are going to have to deal with this somehow because I think open access is going to happen. Looking around the room, I see that most of us are old and not Generation Xers. Most of us join these organizations because we just think it's part of being a professional in that field. The trouble is that Generation Xers don't join organizations.

WHAT HAPPENS TO PEER REVIEW?

This is not a question that has concerned you, but many people say, "Why do we need peer review at all? Why don't we just have a wiki?" And I think the answer is that peer review is different. It's very structured, it's moderated, and there is a degree of confidentiality about what people say. The wiki is much more egalitarian.

I think wikis make good sense for collecting comments about the literature after the paper has been published. One needs some structure like CMT provides for the peer review process.

PUBLISHING DATA

I had better move on and go very quickly through publishing data. I've talked about publishing literature, but if the answer is 42, what are the units? You put some data in a file up on the Internet, but this brings us back to the problem of files. The important record to show your work in context is called the data provenance. How did you get the number 42?

Here is a thought experiment. You've done some science, and you want to publish it. How do you publish it so that others can read it and reproduce your results in a hundred years' time? Mendel did this, and Darwin did this, but barely. We are now further behind than Mendel and Darwin in terms of techniques to do this. It's a mess, and we've got to work on this problem.

DATA, INFORMATION, AND KNOWLEDGE: ONTOLOGIES AND SEMANTICS

We are trying to objectify knowledge. We can help with basic things like units, and what is a measurement, who took the measurement, and when the measurement was taken. These are generic things and apply to all fields. Here [at Microsoft Research] we do computer science. What do we mean by planet, star, and galaxy? That's astronomy. What's the gene? That's biology. So what are the objects, what are the attributes, and what are the methods in the object-oriented sense on these objects? And note, parenthetically, that the Internet is really turning into an object-oriented system where people fetch objects. In the business world, they're objectifying what a customer is, what an invoice is, and so on. In the sciences, for example, we need similarly to objectify what a gene is—which is what GenBank[15] does.

And here we need a warning that to go further, you are going to bump into the O word for "ontology," the S word for "schema," and "controlled vocabularies." That is to say, in going down this path, you're going to start talking about semantics, which is to say, "What do things mean?" And of course everybody has a different opinion of what things mean, so the conversations can be endless.

The best example of all of this is Entrez,[16] the Life Sciences Search Engine,

[15] www.ncbi.nlm.nih.gov/Genbank
[16] www.ncbi.nlm.nih.gov/Entrez

created by the National Center for Biotechnology Information for the NLM. Entrez allows searches across PubMed Central, which is the literature, but they also have phylogeny data, they have nucleotide sequences, they have protein sequences and their 3-D structures, and then they have GenBank. It is really a very impressive system. They have also built the PubChem database and a lot of other things. This is all an example of the data and the literature interoperating. You can be looking at an article, go to the gene data, follow the gene to the disease, go back to the literature, and so on. It is really quite stunning!

So in this world, we have traditionally had authors, publishers, curators, and consumers. In the new world, individual scientists now work in collaborations, and journals are turning into Web sites for data and other details of the experiments. Curators now look after large digital archives, and about the only thing the same is the individual scientist. It is really a pretty fundamental change in the way we do science.

One problem is that all projects end at a certain point and it is not clear what then happens to the data. There is data at all scales. There are anthropologists out collecting information and putting it into their notebooks. And then there are the particle physicists at the LHC. Most of the bytes are at the high end, but most of the datasets are at the low end. We are now beginning to see mashups where people take datasets from various places and glue them together to make a third dataset. So in the same sense that we need archives for journal publications, we need archives for the data.

So this is my last recommendation to the CSTB: foster digital data libraries. Frankly, the NSF Digital Library effort was all about metadata for libraries and not about actual digital libraries. We should build actual digital libraries both for data and for the literature.

SUMMARY

I wanted to point out that almost everything about science is changing because of the impact of information technology. Experimental, theoretical, and computational science are all being affected by the data deluge, and a fourth, "data-intensive" science paradigm is emerging. The goal is to have a world in which all of the science literature is online, all of the science data is online, and they interoperate with each other. Lots of new tools are needed to make this happen.

EDITORS' NOTE

The full transcript and PowerPoint slides from Jim's talk may be found at the Fourth Paradigm Web site.[17] The questions and answers during the talk have been extracted from this text and are available on the Web site. (Note that the questioners have not been identified by name.) The text presented here includes minor edits to improve readability, as well as our added footnotes and references, but we believe that it remains faithful to Jim's presentation.

REFERENCES

[1] G. Bell, T. Hey, and A. Szalay, "Beyond the Data Deluge," *Science*, vol. 323, no. 5919, pp. 1297–1298, 2009, doi: 10.1126/science.1170411.

[2] J. Wing, "Computational Thinking," *Comm. ACM*, vol. 49, no. 3, Mar. 2006, doi: 10.1145/1118178.1118215.

[3] NSF Regional Scale Nodes, http://rsn.apl.washington.edu.

[4] Large Hadron Collider (LHC) experiments, http://public.web.cern.ch/Public/en/LHC/ LHCExperiments-en.html.

[5] BaBar, www.slac.stanford.edu/BFROOT.

[6] G. Bell, J. Gray, and A. Szalay, "Petascale Computational Systems," *IEEE Computer*, pp. 110–112, vol. 39, 2006, doi: 10.1109/MC.2006.29.

[17] www.fourthparadigm.org

1. EARTH AND ENVIRONMENT

Introduction

DAN FAY | Microsoft Research

C HANGE IS INEVITABLE—the Universe expands, nature adapts and evolves, and so must the scientific tools and technologies that we employ to feed our unrelenting quest for greater knowledge in space, Earth, and environmental sciences. The opportunities and challenges are many. New computing technologies such as cloud computing and multicore processors cannot provide the entire solution in their generic forms. But effective and timely application of such technologies can help us significantly advance our understanding of our world, including its environmental challenges and how we might address them.

With science moving toward being computational and data based, key technology challenges include the need to better capture, analyze, model, and visualize scientific information. The ultimate goal is to aid scientists, researchers, policymakers, and the general public in making informed decisions. As society demands action and responsiveness to growing environmental issues, new types of applications grounded in scientific research will need to move from raw discovery and eliciting basic data that leads to knowledge to informing practical decisions. Active issues such as climate change will not wait until scientists have all the data to fill their knowledge gaps.

As evidenced by the articles in this part of the book, scientists are indeed actively pursuing scientific understanding through the use of new computing technologies. Szalay and Blakeley describe Jim Gray's informal rules for data-centric development and how they serve as a blueprint for making large-scale datasets available through the use of databases, leveraging the built-in data management as well as the parallel processing inherent in SQL servers.

In order to facilitate informed decisions based on reliable scientific evidence, Dozier and Gail explore how the applied use of technology and current scientific knowledge is key to providing tools to policy and decision makers. Hunt, Baldocchi, and van Ingen describe the changes under way in ecological science in moving from "science in the small" to large collaborations based on synthesis of data. These aggregated datasets expose the need for collaborative tools in the cloud as well as easy-to-use visualization and analysis tools. Delaney and Barga then provide compelling insights into the need for real-time monitoring of the complex dynamics in the sea by creating an interactive ocean laboratory. This novel cyberinfrastructure will enable new discoveries and insights through improved ocean models.

The need for novel scientific browsing technologies is highlighted by Goodman and Wong. To advance the linkage across existing resources, astronomers can use a new class of visualization tools, such as the WorldWide Telescope (WWT). This new class of tool offers access to data and information not only to professional scientists but also the general public, both for education and possibly to enable new discoveries by anyone with access to the Internet. Finally, Lehning et al. provide details about the use of densely deployed real-time sensors combined with visualization for increased understanding of environmental dynamics—like a virtual telescope looking back at the Earth. These applications illustrate how scientists and technologists have the opportunity to embrace and involve citizen scientists in their efforts.

In Part 1 and throughout the book, we see new sensors and infrastructures enabling real-time access to potentially enormous quantities of data, but with experimental repeatability through the use of workflows. Service-oriented architectures are helping to mitigate the transition to new underlying technologies and enable the linkage of data and resources. This rapidly evolving process is the only mechanism we have to deal with the data deluge arising from our instruments.

The question before us is how the world's intellectual and technological resources can be best orchestrated to authoritatively guide our responses to current and future societal challenges. The articles that follow provide some great answers.

Gray's Laws: Database-centric Computing in Science

ALEXANDER S. SZALAY
The Johns Hopkins University

JOSÉ A. BLAKELEY
Microsoft

THE EXPLOSION IN SCIENTIFIC DATA has created a major challenge for cutting-edge scientific projects. With datasets growing beyond a few tens of terabytes, scientists have no off-the-shelf solutions that they can readily use to manage and analyze the data [1]. Successful projects to date have deployed various combinations of flat files and databases [2]. However, most of these solutions have been tailored to specific projects and would not be easy to generalize or scale to the next generation of experiments. Also, today's computer architectures are increasingly imbalanced; the latency gap between multi-core CPUs and mechanical hard disks is growing every year, making the challenges of data-intensive computing harder to overcome [3]. What is needed is a systematic and general approach to these problems with an architecture that can scale into the future.

GRAY'S LAWS

Jim Gray formulated several informal rules—or laws—that codify how to approach data engineering challenges related to large-scale scientific datasets. The laws are as follows:

1. Scientific computing is becoming increasingly data intensive.
2. The solution is in a "scale-out" architecture.
3. Bring computations to the data, rather than data to the computations.

4. Start the design with the "20 queries."
5. Go from "working to working."

It is important to realize that the analysis of observational datasets is severely limited by the relatively low I/O performance of most of today's computing platforms. High-performance numerical simulations are also increasingly feeling the "I/O bottleneck." Once datasets exceed the random access memory (RAM) capacity of the system, locality in a multi-tiered cache no longer helps [4]. Yet very few high-end platforms provide a fast enough I/O subsystem.

High-performance, scalable numerical computation also presents an algorithmic challenge. Traditional numerical analysis packages have been designed to operate on datasets that fit in RAM. To tackle analyses that are orders of magnitude larger, these packages must be redesigned to work in a multi-phase, divide-and-conquer manner while maintaining their numerical accuracy. This suggests an approach in which a large-scale problem is decomposed into smaller pieces that can be solved in RAM, whereas the rest of the dataset resides on disk. This approach is analogous to the way in which database algorithms such as sorts or joins work on datasets larger than RAM. These challenges are reaching a critical stage.

Buying larger network storage systems and attaching them to clusters of compute nodes will not solve the problem because network/interconnect speeds are not growing fast enough to cope with the yearly doubling of the necessary storage. Scale-out solutions advocate simple building blocks in which the data is partitioned among nodes with locally attached storage [5]. The smaller and simpler these blocks are, the better the balance between CPUs, disks, and networking can become. Gray envisaged simple "CyberBricks" where each disk drive has its own CPU and networking [6]. While the number of nodes on such a system would be much larger than in a traditional "scale-up" architecture, the simplicity and lower cost of each node and the aggregate performance would more than make up for the added complexity. With the emergence of solid-state disks and low-power motherboards, we are on the verge of being able to build such systems [7].

DATABASE-CENTRIC COMPUTING

Most scientific data analyses are performed in hierarchical steps. During the first pass, a subset of the data is extracted by either filtering on certain attributes (e.g., removing erroneous data) or extracting a vertical subset of the columns. In the next step, data are usually transformed or aggregated in some way. Of course, in more complex datasets, these patterns are often accompanied by complex joins among multiple datasets, such as external calibrations or extracting and analyzing different parts of a gene sequence [8]. As datasets grow ever larger, the most efficient way to perform most of these computations is clearly to move the analysis functions as close to the data as possible. It also turns out that most of these patterns are easily expressed by a set-oriented, declarative language whose execution can benefit enormously from cost-based query optimization, automatic parallelism, and indexes.

Gray and his collaborators have shown on several projects that existing relational database technologies can be successfully applied in this context [9]. There are also seamless ways to integrate complex class libraries written in procedural languages as an extension of the underlying database engine [10, 11].

MapReduce has become a popular distributed data analysis and computing paradigm in recent years [12]. The principles behind this paradigm resemble the distributed grouping and aggregation capabilities that have existed in parallel relational database systems for some time. New-generation parallel database systems such as Teradata, Aster Data, and Vertica have rebranded these capabilities as "MapReduce in the database." New benchmarks comparing the merits of each approach have been developed [13].

CONNECTING TO THE SCIENTISTS

One of the most challenging problems in designing scientific databases is to establish effective communication between the builder of the database and the domain scientists interested in the analysis. Most projects make the mistake of trying to be "everything for everyone." It is clear that that some features are more important than others and that various design trade-offs are necessary, resulting in performance trade-offs.

Jim Gray came up with the heuristic rule of "20 queries." On each project he was involved with, he asked for the 20 most important questions the researchers wanted the data system to answer. He said that five questions are not enough to see a broader pattern, and a hundred questions would result in a shortage of focus. Since most selections involving human choices follow a "long tail," or so-called 1/f distribution, it is clear that the relative information in the queries ranked by importance is logarithmic, so the gain realized by going from approximately 20 ($2^{4.5}$) to 100 ($2^{6.5}$) is quite modest [14].

The "20 queries" rule is a moniker for a design step that engages the domain scientist and the database engineer in a conversation that helps bridge the semantic gap between nouns and verbs used in the scientific domain and the entities and relationships stored in the database. Queries define the precise set of questions in terms of entities and relationships that domain scientists expect to pose to the database. At the end of a full iteration of this exercise, the domain scientist and the database speak a common language.

This approach has been very successful in keeping the design process focused on the most important features the system must support, while at the same time helping the domain scientists understand the database system trade-offs, thereby limiting "feature creep."

Another design law is to move from working version to working version. Gray was very much aware of how quickly data-driven computing architecture changes, especially if it involves distributed data. New distributed computing paradigms come and go every other year, making it extremely difficult to engage in a multi-year top-down design and implementation cycle. By the time such a project is completed, the starting premises have become obsolete. If we build a system that starts working only if every one of its components functions correctly, we will never finish.

The only way to survive and make progress in such a world is to build modular systems in which individual components can be replaced as the underlying technologies evolve. Today's service-oriented architectures are good examples of this. Web services have already gone through several major evolutionary stages, and the end is nowhere in sight.

FROM TERASCALE TO PETASCALE SCIENTIFIC DATABASES

By using Microsoft SQL Server, we have successfully tackled several projects on a scale from a few terabytes (TB) to tens of terabytes [15-17]. Implementing databases that will soon exceed 100 TB also looks rather straightforward [18], but it is not entirely clear how science will cross the petascale barrier. As databases become larger and larger, they will inevitably start using an increasingly scaled-out architecture. Data will be heavily partitioned, making distributed, non-local queries and distributed joins increasingly difficult.

For most of the petascale problems today, a simple data-crawling strategy over massively scaled-out, share-nothing data partitions has been adequate (MapReduce, Hadoop, etc.). But it is also clear that this layout is very suboptimal when a good index might provide better performance by orders of magnitude. Joins between tables of very different cardinalities have been notoriously difficult to use with these crawlers.

Databases have many things to offer in terms of more efficient plans. We also need to rethink the utility of expecting a monolithic result set. One can imagine crawlers over heavily partitioned databases implementing a construct that can provide results one bucket at a time, resulting in easier checkpointing and recovery in the middle of an extensive query. This approach is also useful for aggregate functions with a clause that would stop when the result is estimated to be within, for example, 99% accuracy. These simple enhancements would go a long way toward sidestepping huge monolithic queries—breaking them up into smaller, more manageable ones.

Cloud computing is another recently emerging paradigm. It offers obvious advantages, such as co-locating data with computations and an economy of scale in hosting the services. While these platforms obviously perform very well for their current intended use in search engines or elastic hosting of commercial Web sites, their role in scientific computing is yet to be clarified. In some scientific analysis scenarios, the data needs to be close to the experiment. In other cases, the nodes need to be tightly integrated with a very low latency. In yet other cases, very high I/O bandwidth is required. Each of these analysis strategies would be suboptimal in current virtualization environments. Certainly, more specialized data clouds are bound to emerge soon. In the next few years, we will see if scientific computing moves from universities to commercial service providers or whether it is necessary for the largest scientific data stores to be aggregated into one.

CONCLUSIONS

Experimental science is generating vast volumes of data. The Pan-STARRS project will capture 2.5 petabytes (PB) of data each year when in production [18]. The Large Hadron Collider will generate 50 to 100 PB of data each year, with about 20 PB of that data stored and processed on a worldwide federation of national grids linking 100,000 CPUs [19]. Yet generic data-centric solutions to cope with this volume of data and corresponding analyses are not readily available [20].

Scientists and scientific institutions need a template and collection of best practices that lead to balanced hardware architectures and corresponding software to deal with these volumes of data. This would reduce the need to reinvent the wheel. Database features such as declarative, set-oriented languages and automatic parallelism, which have been successful in building large-scale scientific applications, are clearly needed.

We believe that the current wave of databases can manage at least another order of magnitude in scale. So for the time being, we can continue to work. However, it is time to start thinking about the next wave. Scientific databases are an early predictor of requirements that will be needed by conventional corporate applications; therefore, investments in these applications will lead to technologies that will be broadly applicable in a few years. Today's science challenges are good representatives of the data management challenges for the 21st century. Gray's Laws represent an excellent set of guiding principles for designing the data-intensive systems of the future.

REFERENCES

[1] A. S. Szalay and J. Gray, "Science in an Exponential World," *Nature*, vol. 440, pp. 23–24, 2006, doi: 10.1038/440413a.

[2] J. Becla and D. Wang, "Lessons Learned from Managing a Petabyte," CIDR 2005 Conference, Asilomar, 2005, doi: 10.2172/839755.

[3] G. Bell, J. Gray, and A. Szalay, "Petascale Computational Systems: Balanced Cyber-Infrastructure in a Data-Centric World," *IEEE Computer,* vol. 39, pp. 110–112, 2006, doi: 10.1109/MC.2006.29.

[4] W. W. Hsu and A. J. Smith, "Characteristics of I/O traffic in personal computer and server workloads," *IBM Sys. J.,* vol. 42, pp. 347–358, 2003, doi: 10.1147/sj.422.0347.

[5] A. Szalay, G. Bell, et al., "GrayWulf: Scalable Clustered Architecture for Data Intensive Computing," Proc. HICSS-42 Conference, Hawaii, 2009, doi: 10.1109/HICSS.2009.750.

[6] J. Gray, Cyberbricks Talk at DEC/NT Wizards Conference, http://research.microsoft.com/en-us/um/people/gray/talks/DEC_Cyberbrick.ppt; T. Barclay, W. Chong, and J. Gray, "TerraServer Bricks – A High Availability Cluster Alternative," Microsoft Technical Report, MSR-TR-2004-107, 2004.

[7] A. S. Szalay, G. Bell, A. Terzis, A. S. White, and J. Vandenberg, "Low Power Amdahl Blades for Data-Intensive Computing," http://perspectives.mvdirona.com/content/binary/AmdahlBladesV3.pdf.

[8] U. Roehm and J. A. Blakeley, "Data Management for High-Throughput Genomics," *Proc. CIDR,* 2009.

[9] J. Gray, D. T. Liu, M. A. Nieto-Santisteban, A. S. Szalay, G. Heber, and D. DeWitt, "Scientific Data Management in the Coming Decade," *ACM SIGMOD Record,* vol. 34, no. 4, pp. 35–41, 2005; also MSR-TR-2005-10, doi: 10.1145/1107499.1107503.

[10] A. Acheson et al., "Hosting the .NET Runtime in Microsoft SQL Server," ACM SIGMOD Conf., 2004, doi: 10.1145/1007568.1007669.

[11] J. A. Blakeley, M. Henaire, C. Kleinerman, I. Kunen, A. Prout, B. Richards, and V. Rao, ".NET Database Programmability and Extensibility in Microsoft SQL Server," ACM SIGMOD Conf., 2008, doi: 10.1145/1376616.1376725.

[12] J. Dean and S. Ghemawat, "MapReduce: Simplified Data Processing on Large Clusters," OSDI, 2004, doi: 10.1145/1327452.1327492.

[13] A. Pavlo et al., "A Comparison of Approaches to Large-Scale Data Analysis," ACM SIGMOD Conf., 2009, doi: 10.1145/1559845.1559865.

[14] C. Anderson. *The Long Tail.* New York: Random House, 2007.

[15] A. R. Thakar, A. S. Szalay, P. Z. Kunszt, and J. Gray, "The Sloan Digital Sky Survey Science Archive: Migrating a Multi-Terabyte Astronomical Archive from Object to Relational DBMS," *Comp. Sci. and Eng.,* vol. 5, no. 5, pp. 16–29, Sept. 2003.

[16] A. Terzis, R. Musaloiu-E., J. Cogan, K. Szlavecz, A. Szalay, J. Gray, S. Ozer, M. Liang, J. Gupchup, and R. Burns, "Wireless Sensor Networks for Soil Science," *Int. J. Sensor Networks,* to be published 2009.

[17] Y. Li, E. Perlman, M. Wan, Y. Yang, C. Meneveau, R. Burns, S. Chen, A. Szalay, and G. Eyink, "A public turbulence database cluster and applications to study Lagrangian evolution of velocity increments in turbulence," *J. Turbul.,* vol. 9, no. 31, pp. 1–29, 2008, doi: 10.1080/14685240802376389.

[18] Pan-STARRS: Panoramic Survey Telescope and Rapid Response System, http://pan-starrs.ifa.hawaii.edu.

[19] A. M. Parker, "Understanding the Universe," in *Towards 2020 Science,* Microsoft Corporation, 2006, http://research.microsoft.com/towards2020science/background_overview.htm.

[20] G. Bell, T. Hey, and A. Szalay, "Beyond the Data Deluge," *Science,* vol. 323, no. 5919, pp. 1297–1298, 2009, doi: 10.1126/science.1170411.

The Emerging Science of Environmental Applications

JEFF DOZIER
University of California,
Santa Barbara

WILLIAM B. GAIL
Microsoft Corporation

THE SCIENCE OF EARTH AND ENVIRONMENT has matured through two major phases and is entering a third. In the first phase, which ended two decades ago, Earth and environmental science was largely discipline oriented and focused on developing knowledge in geology, atmospheric chemistry, ecosystems, and other aspects of the Earth system. In the 1980s, the scientific community recognized the close coupling of these disciplines and began to study them as interacting elements of a single system. During this second phase, the paradigm of Earth system science emerged. With it came the ability to understand complex, system-oriented phenomena such as climate change, which links concepts from atmospheric sciences, biology, and human behavior. Essential to the study of Earth's interacting systems was the ability to acquire, manage, and make available data from satellite observations; in parallel, new models were developed to express our growing understanding of the complex processes in the dynamic Earth system [1].

In the emerging third phase, knowledge developed primarily for the purpose of scientific understanding is being complemented by knowledge created to target practical decisions and action. This new knowledge endeavor can be referred to as the *science of environmental applications*. Climate change provides the most prominent example of the importance of this shift. Until now, the climate science community has focused on critical questions involving basic knowledge, from measuring the amount of change to determining the causes. With the basic understanding now well established, the demand for climate applications knowledge is emerging. How do we quantify and monitor total forest biomass so that carbon markets can characterize supply? What are the implications of regional shifts in water resources for demographic trends, agricultural output, and energy production? To what extent will seawalls and other adaptations to rising sea level impact coasts?

These questions are informed by basic science, but they raise additional issues that can be addressed only by a new science discipline focused specifically on applications—a discipline that integrates physical, biogeochemical, engineering, and human processes. Its principal questions reflect a fundamental curiosity about the nature of the world we live in, tempered by the awareness that a question's importance scales with its relevance to a societal imperative. As Nobel laureate and U.S. Secretary of Energy Steven Chu has remarked, "We seek solutions. We don't seek—dare I say this?—just scientific papers anymore" [2].

To illustrate the relationships between basic science and applications, consider the role of snowmelt runoff in water supplies. Worldwide, 1 billion people depend on snow or glacier melt for their water resources [3]. Design and operations of water systems have traditionally relied on historical measurements in a stationary climate, along with empirical relationships and models. As climates and land use change, populations grow and relocate, and our built systems age and decay, these empirical methods of managing our water become inaccurate—a conundrum characterized as "stationarity is dead" [4]. Snowmelt commonly provides water for competing uses: urban and agricultural supply, hydropower, recreation, and ecosystems. In many areas, both rainfall and snowfall occur, raising the concern that a future warmer climate will lead to a greater fraction of precipitation as rain, with the water arriving months before agricultural demand peaks and with more rapid runoff leading to more floods. In these mixed rain and snow systems, the societal need is: How do we sustain flood control and the benefits that water provides to humans and ecosystems when changes in the timing and magnitude of runoff are likely to render existing infrastructure inadequate?

The solution to the societal need requires a more fundamental, process-based understanding of the water cycle. Currently, historical data drive practices and decisions for flood control and water supply systems. Flood operations and reservoir flood capacity are predetermined by regulatory orders that are static, regardless of the type of water year, current state of the snowpack, or risk of flood. In many years, early snowmelt is not stored because statistically based projections anticipate floods that better information might suggest cannot materialize because of the absence of snow. The more we experience warming, the more frequently this occurrence will impact the water supply [5]. The related science challenges are: (1) The statistical methods in use do not try to estimate the basin's water balance, and with the current measurement networks even in the U.S., we lack adequate knowledge of the amount of snow in the basins; (2) We are unable to partition the input between rain and snow, or to partition that rain or snow between evapotranspiration and runoff; (3) We lack the knowledge to manage the relationship between snow cover, forests, and carbon stocks; (4) Runoff forecasts that are not based on physical principles relating to snowmelt are often inaccurate; and (5) We do not know what incentives and institutional arrangements would lead to better management of the watershed for ecosystem services.

Generally, models do not consider these kinds of interactions; hence the need for a *science of environmental applications*. Its core characteristics differentiate it from the basic science of Earth and environment:

- **Need driven versus curiosity driven.** Basic science is question driven; in contrast, the new applications science is guided more by societal needs than scientific curiosity. Rather than seeking answers to questions, it focuses on creating the ability to seek courses of action and determine their consequences.

- **Externally constrained.** External circumstances often dictate when and how applications knowledge is needed. The creation of carbon trading markets will not wait until we fully quantify forest carbon content. It will happen on a schedule dictated by policy and economics. Construction and repair of the urban water infrastructure will not wait for an understanding of evolving rainfall patterns. Applications science must be prepared to inform actions subject to these external drivers, not according to academic schedules based on when and how the best knowledge can be obtained.

- **Consequential and recursive.** Actions arising from our knowledge of the Earth often change the Earth, creating the need for new knowledge about what we have changed. For example, the more we knew in the past about locations of fish populations, the more the populations were overfished; our original knowledge about them became rapidly outdated through our own actions. Applications science seeks to understand not just those aspects of the Earth addressed by a particular use scenario, but also the consequences and externalities that result from that use scenario. A recent example is the shift of agricultural land to corn-for-ethanol production—an effort to reduce climate change that we now recognize as significantly stressing scarce water resources.

- **Useful even when incomplete.** As the snowpack example illustrates, actions are often needed despite incomplete data or partial knowledge. The difficulty of establishing confidence in the quality of our knowledge is particularly disconcerting given the loss of stationarity associated with climate change. New means of making effective use of partial knowledge must be developed, including robust inference engines and statistical interpretation.

- **Scalable.** Basic science knowledge does not always scale to support applications needs. The example of carbon trading presents an excellent illustration. Basic science tells us how to relate carbon content to measurements of vegetation type and density, but it does not give us the tools that scale this to a global inventory. New knowledge tools must be built to accurately create and update this inventory through cost-effective remote sensing or other means.

- **Robust.** The decision makers who apply applications knowledge typically have limited comprehension of how the knowledge was developed and in what situations it is applicable. To avoid misuse, the knowledge must be characterized in highly robust terms. It must be stable over time and insensitive to individual interpretations, changing context, and special conditions.

- **Data intensive.** Basic science is data intensive in its own right, but data sources that support basic science are often insufficient to support applications. Localized impacts with global extent, such as intrusion of invasive species, are often difficult for centralized projects with small numbers of researchers to ascertain. New applications-appropriate sources must be identified, and new ways of observing (including the use of communities as data gatherers) must be developed.

Each of these characteristics implies development of *new knowledge types* and *new tools for acquiring that knowledge*. The snowpack example illustrates what this requirement means for a specific application area. Four elements have recently come together that make deployment of a measurement and information system that can support decisions at a scale of a large river basin feasible: (1) accurate, sustained satellite estimates of snow-covered area across an entire mountain range; (2) reliable, low-cost sensors and telemetry systems for snow and soil moisture; (3) social science data that complement natural and engineered systems data to enable analysis of human decision making; and (4) cyberinfrastructure advances to integrate data and deliver them in near real time.

For snow-dominated drainage basins, the highest-priority scientific challenge is to estimate the spatial distribution and heterogeneity of the *snow water equivalent*— i.e., the amount of water that would result if the snow were to melt. Because of wind redistribution of snow after it falls, snow on the ground is far more heterogeneous than rainfall, with several meters of differences within a 10 to 100 m distance. Heterogeneity in snow depth smooths the daily runoff because of the variability of the duration of meltwater in the snowpack [6]; seasonally, it produces quasi-riparian zones of increased soil moisture well into the summer. The approach to estimating the snow water equivalent involves several tasks using improved data: (1) extensive validation of the satellite estimates of snow cover and its reflectivity, as Figure 1 on the next page shows; (2) using results from an energy balance reconstruction of snow cover to improve interpolation from more extensive ground measurements and satellite data [7]; (3) development of innovative ways to characterize heterogeneity [8]; and (4) testing the interpolated estimates with a spatially distributed runoff model [9]. The measurements would also help clarify the accuracy in precipitation estimates from regional climate models.

This third phase of Earth and environmental science will evolve over the next decade as the scientific community begins to pursue it. Weather science has already built substantial capability in applications science; the larger field of Earth science will need to learn from and extend those efforts. The need for basic science and further discovery will not diminish, but instead will be augmented and extended by this new phase. The questions to address are both practically important and intellectually captivating. Will our hydrologic forecasting skill decline as changes in precipitation diminish the value of statistics obtained from historic patterns? Where will the next big climate change issue arise, and what policy actions taken today could allow us to anticipate it?

Equally important is improving how we apply this knowledge in our daily lives. The Internet and mobile telephones, with their global reach, provide new ways to disseminate information rapidly and widely. Information was available to avoid much of the devastation from the Asian tsunami and Hurricane Katrina, but we

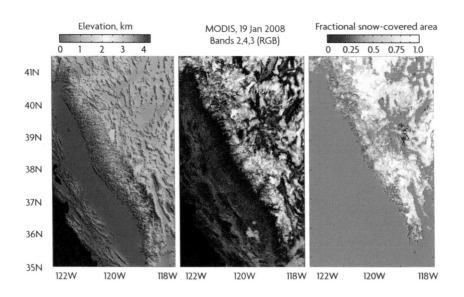

FIGURE 1.

An illustration of the type of data that are useful in analyzing the snow cover. The left panel shows elevations of the Sierra Nevada and Central Valley of California, along with a portion of northwestern Nevada. The middle panel shows the raw satellite data in three spectral bands (0.841–0.876, 0.545–0.565, and 0.459–0.479μm) from NASA's Moderate Resolution Imaging Spectroradiometer (MODIS), which provides daily global data at 250 to 1000 m resolution in 36 spectral bands. From seven "land" bands at 500 m resolution, we derive the fractional snow-covered area—i.e., the fraction of each 500 m grid cell covered by snow, shown in the right panel [10].

lacked the tools for rapid decision making and communication of needed actions. Applications science is therefore integrative; it couples understanding of physical phenomena and research into the ways that people and organizations can use better knowledge to make decisions. The public as a whole can also become an important contributor to localized Earth observation, augmenting our limited satellite and sensor networks through devices as simple as mobile phone cameras. The ability to leverage this emerging data-gathering capability will be an important challenge for the new phase of environmental science.

The security and prosperity of nearly 7 billion people depend increasingly on our ability to gather and apply information about the world around us. Basic environmental science has established an excellent starting point. We must now develop this into a robust science of environmental applications.

REFERENCES

[1] National Research Council, *Earth Observations from Space: The First 50 Years of Scientific Achievement*. Washington, D.C.: National Academies Press, 2007.

[2] R. DelVecchio, "UC Berkeley: Panel looks at control of emissions," *S.F. Chronicle*, March 22, 2007.

[3] T. P. Barnett, J. C. Adam, and D. P. Lettenmaier, "Potential impacts of a warming climate on water availability in snow-dominated regions," *Nature*, vol. 438, pp. 303–309, doi: 10.1038/nature04141, 2005.

[4] P. C. D. Milly, J. Betancourt, M. Falkenmark, R. M. Hirsch, Z. W. Kundzewicz, D. P. Lettenmaier, and R. J. Stouffer, "Stationarity is dead: whither water management?" *Science*, vol. 319, pp. 573–574, 2008, doi: 10.1126/science.1151915.

[5] R. C. Bales, N. P. Molotch, T. H. Painter, M. D. Dettinger, R. Rice, and J. Dozier, "Mountain hydrology of the western United States," *Water Resour. Res.*, vol. 42, W08432, 2006, doi: 10.1029/2005WR004387.

[6] J. D. Lundquist and M. D. Dettinger, "How snowpack heterogeneity affects diurnal streamflow timing," *Water Resour. Res.*, vol. 41, W05007, 2005, doi: 10.1029/2004WR003649.

[7] D. W. Cline, R. C. Bales, and J. Dozier, "Estimating the spatial distribution of snow in mountain basins using remote sensing and energy balance modeling," *Water Resour. Res.*, vol. 34, pp. 1275–1285, 1998, doi: 10.1029/97WR03755.

[8] N. P. Molotch and R. C. Bales, "Scaling snow observations from the point to the grid element: implications for observation network design," *Water Resour. Res.*, vol. 41, W11421, 2005, doi: 10.1029/2005WR004229.

[9] C. L. Tague and L. E. Band, "RHESSys: regional hydro-ecologic simulation system—an object-oriented approach to spatially distributed modeling of carbon, water, and nutrient cycling," *Earth Int.*, vol. 19, pp. 1–42, 2004.

[10] T. H. Painter, K. Rittger, C. McKenzie, R. E. Davis, and J. Dozier, "Retrieval of subpixel snow-covered area, grain size, and albedo from MODIS," *Remote Sens. Environ.*, vol. 113, pp. 868–879, 2009, doi: 10.1016/j.rse.2009.01.001.

Redefining Ecological Science Using Data

JAMES R. HUNT
University of California,
Berkeley, and the Berkeley
Water Center

DENNIS D. BALDOCCHI
University of California,
Berkeley

CATHARINE VAN INGEN
Microsoft Research

E COLOGY IS THE STUDY OF LIFE and its interactions with the physical environment. Because climate change requires rapid adaptation, new data analysis tools are essential to quantify those changes in the midst of high natural variability. Ecology is a science in which studies have been performed primarily by small groups of individuals, with data recorded and stored in notebooks. But large synthesis studies are now being attempted by collaborations involving hundreds of scientists. These larger efforts are essential because of two developments: one in how science is done and the other in the resource management questions being asked. While collaboration synthesis studies are still nascent, their ever-increasing importance is clear. Computational support is integral to these collaborations and key to the scientific process.

HOW GLOBAL CHANGES ARE CHANGING ECOLOGICAL SCIENCE

The global climate and the Earth's landscape are changing, and scientists must quantify significant linkages between atmospheric, oceanic, and terrestrial processes to properly study the phenomena. For example, scientists are now asking how climate fluctuations in temperature, precipitation, solar radiation, length of growing season, and extreme weather events such as droughts affect the net carbon exchange between vegetation and the atmosphere. This question spans many Earth science disciplines with their respective data, models, and assumptions.

These changes require a new approach to resolving resource management questions. In the short run of the next few decades, ecosystems cannot be restored to their former status. For example, with a warming climate on the West Coast of the United States, can historical data from coastal watersheds in southern California be used to predict the fish habitats of northern California coastal watersheds? Similarly, what can remote sensing tell us about deforestation? Addressing these challenges requires a synthesis of data and models that spans length scales from the very local (river pools) to the global (oceanic circulations) and spans time scales from a few tens of milliseconds to centuries.

AN EXAMPLE OF ECOLOGICAL SYNTHESIS

Figure 1 shows a simple "science mash-up" example of a synthesis study. The graph compares annual runoff from relatively small watersheds in the foothills of the Sierra Nevada in California to local annual precipitation over multiple years. Annual runoff values were obtained from the U.S. Geological Survey (USGS) for three of the gauging stations along Dry Creek and the Schubert University of California experimental field site.[1] Long-term precipitation records from nearby rain gauges were obtained from the National Climatic Data Center.[2] The precipitation that does not run off undergoes evapotranspiration (ET) that is largely dominated by watershed vegetation. In these watersheds, a single value of 400 mm is observed over all years of data. A similar value of annual ET was obtained by independent

[1] http://waterdata.usgs.gov/nwis
[2] www.ncdc.noaa.gov

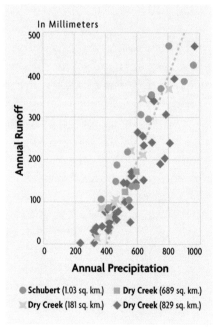

FIGURE 1.
Simple annual water balance to estimate evapotranspiration in Sierra Nevada foothill watersheds. The dashed line represents an annual ET of 400 mm.

measurement from atmospheric sensors deployed over an oak savannah ecosystem at the AmeriFlux Tonzi Ranch tower.[3] This synthesis of historical data defines a watershed model appropriate for historical conditions and provides a reference frame for addressing climate change effects in a highly variable system.

THE COMING FLOOD OF ECOLOGICAL DATA

These new synthesis studies are enabled by the confluence of low-cost sensors, remote sensing, Internet connectivity, and commodity computing. Sensor deployments by research groups are shifting from short campaigns to long-term monitoring with finer-scale and more diverse instruments. Satellites give global coverage particularly to remote or harsh regions where field research is hampered by physical and political logistics. Internet connectivity is enabling data sharing across organizations and disciplines. The result of these first three factors is a data flood. Commodity computing provides part of the solution, by allowing for the flood to be paired with models that incorporate different physical and biological processes and allowing for different models to be linked to span the length and time scales of interest.

The flood of ecological data and ecological science synthesis presents unique computing infrastructure challenges and new opportunities. Unlike sciences such as physics or astronomy, in which detectors are shared, in ecological science data are generated by a wide variety of groups using a wide variety of sampling or simulation methodologies and data standards. As shown earlier in Figure 1, the use of published data from two different sources was essential to obtain evapotranspiration. This synthesis required digital access to long records, separate processing of those datasets to arrive at ET, and finally verification with independent flux tower measurements. Other synthetic activities will require access to evolving resources from government organizations such as NASA or USGS, science collaborations such as the National Ecological Observatory Network and the WATERS Network,[4] individual university science research groups such as Life Under Your Feet,[5] and even citizen scientist groups such as the Community Collaborative Rain, Hail and Snow Network[6] and the USA National Phenology Network.[7]

While the bulk of the data start out as digital, originating from the field sensor,

---

[3] www.fluxdata.org:8080/SitePages/siteInfo.aspx?US-Ton
[4] www.watersnet.org
[5] www.lifeunderyourfeet.org
[6] www.cocorahs.org
[7] www.usanpn.org

radar, or satellite, the historic data and field data, which are critical for the science, are being digitized. The latter data are not always evenly spaced time series; they can include the date of leaf budding, or aerial imagery at different wavelengths and resolutions to assess quantities throughout the watershed such as soil moisture, vegetation, and land use. Deriving science variables from remote sensing remains an active area of research; as such, hard-won field measurements often form the ground truth necessary to develop conversion algorithms. Citizen science field observations such as plant species, plant growth (budding dates or tree ring growth, for example), and fish and bird counts are becoming increasingly important. Integrating such diverse information is an ever-increasing challenge to science analysis.

NAVIGATING THE ECOLOGICAL DATA FLOOD

The first step in any ecological science analysis is data discovery and harmonization. Larger datasets are discoverable today; smaller and historic datasets are often found by word of mouth. Because of the diversity of data publishers, no single reporting protocol exists. Unit conversions, geospatial reprojections, and time/length scale regularizations are a way of life. Science data catalog portals such as SciScope[8] and Web services with common data models such as those from the Open Geospatial Consortium[9] are evolving.

Integral to these science data search portals is knowledge of geospatial features and variable namespace mediation. The first enables searches across study watersheds or geological regions as well as simple polygon bounding boxes. The second enables searches to include multiple search terms—such as "rainfall," "precipitation," and "precip"—when searching across data repositories with different naming conventions. A new generation of metadata registries that use semantic Web technologies will enable richer searches as well as automated name and unit conversions. The combination of both developments will enable science data searches such as "Find me the daily river flow and suspended sediment discharge data from all watersheds in Washington State with more than 30 inches of annual rainfall."

MOVING ECOLOGICAL SYNTHESIS INTO THE CLOUD

Large synthesis datasets are also leading to a migration from the desktop to cloud computing. Most ecological science datasets have been collections of files. An example is the Fluxnet LaThuile synthesis dataset, containing 966 site-years of sensor

[8] www.sciscope.org
[9] www.opengeospatial.org

data from 253 sites around the world. The data for each site-year is published as a simple comma-separated or MATLAB-ready file of either daily aggregates or half-hourly aggregates. Most of the scientists download some or all of the files and then perform analyses locally. Other scientists are using an alternative cloud service that links MATLAB on the desktop to a SQL Server Analysis Services data cube in the cloud. The data appears local, but the scientists need not be bothered with the individual file handling. Local download and manipulation of the remote sensing data that would complement that sensor data are not practical for many scientists. A cloud analysis now in progress using both to compute changes in evapotranspiration across the United States over the last 10 years will download 3 terabytes of imagery and use 4,000 CPU hours of processing to generate less than 100 MB of results. Doing the analysis off the desktop leverages the higher bandwidth, large temporary storage capacity, and compute farm available in the cloud.

Synthesis studies also create a need for collaborative tools in the cloud. Science data has value for data-owner scientists in the form of publications, grants, reputation, and students. Sharing data with others should increase rather than decrease that value. Determining the appropriate citations, acknowledgment, and/or co-authorship policies for synthesis papers remains an open area of discussion in larger collaborations such as Fluxnet[10] and the North American Carbon Program.[11] Journal space and authorship limitations are an important concern in these discussions. Addressing the ethical question of what it means to be a co-author is essential: Is contributing data sufficient when that contribution is based on significant intellectual and physical effort? Once such policies are agreed upon, simple collaborative tools in the cloud can greatly reduce the logistics required to publish a paper, provide a location for the discovery of collaboration authors, and enable researchers to track how their data are used.

HOW CYBERINFRASTRUCTURE IS CHANGING ECOLOGICAL SCIENCE

The flood of ecological data will break down scientific silos and enable a new generation of scientific research. The goal of understanding the impacts of climate change is driving research that spans disciplines such as plant physiology, soil science, meteorology, oceanography, hydrology, and fluvial geomorphology. Bridging the diverse length and time scales involved will require a collection of cooperating models. Synthesizing the field observations with those model results at key length

[10] www.fluxdata.org
[11] www.nacarbon.org/nacp

and time scales is crucial to the development and validation of such models.

The diversity of ecological dataset size, dataset semantics, and dataset publisher concerns poses a cyberinfrastructure challenge that will be addressed over the next several years. Synthesis science drives not only direct conversations but also virtual ones between scientists of different backgrounds. Advances in metadata representation can break down the semantic and syntactic barriers to those conversations. Data visualizations that range from our simple mashup to more complex virtual worlds are also key elements in those conversations. Cloud access to discoverable, distributed datasets and, perhaps even more important, enabling cloud data analyses near the more massive datasets will enable a new generation of cross-discipline science.

A 2020 Vision for Ocean Science

JOHN R. DELANEY
University of Washington

ROGER S. BARGA
Microsoft Research

T HE GLOBAL OCEAN is the last physical frontier on Earth. Covering 70 percent of the planetary surface, it is the largest, most complex biome we know. The ocean is a huge, mobile reservoir of heat and chemical mass. As such, it is the "engine" that drives weather-climate systems across the ocean basins and the continents, directly affecting food production, drought, and flooding on land. Water is effectively opaque to electromagnetic radiation, so the seafloor has not been as well mapped as the surfaces of Mars and Venus, and although the spatial relationships within the ocean basins are well understood to a first order, the long- and short-term temporal variations and the complexities of ocean dynamics are poorly understood.

The ultimate repository of human waste, the ocean has absorbed nearly half of the fossil carbon released since 1800. The ocean basins are a source of hazards: earthquakes, tsunamis, and giant storms. These events are episodic, powerful, often highly mobile, and frequently unpredictable. Because the ocean basins are a vast, but finite, repository of living and non-living resources, we turn to them for food, energy, and the many minerals necessary to sustain a broad range of human lifestyles. Many scientists believe that underwater volcanoes were the crucible in which early life began on Earth and perhaps on other planets. The oceans connect all continents; they are owned by no one, yet they belong to all of us by virtue of their mobile nature. The oceans may be viewed as the common heritage of humankind, the responsibility and life support of us all.

OCEAN COMPLEXITY

Our challenge is to optimize the benefits and mitigate the risks of living on a planet dominated by two major energy sources: sunlight driving the atmosphere and much of the upper ocean, and internal heat driving plate tectonics and portions of the lower ocean. For more than 4 billion years, the global ocean has responded to and integrated the impacts of these two powerful driving forces as the Earth, the oceans, the atmosphere, and life have co-evolved. As a consequence, our oceans have had a long, complicated history, producing today's immensely complex system in which thousands of physical, chemical, and biological processes continually interact over many scales of time and space as the oceans maintain our planetary-scale ecological "comfort zone."

Figure 1 captures a small fraction of this complexity, which is constantly driven by energy from above and below. Deeper understanding of this "global life-support system" requires entirely novel research approaches that will allow broad spectrum, interactive ocean processes to be studied simultaneously and interactively by many scientists—approaches that enable continuous *in situ* examination of linkages among many processes in a coherent time and space framework. Implementing these powerful new approaches is both the challenge and the vision of next-generation ocean science.

HISTORICAL PERSPECTIVE

For thousands of years, humans have gone to sea in ships to escape, to conquer, to trade, and to explore. Between October 1957 and January 1960, we launched the first Earth-orbiting satellite and dove to the deepest part of the ocean. Ships, satellites, and submarines have been the mainstays of spatially focused oceanographic research and exploration for the past 50 years. We are now poised on the next threshold of technological breakthrough that will advance oceanic discovery; this time, exploration will be focused on the time domain and interacting processes. This new era will draw deeply on the emergence, and convergence, of many rapidly evolving new technologies. These changes are setting the scene for what Marcel Proust called "[t]he real voyage of discovery, [which] lies not in seeking new landscapes, but in having new eyes."

In many ways, this "vision" of next-generation oceanographic research and

FIGURE 1.

Two primary energy sources powerfully influence the ocean basins: sunlight and its radiant energy, and internal heat with its convective and conductive input. Understanding the complexity of the oceans requires documenting and quantifying—in a well-defined time-space framework over decades—myriad processes that are constantly changing and interacting with one another.

Illustration designed by John Delaney and Mark Stoermer;
created by the Center for Environmental Visualization (CEV) for the NEPTUNE Program.

education involves utilizing a wide range of innovative technologies to simultaneously and continuously "see," or sense, many different processes operating throughout entire volumes of the ocean *from a perspective within the ocean*. Some of these same capabilities will enable remote *in situ* detection of critical changes taking place within selected ocean volumes. Rapid reconfiguration of key sensor arrays linked to the Internet via submarine electro-optical cables will allow us to capture, image, document, and measure energetic and previously inaccessible phenomena such as erupting volcanoes, major migration patterns, large submarine slumps, big earthquakes, giant storms, and a host of other complex phenomena that have been largely inaccessible to scientific study.

THE FOURTH PARADIGM

The ocean has been chronically under-sampled for as long as humans have been trying to characterize its innate complexity. In a very real sense, the current suite of computationally intensive numerical/theoretical models of ocean behavior has outstripped the requisite level of actual data necessary to ground those models in reality. As a consequence, we have been unable to even come close to useful predictive models of the real behavior of the oceans. Only by quantifying powerful episodic events, like giant storms and erupting volcanoes, within the context of longer-term decadal changes can we begin to approach dependable predictive models of ocean behavior. Over time, as the adaptive models are progressively refined by continual comparison with actual data flowing from real systems, we slowly gain the ability to predict the future behavior of these immensely complex natural systems. To achieve that goal, we must take steps to fundamentally change the way we approach oceanography.

This path has several crucial steps. We must be able to document conditions and measure fluxes *within the volume of the ocean, simultaneously and in real time,* over many scales of time and space, regardless of the depth, energy, mobility, or complexity of the processes involved. These measurements must be made using co-located arrays of many sensor types, operated by many investigators over periods of decades to centuries. And the data must be collected, archived, visualized, and compared immediately to model simulations that are explicitly configured to address complexity at scales comparable in time and space to the actual measurements.

This approach offers three major advantages: (1) The models must progressively emulate the measured reality through constant comparison with data to capture the real behavior of the oceans in "model space" to move toward more predictive

---

Ø

---

simulations; (2) When the models and the data disagree, assuming the data are valid, we must immediately adapt at-sea sensor-robot systems to fully characterize the events that are unfolding because they obviously offer new insights into the complexities we seek to capture in the failed models; (3) By making and archiving all observations and measurements in coherently indexed time and space frameworks, we can allow many investigators (even those not involved in the data collection) to examine correlations among any number of selected phenomena during, or long after, the time that the events or processes occur. If the archived data are immediately and widely available via the Internet, the potential for discovery rises substantially because of the growing number of potential investigators who can explore a rapidly expanding spectrum of "parameter space." For scientists operating in this data-intensive environment, there will be a need for development of a new suite of scientific workflow products that can facilitate the archiving, assimilation, visualization, modeling, and interpretation of the information about all scientific systems of interest. Several workshop reports that offer examples of these "workflow products" are available in the open literature [1, 2].

EMERGENCE AND CONVERGENCE

Ocean science is becoming the beneficiary of a host of powerful *emergent* technologies driven by many communities that are entirely external to the world of ocean research—they include, but are not limited to, nanotechnology, biotechnology, information technology, computational modeling, imaging technologies, and robotics. More powerful yet will be the progressive *convergence* of these enabling capabilities as they are adapted to conduct sophisticated remote marine operations in novel ways by combining innovative technologies into appropriate investigative or experimental systems.

For example, computer-enabled support activities must include massive data storage systems, cloud computing, scientific workflow, advanced visualization displays, and handheld supercomputing. Instead of batteries and satellites being used to operate remote installations, electrical power and the vast bandwidth of optical fiber will be used to transform the kinds of scientific and educational activities that can be conducted within the ocean. Adaptation of industry-standard electro-optical cables for use in oceanographic research can fundamentally change the nature of human telepresence throughout the full volume of the oceans by introducing unprecedented but routinely available power and bandwidth into "ocean space." High-resolution optical and acoustic sensing will be part of the broader technology of "ocean imaging systems." These approaches will include routine use of high-definition video, in stereo if needed, as well as high-resolution sonar, acoustic lenses, laser imaging, and volumetric sampling. Advanced sensor technologies will include chemical sensing using remote, and mobile, mass spectrometers and gas chromatographs, eco-genomic analysis, and adaptive sampling techniques.

AN INTEGRATED APPROACH

After decades of planning [3, 4], the U.S. National Science Foundation (NSF) is on the verge of investing more than US$600 million over 6 years in the construction and early operation of an innovative infrastructure known as the Ocean Observatories Initiative (OOI) [4]. The design life of the program is 25 years. In addition to making much-needed high-latitude and coastal measurements supported by relatively low-bandwidth satellite communications systems, this initiative will include a transformative undertaking to implement electro-optically cabled observing systems in the northeast Pacific Ocean [5-7] off the coasts of Washington, Oregon, and British Columbia, as illustrated in Figure 2.[1]

These interactive, distributed sensor networks in the U.S. and Canada will create a large-aperture "natural laboratory" for conducting a wide range of long-term innovative experiments within the ocean volume using real-time control over the entire "laboratory" system. Extending unprecedented power and bandwidth to a wide range of interactive sensors, instruments, and robots distributed throughout the ocean water, at the air-sea interface, on the seafloor, and below the seafloor within drill holes will empower next-generation creativity and exploration of the time domain among a broad spectrum of investigators. The University of Washington leads the cabled component of the NSF initiative, known as the Regional Scale Nodes (formerly known, and funded, as NEPTUNE); the University of Victoria leads the effort in Canada, known as NEPTUNE Canada. The two approaches were conceived jointly in 2000 as a collaborative U.S.-Canadian effort. The Consortium for Ocean Leadership in Washington, D.C., is managing and integrating the entire OOI system for NSF. Woods Hole Oceanographic Institution and the University of California, San Diego, are responsible for overseeing the Coastal-Global and Cyber-Infrastructure portions of the program, respectively. Oregon State University and Scripps Institution of Oceanography are participants in the Coastal-Global portion of the OOI.

---

[1] www.interactiveoceans.ocean.washington.edu

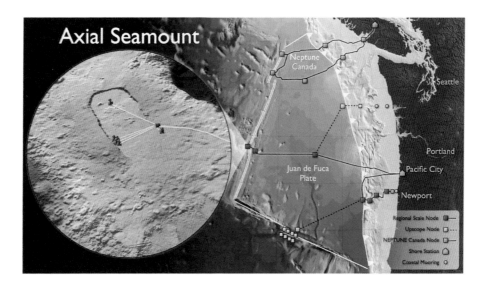

FIGURE 2.

A portion of the OOI focuses on the dynamic behavior of the Juan de Fuca Plate and the energetic processes operating in the overlying ocean and atmosphere. Recent modifications in the Regional Scale Nodes (RSN) have focused on delivery of the elements shown in red, and the pink components are future expansion. The inset shows the crest of Axial Seamount along the active Juan de Fuca Ridge. Each square block site will provide unprecedented electrical power and bandwidth available for research and education. Many of the processes shown in Figure 1 can be examined at the sites here.

Image created by CEV for OOI-RSN.

The cabled ocean observatory approach will revolutionize ocean science by providing interactive access to ocean data and instruments 24/7/365 over two to three decades. More than 1,200 kilometers of electro-optical submarine cable will deliver many tens of kilowatts of power to seafloor nodes, where instruments that might spread over a 50 km radius for each node will be plugged in directly or via secondary extension cables. The primary cable will provide between 2.5 and 10 gigabit/sec bandwidth connectivity between land and a growing number of fixed sensor packages and mobile sensor platforms. We expect that a host of novel approaches to oceanography will evolve based on the availability of *in situ* power and bandwidth. A major benefit will be the real-time data return and command-control of fleets of remotely operated vehicles (ROVs) and autonomous underwater vehicles

FIGURE 3.

Next-generation scientists or citizens. This virtual picture shows a deep ocean octopus, known as Grimpoteuthis, *and a portion of a submarine hydrothermal system on the Juan de Fuca Ridge. Such real-time displays of 3-D HD video will be routine within 5 years.*

Graphic designed by Mark Stoermer and created by CEV for NEPTUNE in 2005.

(AUVs). The infrastructure will be adaptable, expandable, and exportable to interested users. Data policy for the OOI calls for all information to be made available to all interested users via the Internet (with the exception of information bearing on national security).

Hardwired to the Internet, the cabled observatories will provide scientists, students, educators, and the public with virtual access to remarkable parts of our planet that are rarely visited by humans. In effect, the Internet will be extended to the seafloor, with the ability to interact with a host of instruments, including HD video live from the many environments within the oceans, as illustrated in Figure 3. The cabled observatory systems will be able to capture processes at the scale of the tectonic plate, mesoscale oceanic eddies, or even smaller scales. Research into representative activities responsible for climate change, major biological productivity at the base of the food chain, or encroaching ocean acidification (to name a few) will be readily conducted with this new infrastructure. Novel studies of mid-ocean spreading centers, transform faults, and especially processes in the subduction zone at the base of the continental slope, which may trigger massive earthquakes in the Pacific Northwest, will also be addressable using the same investment in the same cabled infrastructure.

This interactive ocean laboratory will be enabled by a common cyberinfrastructure that integrates multiple observatories, thousands of instruments, tens of thousands of users, and petabytes of data. The goals of the cabled ocean observatory can be achieved only if the at-sea portion is complemented by state-of-the-art information technology infrastructure resulting from a strong collaborative effort between computer scientists and ocean scientists. Such collaboration will allow scientists to interact with the ocean through real-time command and control of sensors; provide models with a continuous data feed; automate data quality control and calibration; and support novel approaches to data management, analysis, and visualization.

WHAT IS POSSIBLE?

Figure 4 on the next page depicts some of the potentially transformative capabilities that could emerge in ocean science by 2020. In the long term, a key element of the introduction of unprecedented power and bandwidth for use within the ocean basins will be the potential for bold and integrative designs and developments that enhance our understanding of, and perhaps our ability to predict, the behavior of Earth, ocean, and atmosphere interactions and their bearing on a sustainable planetary habitat.

CONCLUSION

The cabled ocean observatory merges dramatic technological advancements in sensor technologies, robotic systems, high-speed communication, eco-genomics, and nanotechnology with ocean observatory infrastructure in ways that will substantially transform the approaches that scientists, educators, technologists, and policymakers take in interacting with the dynamic global ocean. Over the coming decades, most nations will implement systems of this type in the offshore extensions of their territorial seas. As these systems become more sophisticated and data become routinely available via the Internet, the Internet will emerge as the most powerful oceanographic research tool on the planet. In this fashion, the legacy of Jim Gray will continue to grow as we learn to discover truths and insights within the data we already have "in the can."

While the cabled observatory will have profound ramifications for the manner

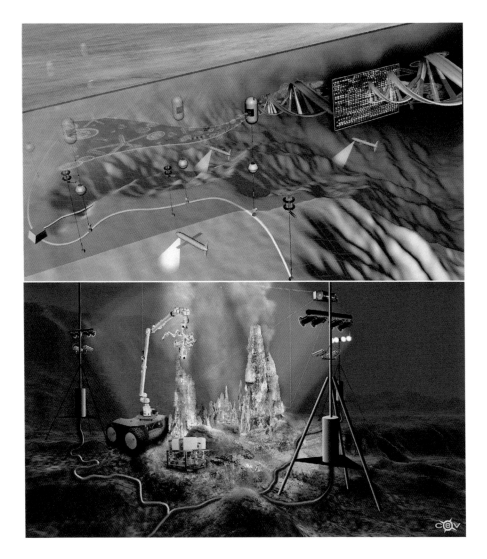

FIGURE 4.

Some of the transformative developments that could become routine within 5 years with the added power of a cabled support system. The top image shows miniaturized genomic analysis systems adapted from land laboratories to the ocean to allow scientists, with the flip of a switch in their lab hundreds of miles away, to sample ambient flow remotely and run in situ gene sequencing operations within the ocean. The data can be made available on the Internet within minutes of the decision to sample microbes in an erupting submarine volcanic plume or a seasonally driven phytoplankton bloom. The lower part shows a conceptual illustration of an entire remote analytical-biological laboratory on the seafloor that allows a variety of key measurements or dissections to be made in situ using stereo high-definition video to guide high-precision remote manipulations.

Scientific concepts by Ginger Armbrust and John Delaney; graphic design by Mark Stoermer for CEV.

in which scientists, engineers, and educators conduct their professional activities, the most far-reaching effects may be a significant shift in public attitudes toward the oceans as well as toward the scientific process. The real-time data and high-speed communications inherent in cabled remote observing systems will also open entirely new avenues for the public to interact with the natural world.

In the final analysis, having predictive models of how the ocean functions based on decades of refining sophisticated computer simulations against high-quality observations from distributed sensor networks will form the basis for learning to manage, or at least adapt to, the most powerful climate modulating system on the planet—the global ocean.

ACKNOWLEDGMENTS

We gratefully acknowledge the significant influence of Jim Gray, who unflinchingly stated that this cabled ocean observing approach using high-bandwidth and real-time data flow would be integral to human progress and understanding of the world we live in. We are also pleased to acknowledge the support of the University of Washington, the National Science Foundation, the Consortium for Ocean Leadership, and the Microsoft External Research group for technical collaboration and financial support. NSF and the National Oceanographic Partnership Program were particularly supportive of the early development of the NEPTUNE concept from 1998 to 2005, through grants to J. R. Delaney. Deborah Kelley, Nancy Penrose, and Mark Stoermer contributed significantly to the preparation of this manuscript and to conversations bearing on the content.

REFERENCES

[1] "Project Trident: A Scientific Workflow Workbench Brings Clarity to Data," http://research.microsoft.com/en-us/collaboration/focus/e3/workflowtool.aspx.
[2] Two URLs for the NSF Workshop on Challenges of Scientific Workflows: http://grids.ucs.indiana.edu/ptliupages/publications/IEEEComputer-gil.pdf http://vtcpc.isi.edu/wiki/index.php/Main_Page.
[3] National Research Council of the National Academies, *Enabling Ocean Research in the 21st Century: Implementation of a Network of Ocean Observatories*. Washington, D.C.: National Academies Press, 2003, p. 220.
[4] "Ocean Observatories Initiative (OOI) Scientific Objectives and Network Design: A Closer Look," 2007, http://ooi.ocean.washington.edu/cruise/cruiseFile/show/40. Ocean Leadership Web site for the Ocean Observatories Initiative: www.oceanleadership.org/programs-and-partnerships/ocean-observing/ooi.
[5] J. R. Delaney, F. N. Spiess, S. C. Solomon, R. Hessler, J. L. Karsten, J. A. Baross, R. T. Holcomb, D. Norton, R. E. McDuff, F. L. Sayles, J. Whitehead, D. Abbott, and L. Olson, "Scientific rationale for establishing long-term ocean bottom observatory/laboratory systems," in *Marine Minerals:*

Resource Assessment Strategies, P. G. Teleki, M. R. Dobson, J. R. Moor, and U. von Stackelberg, Eds., pp. 389–411, 1987.

[6] J. R. Delaney, G. R. Heath, A. D. Chave, B. M. Howe, and H. Kirkham, "NEPTUNE: Real-time ocean and earth sciences at the scale of a tectonic plate," *Oceanography,* vol. 13, pp. 71–83, 2000, doi: 10.1109/OCEANS.2001.968033.

[7] A. D. Chave, B. St. Arnaud, M. Abbott, J. R. Delaney, R. Johnson, E. Lazowska, A. R. Maffei, J. A. Orcutt, and L. Smarr, "A management concept for ocean observatories based on web services," *Proc. Oceans'04/Techno-Ocean'04,* Kobe, Japan, Nov. 2004, p. 7, doi: 10.1109/OCEANS.2004.1406486.

Bringing the Night Sky Closer: Discoveries in the Data Deluge

ALYSSA A. GOODMAN
Harvard University

CURTIS G. WONG
Microsoft Research

THROUGHOUT HISTORY, ASTRONOMERS have been accustomed to data falling from the sky. But our relatively newfound ability to store the sky's data in "clouds" offers us fascinating new ways to access, distribute, use, and analyze data, both in research and in education. Here we consider three interrelated questions: (1) What trends have we seen, and will soon see, in the growth of image and data collection from telescopes? (2) How might we address the growing challenge of finding the proverbial needle in the haystack of this data to facilitate scientific discovery? (3) What visualization and analytic opportunities does the future hold?

TRENDS IN DATA GROWTH

Astronomy has a history of data collection stretching back at least to Stonehenge more than three millennia ago. Over time, the format of the information recorded by astronomers has changed, from carvings in stone to written records and hand-drawn illustrations to photographs to digital media.

While the telescope (c. 1600) and the opening up of the electromagnetic spectrum beyond wavelengths visible to the human eye (c. 1940) led to qualitative changes in the nature of astronomical investigations, they did not increase the volume of collected data nearly as much as did the advent of the Digital Age.

Charge-coupled devices (CCDs), which came into widespread use by the 1980s, and equivalent detectors at non-optical wavelengths became much more efficient than traditional analog media (such as photographic plates). The resulting rise in the rate of photon collection caused the ongoing (and potentially perpetually accelerating) increase in data available to astronomers. The increasing capabilities and plummeting price of the digital devices used in signal processing, data analysis, and data storage, combined with the expansion of the World Wide Web, transformed astronomy from an observational science into a digital and computational science.

For example, the Large Synoptic Survey Telescope (LSST), coming within the decade, will produce more data in its first year of operation—1.28 petabytes—than any other telescope in history by a significant margin. The LSST will accomplish this feat by using very sensitive CCDs with huge numbers of pixels on a relatively large telescope with very fast optics (f/1.234) and a wide field of view (9.6 square degrees), and by taking a series of many shorter exposures (rather than the traditional longer exposures) that can be used to study the temporal behavior of astronomical sources. And while the LSST, Pan-STARRS, and other coming astronomical megaprojects—many at non-optical wavelengths—will produce huge datasets covering the whole sky, other groups and individuals will continue to add their own smaller, potentially more targeted, datasets.

For the remainder of this article, we will assume that the challenge of managing this explosive growth in data will be solved (likely through the clever use of "cloud" storage and novel data structures), and we will focus instead on how to offer better tools and novel technical and social analytics that will let us learn more about our universe.

A number of emerging trends can help us find the "needles in haystacks" of data available over the Internet, including crowdsourcing, democratization of access via new browsing technologies, and growing computational power.

CROWDSOURCING

The Sloan Digital Sky Survey was undertaken to image, and measure spectra for, millions of galaxies. Most of the galaxy images had never been viewed by a human because they were automatically extracted from wide-field images reduced in an automated pipeline. To test a claim that more galaxies rotate in an anticlockwise direction than clockwise, the Sloan team used custom code to create a Web page that served up pictures of galaxies to members of the public willing to play the online Galaxy Zoo game, which consists primarily of classifying the handedness of the galaxies. Clever algorithms within the "Zoo" serve the same galaxy to multiple users as a reference benchmark and to check up on players to see how accurate they are.

The results from the first year's aggregated classification of galaxies by the public proved to be just as accurate as that done by astronomers. More than 50 million classifications of a million galaxies were done by the public in the first year, and the claim about right/left handed preference was ultimately refuted. Meanwhile, Hanny Van Arkel, a schoolteacher in Holland, found a galaxy that is now the bluest known galaxy in the universe. It has come under intense scrutiny by major telescopes, including the Very Large Array (VLA) radio telescope, and will soon be scrutinized by the Hubble Space Telescope.

DEMOCRATIZING ACCESS VIA NEW BROWSING TECHNOLOGIES

The time needed to acquire data from any astronomical object increases at least as quickly as the square of the distance to that object, so any service that can accumulate custom ensembles of already captured images and data effectively brings the night sky closer. The use of archived online data stored in a "data cloud" is facilitated by new software tools, such as Microsoft's WorldWide Telescope (WWT), which provide intuitive access to images of the night sky that have taken astronomers thousands and thousands of hours of telescope time to acquire.

Using WWT (shown in Figure 1 on the next page), anyone can pan and zoom around the sky, at wavelengths from X-ray through radio, and anyone can navigate through a three-dimensional model of the Universe constructed from real observations, just to see what's there. Anyone can notice an unusual correspondence between features at multiple wavelengths at some position in the sky and click right through to all the published journal articles that discuss that position. Anyone can hook up a telescope to the computer running WWT and overlay live, new images on top of online images of the same piece of sky at virtually any wavelength. Anyone can be guided in their explorations via narrated "tours" produced by WWT users. As more and more tours are produced, WWT will become a true "sky browser," with the sky as the substrate for conversations about the universe. Explorers will navigate along paths that intersect at objects of common interest, linking ideas and individuals. Hopping from tour to tour will be like surfing from Web page to Web page now.

But the power of WWT goes far beyond its standalone ability. It is, and will continue to be, part of an ecosystem of online astronomy that will speed the progress of both "citizen" and "professional" science in the coming years.

FIGURE 1.

WorldWide Telescope view of the 30 Doradus region near the Large Magellanic Cloud.

Image courtesy of the National Optical Astronomy Observatory/National Science Foundation.

Microsoft, through WWT, and Google, through Google Sky, have both created API (application programming interface) environments that allow the sky-browsing software to function inside a Web page. These APIs facilitate the creation of everything from educational environments for children to "citizen science" sites and data distribution sites for professional astronomical surveys.

Tools such as Galaxy Zoo are now easy to implement, thanks to APIs. So it now falls to the astronomical and educational communities to capitalize on the public's willingness to help navigate the increasing influx of data. High-school students can now use satellite data that no one has yet analyzed to make real discoveries about the Universe, rather than just sliding blocks down inclined planes in their physics class. Amateur astronomers can gather data on demand to fill in missing information that students, professionals, and other astronomers ask for online. The collaborative and educational possibilities are truly limitless.

The role of WWT and tools like it in the professional astronomy community will

WT in particular has already become a better way to any extant professional tool. WWT, as part of interna- y" efforts, is being seamlessly linked to quantitative and nomers are accustomed to, in order to provide a beautiful nformation that is usually served only piecemeal. And it has re the kinds of holistic views of data that astronomers were igital Age chopped up the sky into so many small pieces and s.

TIONAL POWER

core processors will enhance commodity computing power two magnitude beyond today's computers. How will all this comput- to address the data deluge? Faster computers and increased stor- dth will of course enable our contemporary approaches to scale to large. s. In addition, fully new ways of handling and analyzing data will be enabled. For example, computer vision techniques are already surfacing in consumer digital cameras with face detection and recognition as common features.

More computational power will allow us to triage and potentially identify unique objects, events, and data outliers as soon as they are detected and route them to citizen-scientist networks for confirmation. Engagement of citizen scientists in the alerting network for this "last leg" of detection can be optimized through better-designed interfaces that can transform work into play. Interfaces could potentially connect human confirmation of objects with global networks of games and simulations where real-time data is broadly distributed and integrated into real-time massive multiplayer games that seamlessly integrate the correct identification of the objects into the games' success metrics. Such games could give kids the opportunity to raise their social stature among game-playing peers while making a meaningful contribution to science.

VISUALIZATION AND ANALYSIS FOR THE FUTURE

WWT offers a glimpse of the future. As the diversity and scale of collected data expand, software will have to become more sophisticated in terms of how it accesses data, while simultaneously growing more intuitive, customizable, and compatible.

The way to improve tools like WWT will likely be linked to the larger challenge of how to improve the way visualization and data analysis tools can be used together in all fields—not just in astronomy.

Visualization and analysis challenges are more common across scientific fields than they are different. Imagine, for example, an astronomer and a climate scientist working in parallel. Both want to study the properties of physical systems as observed within a spherical coordinate system. Both want to move seamlessly back and forth between, for example, spectral line observations of some sources at some specific positions on a sphere (e.g., to study the composition of a stellar atmosphere or the CO_2 in the Earth's atmosphere), the context for those positions on the sphere, and journal articles and online discussions about these phenomena.

Today, even within a discipline, scientists are often faced with many choices of how to accomplish the same subtask in analysis, but no package does all the subtasks the way they would prefer. What the future holds is the potential for scientists, or data specialists working with scientists, to design their own software by linking componentized, modular applications on demand. So, for example, the astronomer and the climate scientist could both use some generalized version of WWT as part of a separate, customized system that would link to their favorite discipline- or scientist-specific packages for tasks such as spectral-line analysis.

CONCLUSION

The question linking the three topics we have discussed here is, "How can we design new tools to enhance discovery in the data deluge to come in astronomy?" The answer seems to revolve around improved *linkage* between and among existing *resources*—including citizen scientists willing to help analyze data; accessible image browsers such as WWT; and more customized visualization tools that are mashed up from common components. This approach, which seeks to more seamlessly connect (and reuse) diverse components, will likely be common to many fields of science—not just astronomy—in the coming decade.

Instrumenting the Earth: Next-Generation Sensor Networks and Environmental Science

MICHAEL LEHNING
NICHOLAS DAWES
MATHIAS BAVAY
WSL Institute for
Snow and Avalanche
Research SLF

MARC PARLANGE
École Polytechnique
Fédérale de Lausanne

SUMAN NATH
FENG ZHAO
Microsoft Research

I NCREASING ENVIRONMENTAL CHALLENGES WORLDWIDE and a growing awareness of global climate change indicate an urgent need for environmental scientists to conduct science in a new and better way. Existing large-scale environmental monitoring systems, with their coarse spatiotemporal resolution, are not only expensive, but they are incapable of revealing the complex interactions between atmospheric and land surface components with enough precision to generate accurate environmental system models.

This is especially the case in mountainous regions with highly complex surfaces—the source of much of the world's fresh water and weather patterns. The amount of data required to understand and model these interactions is so massive (terabytes, and increasing) that no off-the-shelf solution allows scientists to easily manage and analyze it. This has led to rapidly growing global collaboration among environmental scientists and computer scientists to approach these problems systematically and to develop sensing and database solutions that will enable environmental scientists to conduct their next-generation experiments.

NEXT-GENERATION ENVIRONMENTAL SCIENCE

The next generation of environmental science, as shown in Figure 1, is motivated by the following observations by the atmospheric science community: First, the most prominent challenge in weather and climate prediction is represented by land-atmosphere interaction processes. Second, the average effect of a patchy surface on the atmosphere can be very different from an effect that is calculated by averaging a particular surface property such as temperature or moisture [1-3]—particularly in the mountains, where surface variability is typically very high.

Figure 2 shows an example of this—a highly complex mountain surface with bare rocks, debris-covered permafrost, patchy snow cover, sparse trees, and shallow and deep soils with varying vegetation. All of these surface features can occur within a single kilometer—a resolution that is typically not reached by weather forecast models of even the latest generation. Existing models of weather prediction and climate change still operate using a grid resolution, which is far too coarse (multiple kilometers) to explicitly and correctly map the surface heterogeneity in the mountains (and elsewhere). This can lead to severe errors in understanding and prediction.

In next-generation environmental

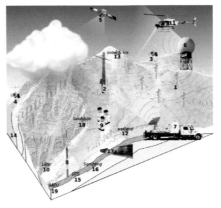

FIGURE 1.

A typical data source context for next-generation environmental science, with a heterogeneous sensor deployment that includes (1) mobile stations, (2) high-resolution conventional weather stations, (3) full-size snow/weather stations, (4) external weather stations, (5) satellite imagery, (6) weather radar, (7) mobile weather radar, (8) stream observations, (9) citizen-supplied observations, (10) ground LIDAR, (11) aerial LIDAR, (12) nitrogen/methane measures, (13) snow hydrology and avalanche probes, (14) seismic probes, (15) distributed optical fiber temperature sensing, (16) water quality sampling, (17) stream gauging stations, (18) rapid mass movements research, (19) runoff stations, and (20) soil research.

science, data resolution will be addressed using densely deployed (typically wireless) sensor networks. Recent developments in wireless sensing have made it possible to instrument and sense the physical world with high resolution and fidelity over an extended period of time. Wireless connections enable reliable collection of data from remote sensors to send to laboratories for processing, analyzing, and archiving. Such high-resolution sensing enables scientists to understand more precisely the variability and dynamics of environmental parameters. Wireless sensing also provides scientists with safe and convenient visibility of *in situ* sensor deploy-

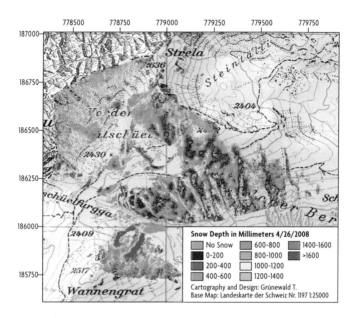

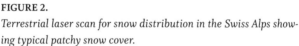

FIGURE 2.

Terrestrial laser scan for snow distribution in the Swiss Alps show-ing typical patchy snow cover.

ments and allows them to enable, debug, and test the deployments from the labo-ratory. This helps minimize site visits, which can be costly, time consuming, and even dangerous.

However, dense sensor deployments in harsh, remote environments remain challenging for several reasons. First, the whole process of sensing, computation, and communication must be extremely energy efficient so that sensors can remain operational for an extended period of time using small batteries, solar panels, or other environmental energy. Second, sensors and their communication links must be fairly robust to ensure reliable data acquisition in harsh outdoor environments. Third, invalid sensor data due to system failures or environmental impacts must be identified and treated accordingly (e.g., flagged or even filtered from the dataset). Although recent research (including the Swiss Experiment and Life Under Your Feet) partially addresses these issues, further research is needed to address them in many production systems.

MANAGING AND EXPLORING MASSIVE VOLUMES OF SENSOR DATA

High-resolution environmental sensing introduces severe data management challenges for scientists. These include reliably archiving large volumes (many terabytes) of data, sharing such data with users within access control policies, and maintaining sufficient context and provenance of sensor data using correct metadata [4].

Environmental scientists can use commercial database tools to address many of the data management and exploratory challenges associated with such a massive influx of data. For example, Microsoft's SenseWeb project [5] provides an infrastructure, including an underlying Microsoft SQL Server database, for archiving massive amounts of sensor data that might be compressed and distributed over multiple computers. SenseWeb also maintains suitable data indexes and enables efficient query processing to help users quickly explore the dataset to find features for detailed analysis [5-7]. But even with these capabilities, SenseWeb hits just the tip of the iceberg of the challenging data management tasks facing environmental scientists. Additional tools are necessary to efficiently integrate sensor data with relevant context and provide data provenance. Querying such data in a unified framework remains challenging. More research is also needed to deal with uncertain data that comes from noisy sensors and to handle the constant data flow from distributed locations.

To better understand environmental phenomena, scientists need to derive and apply various models to transform sensor data into scientific and other practical results. Database technology can help scientists to easily integrate observational data from diverse sources, possibly distributed over the Internet, with model assessments and forecasts—a procedure known as *data assimilation*. Sophisticated data mining techniques can allow scientists to easily explore spatiotemporal patterns of data (both interactively as well as in batch on archived data). Modeling techniques can provide correct and timely prediction of phenomena such as flooding events, landslides, or avalanche cycles, which can be highly useful for intervention and damage prevention, even with just a few hours of lead time. This very short-term forecasting is called *nowcasting* in meteorology.

Scientists in the Swiss Experiment project[1] have made progress in useful data assimilation and nowcasting. One case study in this project applies advanced sensors and models to forecasting alpine natural hazards [8]. A refined nowcast relies on the operational weather forecast to define the target area of a potential storm that

---

[1] www.swiss-experiment.ch

would affect a small-scale region (a few square kilometers) in the mountains. The operational weather forecast should allow sufficient time to install local mobile stations (such as SensorScope stations[2]) and remote sensing devices at the target area and to set up high-resolution hazard models. In the long term, specialized weather forecast models will be developed to allow much more precise local simulation.

FIGURE 3.

SensorMap showing temperature distribution overlaid on 3-D mountain terrain.

To increase the public's environmental awareness and to support decision and policy makers, useful findings from scientific experiments must be presented and disseminated in a practical fashion. For example, SenseWeb provides a Web-based front end called SensorMap[3] that presents real-time and historical environmental factors in an easy-to-understand visual interface. It overlays spatial visualizations (such as icons showing current air pollution at a location or images showing distribution of snowfalls) over a browsable geographic map, plays the visualizations of selected environmental datasets as a movie on top of a geographic map, and shows important trends in historic environmental data as well as useful summaries of real-time environmental data. (See Figure 3.) At present, such platforms support only a limited set of visualizations, and many challenges remain to be solved to support the more advanced visualizations required by diverse audiences.

WORLDWIDE ENVIRONMENTAL MONITORING

We have described the next-generation environmental monitoring system as isolated—focused on a particular region of interest such as a mountain range, ice field, or forest. This is how such environmental systems are starting to be deployed. However, we foresee far more extensive monitoring systems that can allow scientists to share data with one another and combine and correlate data from millions of

[2] www.swiss-experiment.ch/index.php/SensorScope:Home
[3] www.sensormap.org

sensors all over the world to gain an even better understanding of global environmental patterns.

Such a global-scale sensor deployment would introduce unprecedented benefits and challenges. As sensor datasets grow larger, traditional data management techniques (such as loading data into a SQL database and then querying it) will clearly prove inadequate. To avoid moving massive amounts of data around, computations will need to be distributed and pushed as close to data sources as possible [7]. To reduce the storage and communication footprint, datasets will have to be compressed without loss of fidelity. To support data analysis with reasonable latencies, computation should preferably be done over compressed data [9]. Scientific analysis will also most likely require additional metadata, such as sensor specifications, experiment setups, data provenance, and other contextual information. Data from heterogeneous sources will have to be integrated in a unified data management and exploration framework [10].

Obviously, computer science tools can enable this next-generation environmental science only if they are actually used by domain scientists. To expedite adoption by domain scientists, such tools must be intuitive, easy to use, and robust. Moreover, they cannot be "one-size-fits-all" tools for all domains; rather, they should be domain-specific custom tools—or at least custom variants of generic tools. Developing these tools will involve identifying the important problems that domain scientists are trying to answer, analyzing the design trade-offs, and focusing on important features. While such application engineering approaches are common for non-science applications, they tend not to be a priority in science applications. This must change.

CONCLUSION

The close collaboration between environmental science and computer science is providing a new and better way to conduct scientific research through high-resolution and high-fidelity data acquisition, simplified large-scale data management, powerful data modeling and mining, and effective data sharing and visualization. In this paper, we have outlined several challenges to realizing the vision of next-generation environmental science. Some significant progress has been made in this context—such as in the Swiss Experiment and SenseWeb, in which an advanced, integrated environmental data infrastructure is being used by a variety of large environmental research projects, for environmental education, and by individual scientists. Meanwhile, dramatic progress is being made in complementary fields such as basic sensor technology. Our expectation is that all of these advances in instrumenting the Earth will help us realize the dreams of next-generation environmental science—allowing scientists, government, and the public to better understand and live safely in their environment.

REFERENCES

[1] M. Bavay, M. Lehning, T. Jonas, and H. Löwe, "Simulations of future snow cover and discharge in Alpine headwater catchments," *Hydrol. Processes*, vol. 22, pp. 95–108, 2009, doi: 10.1002/hyp.7195.

[2] M. Lehning, H. Löwe, M. Ryser, and N. Raderschall, "Inhomogeneous precipitation distribution and snow transport in steep terrain," *Water Resour. Res.*, vol. 44, 2008, doi: 10.1029/2007WR006545.

[3] N. Raderschall, M. Lehning, and C. Schär, "Fine scale modelling of the boundary layer wind field over steep topography," *Water Resour. Res.*, vol. 44, 2008, doi: 10.1029/2007WR006544.

[4] N. Dawes, A. K. Kumar, S. Michel, K. Aberer, and M. Lehning, "Sensor Metadata Management and Its Application in Collaborative Environmental Research," presented at the 4th IEEE Int. Conf. e-Science, 2008.

[5] A. Kansal, S. Nath, J. Liu, and F. Zhao, "SenseWeb: An Infrastructure for Shared Sensing," *IEEE MultiMedia*, vol. 14, no. 4, pp. 8–13, Oct. 2007, doi: 10.1109/MMUL.2007.82.

[6] Y. Ahmad and S. Nath, "COLR-Tree: Communication Efficient Spatio-Temporal Index for a Sensor Data Web Portal," presented at the Int. Conf. Data Engineering, 2008, doi: 10.1.1.65.6941.

[7] A. Deshpande, S. Nath, P. B. Gibbons, and S. Seshan, "Cache-and-Query for Wide Area Sensor Databases," Proc. 22nd ACM SIGMOD Int. Conf. Management of Data Principles of Database Systems, 2003, doi: 10.1145/872757.872818.

[8] M. Lehning and C. Wilhelm, "Integral Risk Management and Physical Modelling for Mountainous Natural Hazards," in *Extreme Events in Nature and Society*, S. Albeverio, V. Jentsch, and H. Kantz, Eds. Springer, 2005.

[9] G. Reeves, J. Liu, S. Nath, and F. Zhao, "Managing Massive Time Series Streams with MultiScale Compressed Trickles," *Proc. 35th Int. Conf. Very Large Data Bases*, 2009.

[10] S. Nath, J. Liu, and F. Zhao, "Challenges in Building a Portal for Sensors World-Wide," presented at the First Workshop on World-Sensor-Web, 2006, doi: 10.1109/MPRV.2007.27.

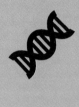

2. HEALTH AND WELLBEING

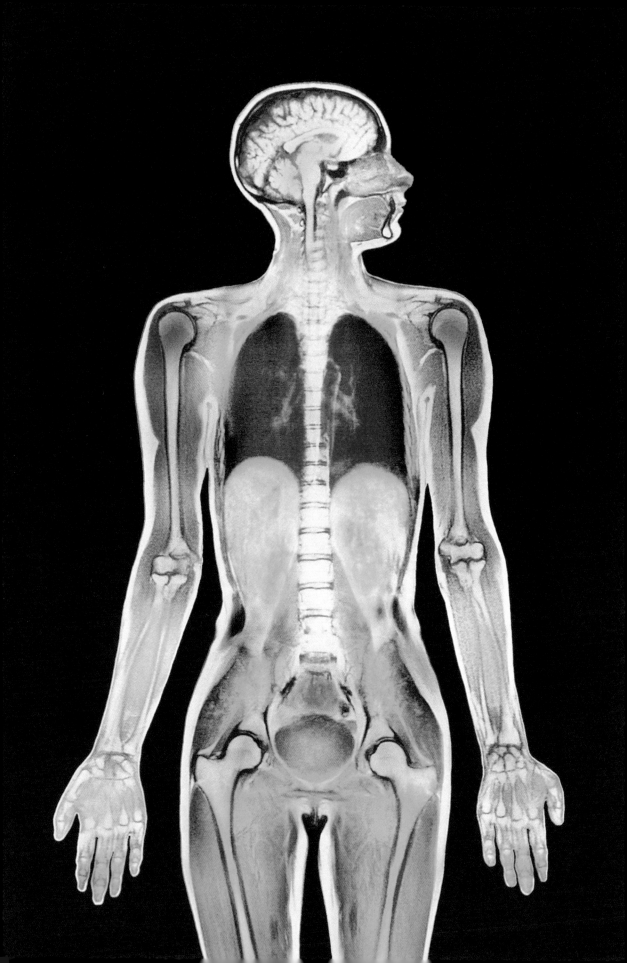

Introduction

SIMON MERCER | Microsoft Research

P ART 2 OF THIS BOOK EXPLORES the remarkable progress and challenges we are seeing in the most intimate and personal of our sciences, the one with the most immediate impact on all of us across the planet: the science of health and medicine.

The first article sets the scene. Gillam et al. describe the progress of medical science over human history and make a strong case for a convergence of technologies that will change the face of healthcare within our lifetime. The remaining articles shed light on the convergent strands that make up this larger picture, by focusing on particular medical science challenges and the technologies being developed to overcome them.

Any assertion that the coming healthcare revolution will be universal is credible only if we can demonstrate how it can cross the economic and social divides of the modern world. Robertson et al. show that a combination of globally pervasive cell phone technology and the computational technique of Bayesian networks can enable collection of computerized healthcare records in regions where medical care is sparse and can also provide automated, accurate diagnoses.

An understanding of the human brain is one of the grand challenges of medicine, and Lichtman et al. describe their approach to the generation of the vast datasets needed to understand this most complex of structures. Even imaging the human brain at the subcellular level, with its estimated 160 trillion synaptic connections, is a challenge that will test the bounds of data storage, and that is merely the first step in deducing function from form.

An approach to the next stage of understanding how we think is presented by Horvitz and Kristan, who describe techniques for recording sequences of neuronal activity and correlating them with behavior in the simplest of organisms. This work will lead to a new generation of software tools, bringing techniques of machine learning/artificial intelligence to generate new insights into medical data.

While the sets of data that make up a personal medical record are orders of magnitude smaller than those describing the architecture of the brain, current trends toward universal electronic healthcare records mean that a large proportion of the global population will soon have records of their health available in a digital form. This will constitute in aggregate a dataset of a size and complexity rivaling those of neuroscience. Here we find parallel challenges and opportunities. Buchan, Winn, and Bishop apply novel machine learning techniques to this vast body of healthcare data to automate the selection of therapies that have the most desirable outcome. Technologies such as these will be needed if we are to realize the world of the "Healthcare Singularity," in which the collective experience of human healthcare is used to inform clinical best practice at the speed of computation.

While the coming era of computerized health records promises more accessible and more detailed medical data, the usability of this information will require the adoption of standard forms of encoding so that inferences can be made across datasets. Cardelli and Priami look toward a future in which medical data can be overlaid onto executable models that encode the underlying logic of biological systems—to not only depict the behavior of an organism but also predict its future condition or reaction to a stimulus. In the case of neuroscience, such models may help us understand how we think; in the case of medical records, they may help us understand the mechanisms of disease and treatment. Although the computational modeling of biological phenomena is in its infancy, it provides perhaps the most intriguing insights into the emerging complementary and synergistic relationship between computational and living systems.

The Healthcare Singularity and the Age of Semantic Medicine

MICHAEL GILLAM
CRAIG FEIED
JONATHAN HANDLER
ELIZA MOODY
Microsoft

BEN SHNEIDERMAN
CATHERINE PLAISANT
University of Maryland

MARK SMITH
MedStar Health Institutes for Innovation

JOHN DICKASON
Private practice

N 1499, WHEN PORTUGUESE EXPLORER VASCO DA GAMA returned home after completing the first-ever sea voyage from Europe to India, he had less than half of his original crew with him—scurvy had claimed the lives of 100 of the 160 men. Throughout the Age of Discovery,[1] scurvy was the leading cause of death among sailors. Ship captains typically planned for the death of as many as half of their crew during long voyages. A dietary cause for scurvy was suspected, but no one had proved it. More than a century later, on a voyage from England to India in 1601, Captain James Lancaster placed the crew of one of his four ships on a regimen of three teaspoons of lemon juice a day. By the halfway point of the trip, almost 40% of the men (110 of 278) on three of the ships had died, while on the lemon-supplied ship, every man survived [1]. The British navy responded to this discovery by repeating the experiment—*146 years later.*

In 1747, a British navy physician named James Lind treated sailors suffering from scurvy using six randomized approaches and demonstrated that citrus reversed the symptoms. The British navy responded, 48 years later, by enacting new dietary guidelines requiring citrus, which virtually eradicated scurvy from the British fleet overnight. The British Board of Trade adopted similar dietary

[1] 15th to 17th centuries.

practices for the merchant fleet in 1865, *an additional 70 years later*. The total time from Lancaster's definitive demonstration of how to prevent scurvy to adoption across the British Empire was 264 years [2].

The translation of medical discovery to practice has thankfully improved substantially. But a 2003 report from the Institute of Medicine found that the lag between significant discovery and adoption into routine patient care still averages 17 years [3, 4]. This delayed translation of knowledge to clinical care has negative effects on both the cost and the quality of patient care. A nationwide review of 439 quality indicators found that only half of adults receive the care recommended by U.S. national standards [5].

THE IMPACT OF THE INFORMATION EXPLOSION IN MEDICINE

Despite the adoption rate of medical knowledge significantly improving, we face a new challenge due to the exponential increase in the rate of medical knowledge discovery. More than 18 million articles are currently catalogued in the biomedical literature, including over 800,000 added in 2008. The accession rate has doubled every 20 years, and the number of articles per year is expected to surpass 1 million in 2012, as shown in Figure 1.

Translating all of this emerging medical knowledge into practice is a staggering challenge. Five hundred years ago, Leonardo da Vinci could be a painter, engineer, musician, and scientist. One hundred years ago, it is said that a physician might have reasonably expected to know everything in the field of medicine.[2] Today, a typical primary care doctor must stay abreast of approximately 10,000 diseases and syndromes, 3,000 medications, and 1,100 laboratory tests [6]. Research librarians estimate that a physician in just one specialty, epidemiology, needs 21 hours of study per day just to stay current [7]. Faced with this flood of medical information, clinicians routinely fall behind, despite specialization and sub-specialization [8].

The sense of information overload in medicine has been present for surprisingly many years. An 1865 speech by Dr. Henry Noyes to the American Ophthalmologic Society is revealing. He said that "medical men strive manfully to keep up their knowledge of how the world of medicine moves on; but too often they are the first to accuse themselves of being unable to meet the duties of their daily calling…." He went on to say, "The preparatory work in the study of medicine is so great, if adequately done, that but few can spare time for its thorough performance…." [9]

---

[2] www.medinfo.cam.ac.uk/miu/papers/Hanka/THIM/default.htm

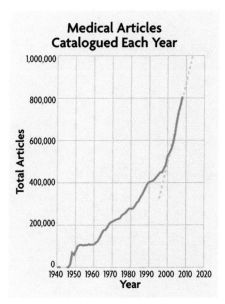

Medical Articles Catalogued Each Year

FIGURE 1.

The number of biomedical articles catalogued each year is increasing precipitously and is expected to surpass 1 million in 2012.

COULD KNOWLEDGE ADOPTION IN HEALTH-CARE BECOME NEARLY INSTANTANEOUS?

The speed at which definitive medical discoveries have broadly reached medical practice over the last two millennia has progressively increased, as shown in Figure 2 on the next page.

Focusing on the last 150 years, in which the effects of industrialization and the information explosion have been most acute, the trajectory flattens slightly but remains largely linear, as the figure shows. (An asymptotic fit yields an r^2 of 0.73, whereas the linear fit is 0.83.)

Given that even the speed of light is finite, this trend will inevitably be asymptotic to the horizontal axis. Yet, if the linearity can be sufficiently maintained for a while, the next 20 years could emerge as a special time for healthcare *as the translation from medical knowledge discovery to widespread medical practice becomes nearly instantaneous.*

The proximity of this trajectory to the axis occurs around the year 2025. In response to the dramatic computational progress observed with Moore's Law and the growth in parallel and distributed computing architectures, Ray Kurzweil, in *The Singularity Is Near*, predicts that 2045 will be the year of the Singularity, when computers meet or exceed human computational ability and when their ability to recursively improve themselves can lead to an "intelligence explosion" that ultimately affects all aspects of human culture and technology [10]. Mathematics defines a "singularity" as a point at which an object changes its nature so as to attain properties that are no longer the expected norms for that class of object. Today, the dissemination path for medical information is complex and multi-faceted, involving commercials, lectures, brochures, colleagues, and journals. In a world with nearly instantaneous knowledge translation, dissemination paths would become almost entirely digital and direct.

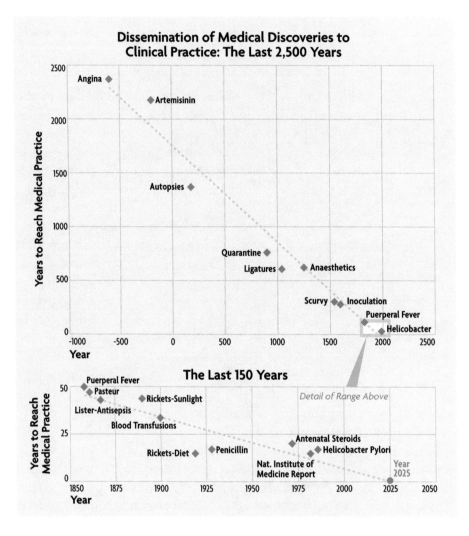

FIGURE 2.

While it took 2,300 years after the first report of angina for the condition to be commonly taught in medical curricula, modern discoveries are being disseminated at an increasingly rapid pace. Focusing on the last 150 years, the trend still appears to be linear, approaching the axis around 2025.

While the ideas around a technological singularity remain controversial,[3] the authors refer to this threshold moment, when medical knowledge becomes "liquid" and its flow from research to practice ("bench to bedside") becomes frictionless and immediate, as the "Healthcare Singularity."

THE PROMISES OF A POST–HEALTHCARE SINGULARITY WORLD

Rofecoxib (Vioxx) was approved as safe and effective by the U.S. Food and Drug Administration (FDA) on May 20, 1999. On September 30, 2004, Merck withdrew it from the market because of concerns about the drug's potential cardiovascular side effects. The FDA estimates that in the 5 years that the drug was on the market, rofecoxib contributed to more than 27,000 heart attacks or sudden cardiac deaths and as many as 140,000 cases of heart disease [11]. Rofecoxib was one of the most widely used medications ever withdrawn; over 80 million people had taken the drug, which was generating US$2.5 billion a year in sales.[4]

Today, it is reasonable to expect that after an FDA announcement of a drug's withdrawal from the market, patients will be informed and clinicians will immediately prescribe alternatives. But current channels of dissemination delay that response. In a post–Healthcare Singularity world, that expectation will be met. To enable instantaneous translation, journal articles will consist of not only words, but also bits. Text will commingle with code, and articles will be considered complete only if they include algorithms.

With this knowledge automation, every new medication will flow through a cascade of post-market studies that are independently created and studied by leading academics across the oceans (effectively "crowdsourcing" quality assurance). Suspicious observations will be flagged in real time, and when certainty is reached, unsafe medications will disappear from clinical prescription systems in a rippling wave across enterprises and clinics. The biomedical information explosion will at last be contained and harnessed.

Other scenarios of knowledge dissemination will be frictionless as well: medical residents can abandon the handbooks they have traditionally carried that list drugs of choice for diseases, opting instead for clinical systems that personalize healthcare and geographically regionalize treatments based on drug sensitivities that are drawn in real time from the local hospital microbiology lab and correlated with the patient's genomic profile.

[3] http://en.wikipedia.org/wiki/Technological_singularity
[4] http://en.wikipedia.org/wiki/Rofecoxib

Knowledge discovery will also be enhanced. Practitioners will have access to high-performance, highly accurate databases of patient records to promote preventive medical care, discover successful treatment patterns [12, 13], and reduce medical errors. Clinicians will be able to generate cause-effect hypotheses, run virtual clinical trials to deliver personalized treatment plans, and simulate interventions that can prevent pandemics.

Looking farther ahead, the instantaneous flow of knowledge from research centers to the front lines of clinical care will speed the treatment and prevention of newly emerging diseases. The moment that research labs have identified the epitopes to target for a new disease outbreak, protein/DNA/RNA/lipid synthesizers placed in every big hospital around the world will receive instructions, remotely transmitted from a central authority, directing the on-site synthesis of vaccines or even directed antibody therapies for rapid administration to patients.

PROGRESS TOWARD THE HEALTHCARE SINGULARITY

Companies such as Microsoft and Google are building new technologies to enable data and knowledge liquidity. Microsoft HealthVault and Google Health are Internet based, secure, and private "consumer data clouds" into which clinical patient data can be pushed from devices and other information systems. Importantly, once the data are in these "patient clouds," they are owned by the patient. Patients themselves determine what data can be redistributed and to whom the data may be released.

A February 2009 study by KLAS reviewed a new class of emerging data aggregation solutions for healthcare. These enterprise data aggregation solutions ("enterprise data clouds") unify data from hundreds or thousands of disparate systems (such as MEDSEEK, Carefx, dbMotion, Medicity, and Microsoft Amalga).[5] These platforms are beginning to serve as conduits for data to fill patient data clouds. A recent example is a link between New York-Presbyterian's hospital-based Amalga aggregation system and its patients' HealthVault service.[6] Through these links, data can flow almost instantaneously from hospitals to patients.

The emergence of consumer data clouds creates new paths by which new medical knowledge can reach patients directly. On April 21, 2009, Mayo Clinic announced the launch of the Mayo Clinic Health Advisory, a privacy- and security-enhanced

---

[5] www.klasresearch.com/Klas/Site/News/PressReleases/2009/Aggregation.aspx
[6] http://chilmarkresearch.com/2009/04/06/healthvault-ny-presbyterian-closing-the-loop-on-care

online application that offers individualized health guidance and recommendations built with the clinical expertise of Mayo Clinic and using secure and private patient health data from Microsoft HealthVault.[7] Importantly, new medical knowledge and recommendations can be computationally instantiated into the advisory and applied virtually instantaneously to patients worldwide.

New technology is bridging research labs and clinical practice. On April 28, 2009, Microsoft announced the release of Amalga Life Sciences, an extension to the data-aggregation class of products for use by scientists and researchers. Through this release, Microsoft is offering scalable "data aggregation and liquidity" solutions that link three audiences: patients, providers, and researchers. Companies such as Microsoft are building the "pipeline" to allow data and knowledge to flow through a *semantically interoperable* network of patients, providers, and researchers. These types of connectivity efforts hold the promise of effectively instantaneous dissemination of medical knowledge throughout the healthcare system. The Healthcare Singularity could be the gateway event to a new Age of Semantic Medicine.

Instantaneous knowledge translation in medicine is not only immensely important, highly desirable, valuable, and achievable in our lifetimes, but perhaps even inevitable.

REFERENCES

[1] F. Mosteller, "Innovation and evaluation," *Science,* vol. 211, pp. 881–886, 1981, doi: 10.1126/ science.6781066.
[2] J. Lind, *A Treatise of the Scurvy* (1753). Edinburgh: University Press, reprinted 1953.
[3] E. A. Balas, "Information Systems Can Prevent Errors and Improve Quality," *J. Am. Med. Inform. Assoc.,* vol. 8, no. 4, pp. 398–399, 2001, PMID: 11418547.
[4] A. C. Greiner and Elisa Knebel, Eds., *Health Professions Education: A Bridge to Quality.* Washington, D.C.: National Academies Press, 2003.
[5] E. A. McGlynn, S. M. Asch, J. Adams, J. Keesey, J. Hicks, A. DeCristofaro, et al., "The quality of health care delivered to adults in the United States," *N. Engl. J. Med.,* vol. 348, pp. 2635–2645, 2003, PMID: 12826639.
[6] T. H. Davenport and J. Glaser, "Just-in-time delivery comes to knowledge management," *Harv. Bus. Rev.,* vol. 80, no. 7, pp. 107–111, 126, July 2002, doi: 10.1225/R0207H.
[7] B. S. Alper, J. A. Hand, S. G. Elliott, S. Kinkade, M. J. Hauan, D. K. Onion, and B. M. Sklar, "How much effort is needed to keep up with the literature relevant for primary care?" *J. Med. Libr. Assoc.,* vol. 92, no. 4, pp. 429–437, Oct. 2004.
[8] C. Lenfant, "Clinical Research to Clinical Practice — Lost in Translation?" *N. Engl. J. Med.,* vol. 349, pp. 868–874, 2003, PMID: 12944573.
[9] H. D. Noyes, *Specialties in Medicine,* June 1865.

[7] www.microsoft.com/presspass/press/2009/apr09/04-21MSMayoConsumerSolutionPR.mspx

[10] R. Kurzweil, *The Singularity Is Near: When Humans Transcend Biology.* New York: Penguin Group, 2005, p. 136.

[11] D. J. Graham, D. Campen, R. Hui, M. Spence, C. Cheetham, G. Levy, S. Shoor, and W. A. Ray, "Risk of acute myocardial infarction and sudden cardiac death in patients treated with cyclo-oxygenase 2 selective and non-selective non-steroidal anti-inflammatory drugs: nested case-control study," *Lancet,* vol. 365, no. 9458, pp. 475–481, Feb. 5–11, 2005.

[12] C. Plaisant, S. Lam, B. Shneiderman, M. S. Smith, D. Roseman, G. Marchand, M. Gillam, C. Feied, J. Handler, and H. Rappaport, "Searching Electronic Health Records for temporal patterns in patient histories: A case study with Microsoft Amalga," *Proc. Am. Med. Inform. Assoc.,* Washington, D.C., Nov. 2008.

[13] T. Wang, C. Plaisant, A. Quinn, R. Stanchak, B. Shneiderman, and S. Murphy, "Aligning temporal data by sentinel events: Discovering patterns in electronic health records," *Proc. ACM CHI2008 Human Factors in Computing Systems Conference,* ACM, New York, Apr. 2008, pp. 457–466, doi: 10.1145/1357054.1357129.

Healthcare Delivery in Developing Countries: Challenges and Potential Solutions

JOEL ROBERTSON
DEL DEHART
Robertson Research
Institute

KRISTIN TOLLE
DAVID HECKERMAN
Microsoft Research

BRINGING INTELLIGENT HEALTHCARE INFORMATICS to bear on the dual problems of reducing healthcare costs and improving quality and outcomes is a challenge even in countries with a reasonably developed technology infrastructure. Much of medical knowledge and information remains in paper form, and even where it is digitized, it often resides in disparate datasets and repositories and in diverse formats. Data sharing is uncommon and frequently hampered by the lack of foolproof de-identification for patient privacy. All of these issues impede opportunities for data mining and analysis that would enable better predictive and preventive medicine.

Developing countries face these same issues, along with the compounding effects of economic and geopolitical constraints, transportation and geographic barriers, a much more limited clinical workforce, and infrastructural challenges to delivery. Simple, high-impact deliverable interventions such as universal childhood immunization and maternal childcare are hampered by poor monitoring and reporting systems. A recent *Lancet* article by Christopher Murray's group concluded that "immunization coverage has improved more gradually and not to the level suggested by countries' official reports of WHO and UNICEF estimates. There is an urgent need for independent and contestable monitoring of health indicators in an era of global initiatives that are target-

The NxOpinion health platform being used by Indian health extension workers.

oriented and disburse funds based on performance." [1]

Additionally, the most recent report on the United Nations Millennium Development Goals notes that "pneumonia kills more children than any other disease, yet in developing countries, the proportion of children under five with suspected pneumonia who are taken to appropriate health-care providers remains low." [2] Providing reliable data gathering and diagnostic decision support at the point of need by the best-trained individual available for care is the goal of public health efforts, but tools to accomplish this have been expensive, unsupportable, and inaccessible.

Below, we elaborate on the challenges facing healthcare delivery in developing countries and describe computer- and cell phone–based technology we have created to help address these challenges. At the core of this technology is the NxOpinion Knowledge Manager[1] (NxKM), which has been under development at the Robertson Research Institute since 2002. This health platform includes a medical knowledge base assembled from the expertise of a large team of experts in the U.S. and developing countries, a diagnostic engine based on Bayesian networks, and cell phones for end-user interaction.

SCALE UP, SCALE OUT, AND SCALE IN

One of the biggest barriers to deployment of a decision support or electronic health record system is the ability to scale. The term "scale up" refers to a system's ability to support a large user base—typically hundreds of thousands or millions. Most systems are evaluated within a narrower scope of users. "Scale out" refers to a system's ability to work in multiple countries and regions as well as the ability to work across disease types. Many systems work only for one particular disease and are not easily regionalized—for example, for local languages, regulations, and processes. "Scale in" refers to the ability of a system to capture and benchmark against a single

[1] www.nxopinion.com/product/knowledgemng

individual. Most systems assume a generic patient and fail to capture unique characteristics that can be effective in individualized treatment.

With respect to scaling up, NxKM has been tested in India, Congo, Dominican Republic, Ghana, and Iraq. It has also been tested in an under-served inner-city community in the United States. In consultation with experts in database scaling, the architecture has been designed to combine multiple individual databases with a central de-identified database, thus allowing, in principle, unlimited scaling options.

As for scaling out to work across many disease types and scaling in to provide accurate individual diagnoses, the amount of knowledge required is huge. For example, INTERNIST-1, an expert system for diagnosis in internal medicine, contains approximately 250,000 relationships among roughly 600 diseases and 4,000 findings [3]. Building on the earlier work of one of us (Heckerman), who developed efficient methods for assessing and representing expert medical knowledge via a Bayesian network [4], we have brought together medical literature, textbook information, and expert panel recommendations to construct a growing knowledge base for NxKM, currently including over 1,000 diseases and over 6,000 discrete findings. The system also scales in by allowing very fine-grained data capture. Each finding within an individual health record or diagnostic case can be tracked and monitored. This level of granularity allows for tremendous flexibility in determining factors relating to outcome and diagnostic accuracy.

With regard to scaling out across a region, a challenge common to developing countries is the exceptionally diverse and region-specific nature of medical conditions. For example, a disease that is common in one country or region might be rare in another. Whereas rule-based expert systems must be completely reengineered in each region, the modular nature of the NxKM knowledge base, which is based on probabilistic similarity networks [4], allows for rapid customization to each region. The current incarnation of NxKM uses region-specific prevalence from expert estimates. It can also update prevalence in each region as it is used in the field. NxKM also incorporates a modular system that facilitates customization to terms, treatments, and language specific to each region. When region-specific information is unknown or unavailable, a default module is used until such data can be collected or identified.

DIAGNOSTIC ACCURACY AND EFFICIENCY

Studies indicate that even highly trained physicians overestimate their diagnostic accuracy. The Institute of Medicine recently estimated that 44,000 to 98,000 preventable deaths occur each year due to medical error, many due to misdiagnosis [5]. In developing countries, the combined challenges of misdiagnoses and missing data not only reduce the quality of medical care for individuals but lead to missed outbreak recognition and flawed population health assessment and planning.

Again, building on the diagnostic methodology from probabilistic similarity networks [4], NxKM employs a Bayesian reasoning engine that yields accurate diagnoses. An important component of the system that leads to improved accuracy is the ability to ask the user additional questions that are likely to narrow the range of possible diagnoses. NxKM has the ability to ask the user for additional findings based on value-of-information computations (such as a cost function) [4]. Also important for clinical use is the ability to identify the confidence in the diagnosis (i.e., the probability of the most likely diagnosis). This determination is especially useful for less-expert users of the system, which is important for improving and supervising the care delivered by health extension workers (HEWs) in developing regions where deep medical knowledge is rare.

GETTING HEALTHCARE TO WHERE IT IS NEEDED: THE LAST MILE

Another key challenge is getting diagnostics to where they are most needed. Because of their prevalence in developing countries, cell phones are a natural choice for a delivery vehicle. Indeed, it is believed that, in many such areas, access to cell phones is better than access to clean water. For example, according to the market database Wireless Intelligence,[2] 80 percent of the world's population was within range of a cellular network in 2008. And figures from the International Telecommunication Union[3] show that by the end of 2006, 68 percent of the world's mobile subscriptions were in developing countries. More recent data from the International Telecommunications Union shows that between 2002 and 2007, cellular subscription was the most rapid growth area for telecommunication in the world, and that the per capita increase was greatest in the developing world.[4]

Consequently, we have developed a system wherein cell phones are used to access a centrally placed NxKM knowledge base and diagnostic engine implemented on a PC. We are now testing the use of this system with HEWs in rural India. In addition to providing recommendations for medical care to the HEWs, the phone/

[2] www.wirelessintelligence.com
[3] www.itu.int
[4] www.itu.int/ITU-D/ict/papers/2009/7.1%20teltscher_IDI%20India%202009.pdf

central-PC solution can be used to create portable personal health records. One of our partner organizations, School Health Annual Report Programme (SHARP), will use it to screen more than 10 million Indian schoolchildren in 2009, creating a unique virtual personal health record for each child.

Another advantage of this approach is that the data collected by this system can be used to improve the NxKM knowledge base. For example, as mentioned above, information about region-specific disease prevalence is important for accurate medical diagnosis. Especially important is time-critical information about the outbreak of a disease in a particular location. As the clinical application is used, validated disease cases, including those corresponding to a new outbreak, are immediately available to NxKM. In addition, individual diagnoses can be monitored centrally. If the uploaded findings of an individual patient are found to yield a low-confidence diagnosis, the patient can be identified for follow-up.

THE USER INTERFACE

A challenge with cellular technology is the highly constrained user interface and the difficulty of entering data using a relatively small screen and keypad. Our system simplifies the process in a number of ways. First, findings that are common for a single location (e.g., facts about a given village) are prepopulated into the system. Also, as mentioned above, the system is capable of generating questions—specifically, simple multiple-choice questions—after only basic information such as the chief complaint has been entered. In addition, questions can be tailored to the organization, location, or skill level of the HEW user.

It is also important that the user interface be independent of the specific device hardware because users often switch between phones of different designs. Our interface application sits on top of a middle-layer platform that we have implemented for multiple devices.

In addition to simple input, the interface allows easy access to important bits of information. For example, it provides a daily summary of patients needing care, including their diagnosis, village location, and previous caregivers.

DATA-SHARING SOLUTIONS

Even beyond traditional legacy data silos (such as EPIC and CERNER) [5], barriers to sharing critical public health data still exist—including concerns about privacy and sovereignty. Data availability can also be limited regionally (e.g., in India and South Africa), by organizations (e.g., the World Health Organization,

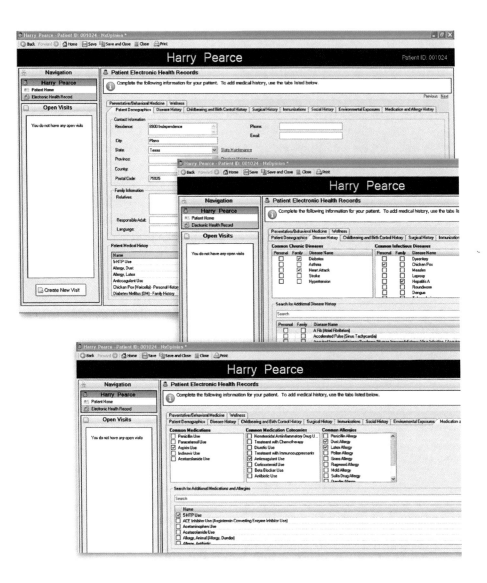

NxOpinion's innovative approach, which shows data when you want it, how you want it, and where you want it, using artificial intelligence.

World Vision, or pharmaceutical companies), or by providers (e.g., insurance companies and medical provider groups). Significant public health value resides in each of these datasets, and efforts should be made to overcome the barriers to gathering data into shared, de-identified global databases. Such public datasets, while useful on their own, also add significant value to proprietary datasets, providing valuable generic context to proprietary information.

NxKM imports, manages, and exports data via *publish sets*. These processes allow various interest groups (governments, public health organizations, primary care providers, small hospitals, laboratory and specialty services, and insurance providers) to share the same interactive de-identified (privacy-preserving) global database while maintaining control of proprietary and protected data.

LOOKING FORWARD

Several challenges remain. While better educated HEWs are able to use these data collection and diagnostic decision support tools readily, other HEWs, such as Accredited Social Health Activists (ASHAs) and other front-line village workers, are often illiterate or speak only a local dialect. We are exploring two potential solutions—one that uses voice recognition technology and another that allows a user to answer multiple-choice questions via the cell phone's numeric keypad. Voice recognition technology provides added flexibility in input, but—at least so far—it requires the voice recognizer to be trained by each user.

Another challenge is unique and reproducible patient identification—verification that the subject receiving treatment is actually the correct patient—when there is no standard identification system for most under-served populations. Voice recognition combined with face recognition and newer methods of biometrics, along with a corroborating GPS location, can help ensure that the patient who needs the care is the one actually receiving treatment.

Another barrier is data integrity. For example, most rural individuals will report diagnoses that have not been substantiated by qualified medical personnel and could be erroneous. We have attempted to mitigate this issue by using an inference engine that allows for down-weighting of unsubstantiated evidence.

Deploying systems that work anywhere in the world can lead to the creation of a massive amount of patient information. Storing, reconciling, and then accessing that information in the field, all while maintaining appropriate privacy and security, are exceptionally challenging when patient numbers are in the millions (instead of tens of thousands, as with most current electronic health record systems). Further, feeding verified data on this scale back into the system to improve its predictive capability while maintaining the ability to analyze and retrieve specific segments (data mine) remains difficult.

A final, and perhaps the greatest, obstacle is that of cooperation. If organizations, governments, and companies are willing to share a de-identified global database while protecting and owning their own database, medical science and healthcare can benefit tremendously. A unified database that allows integration across many monitoring and evaluation systems and databases should help in quickly and efficiently identifying drug resistance or outbreaks of disease and in monitoring the effectiveness of treatments and healthcare interventions. The global database should support data queries that guard against the identification of individuals and yet provide sufficient information for statistical analyses and validation. Such technology is beginning to emerge (e.g., [6]), but the daunting challenge of finding a system of rewards that encourages such cooperation remains.

SUMMARY

We have developed and are beginning to deploy a system for the acquisition, analysis, and transmission of medical knowledge and data in developing countries. The system includes a centralized component based on PC technology that houses medical knowledge and data and has real-time diagnostic capabilities, complemented by a cell phone–based interface for medical workers in the field. We believe that such a system will lead to improved medical care in developing countries through improved diagnoses, the collection of more accurate and timely data across more individuals, and the improved dissemination of accurate and timely medical knowledge and information.

When we stop and think about how a world of connected personal health records can be used to improve medicine, we can see that the potential impact is staggering. By knowing virtually every individual who exists, the diseases affecting that person, and where he or she is located; by improving data integrity; and by collecting the data in a central location, we can revolutionize medicine and perhaps even eradicate more diseases. This global system can monitor the effects of various humanitarian efforts and thereby justify and tailor efforts, medications, and resources to specific areas. It is our hope that a system that can offer high-quality diagnoses as well as collect and rapidly disseminate valid data will save millions of lives. Alerts and responses can become virtually instantaneous and can thus lead to the identification of drug resistance, outbreaks, and effective treatments in a fraction of the time it takes now. The potential for empowering caregivers in developing countries though a global diagnostic and database system is enormous.

REFERENCES

[1] S. S. Lim, D. B. Stein, A. Charrow, and C. J. L. Murray, "Tracking progress towards universal childhood immunisation and the impact of global initiatives: a systematic analysis of three-dose diphtheria, tetanus, and pertussis immunisation coverage," *Lancet,* vol. 372, pp. 2031–2046, 2008, doi: 10.1016/S0140-6736(08)61869-3.

[2] *The Millennium Development Goals Report.* United Nations, 2008.

[3] R. A. Miller, M. A. McNeil, S. M. Challinor, F. E. Masarie, Jr., and J. D. Myers, "The Internist-1/ Quick Medical Reference Project—Status Report," *West. J. Med.* vol. 145, pp. 816–822, 1986.

[4] D. Heckerman. *Probabilistic Similarity Networks.* Cambridge, MA: MIT Press, 1991.

[5] L. Kohn, J. Corrigan, and M. Donaldson, Eds. *To Err Is Human: Building a Safer Health System.* Washington, D.C.: National Academies Press, 2000.

[6] C. Dwork and K. Nissim, "Privacy-Preserving Datamining on Vertically Partitioned Databases," *Proc. CRYPTO,* 2004, doi: 10.1.1.86.8559.

Discovering the Wiring Diagram of the Brain

JEFF W. LICHTMAN
R. CLAY REID
HANSPETER PFISTER
Harvard University

MICHAEL F. COHEN
Microsoft Research

T HE BRAIN, THE SEAT OF OUR COGNITIVE ABILITIES, is perhaps the most complex puzzle in all of biology. Every second in the human brain, billions of cortical nerve cells transmit billions of messages and perform extraordinarily complex computations. How the brain works—how its function follows from its structure—remains a mystery.

The brain's vast numbers of nerve cells are interconnected at synapses in circuits of unimaginable complexity. It is largely assumed that the specificity of these interconnections underlies our ability to perceive and classify objects, our behaviors both learned (such as playing the piano) and intrinsic (such as walking), and our memories—not to mention controlling lower-level functions such as maintaining posture and even breathing. At the highest level, our emotions, our sense of self, our very consciousness are entirely the result of activities in the nervous system.

At a macro level, human brains have been mapped into regions that can be roughly associated with specific types of activities. However, even this building-block approach is fraught with complexity because often many parts of the brain participate in completing a task. This complexity arises especially because most behaviors begin with sensory input and are followed by analysis, decision making, and finally a motor output or action.

At the microscopic level, the brain comprises billions of neurons, each connected to other neurons by up to several thousand synaptic connections. Although the existence of these synaptic circuits has been appreciated for over a century, we have no detailed circuit diagrams of the brains of humans or any other mammals. Indeed, neural circuit mapping has been attempted only once, and that was two decades ago on a small worm with only 300 nerve cells. The central stumbling block is the enormous technical difficulty associated with such mapping. Recent technological breakthroughs in imaging, computer science, and molecular biology, however, allow a reconsideration of this problem. But even if we had a wiring diagram, we would need to know what messages the neurons in the circuit are passing—not unlike listening to the signals on a computer chip. This represents the second impediment to understanding: traditional physiological methods let us listen to only a tiny fraction of the nerves in the circuit.

To get a sense of the scale of the problem, consider the cerebral cortex of the human brain, which contains more than 160 trillion synaptic connections. These connections originate from billions of neurons. Each neuron receives synaptic connections from hundreds or even thousands of different neurons, and each sends information via synapses to a similar number of target neurons. This enormous fan-in and fan-out can occur because each neuron is geometrically complicated, possessing many receptive processes (dendrites) and one highly branched outflow process (an axon) that can extend over relatively long distances.

One might hope to be able to reverse engineer the circuits in the brain. In other words, if we could only tease apart the individual neurons and see which one is connected to which and with what strength, we might at least begin to have the tools to decode the functioning of a particular circuit. The staggering numbers and complex cellular shapes are not the only daunting aspects of the problem. The circuits that connect nerve cells are nanoscopic in scale. The density of synapses in the cerebral cortex is approximately 300 million per cubic millimeter.

Functional magnetic resonance imaging (fMRI) has provided glimpses into the macroscopic 3-D workings of the brain. However, the finest resolution of fMRI is approximately 1 cubic millimeter per voxel—the same cubic millimeter that can contain 300 million synapses. Thus there is a huge amount of circuitry in even the most finely resolved functional images of the human brain. Moreover, the size of these synapses falls below the diffraction-limited resolution of traditional optical imaging technologies.

Circuit mapping could potentially be amenable to analysis based on color coding of neuronal processes [1] and/or the use of techniques that break through the diffraction limit [2]. Presently, the gold standard for analyzing synaptic connections is to use electron microscopy (EM), whose nanometer (nm) resolution is more than sufficient to ascertain the finest details of neural connections. But to map circuits, one must overcome a technical hurdle: EM typically images very thin sections (tens of nanometers in thickness), so reconstructing a volume requires a "serial reconstruction" whereby the image information from contiguous slices of the same volume is recomposed into a volumetric dataset. There are several ways to generate such volumetric data (see, for example, [3-5]), but all of these have the potential to generate astonishingly large digital image data libraries, as described next.

SOME NUMBERS

If one were to reconstruct by EM all the synaptic circuitry in 1 cubic mm of brain (roughly what might fit on the head of a pin), one would need a set of serial images spanning a millimeter in depth. Unambiguously resolving all the axonal and dendritic branches would require sectioning at probably no more than 30 nm. Thus the 1 mm depth would require 33,000 images. Each image should have at least 10 nm lateral resolution to discern all the vesicles (the source of the neurotransmitters) and synapse types. A square-millimeter image at 5 nm resolution is an image that has ~4 x10^{10} pixels, or 10 to 20 gigapixels. So the image data in 1 cubic mm will be in the range of 1 petabyte (2^{50} ~ 1,000,000,000,000,000 bytes). The human brain contains nearly 1 million cubic mm of neural tissue.

SOME SUCCESSES TO DATE

Given this daunting task, one is tempted to give up and find a simpler problem. However, new technologies and techniques provide glimmers of hope. We are pursuing these with the ultimate goal of creating a "connectome"—a complete circuit diagram of the brain. This goal will require intensive and large-scale collaborations among biologists, engineers, and computer scientists.

Three years ago, the Reid and Lichtman labs began working on ways to automate and accelerate large-scale serial-section EM. Focusing specifically on large cortical volumes at high resolution, the Reid group has concentrated on very high throughput as well as highly automated processes. So far, their work has been published only in abstract form [3], but they are confident about soon having the first 10 terabytes of volumetric data on fine-scale brain anatomy. Physiological experiments can now show the function of virtually every neuron in a 300 μm cube. The new EM data has the resolution to show virtually every axon, dendrite, and synapse—the physical connections that underlie neuronal function.

The problem of separating and tracking the individual neurons within the volume remains. However, some successes have already been achieved using exotic means. Lichtman's lab found a way to express various combinations of red, green, and blue fluorescent proteins in genetically engineered mice. These random combinations presently provide about 90 colors or combinations of colors [1]. With this approach, it is possible to track individual neurons as they branch to their eventual synaptic connections to other neurons or to the end-organs in muscle. The multi-color labeled nerves (dubbed "brainbow"), shown in Figure 1, are reminiscent of the rainbow cables in computers and serve the same purpose: to disambiguate wires traveling over long distances.

Because these colored labels are present in the living mouse, it is possible to track synaptic wiring changes by observing the same sites multiple times over minutes, days, or even months.

Reid's lab has been able to stain neurons of rat and cat visual cortices such that they "light up" when activated. By stimulating the cat with lines of different orientations, they have literally been able to see which neurons are firing, depending on the specific visual stimulus. By comparing the organization of the rat's visual cortex to that of the cat, they have found that while a rat's neurons appear to be randomly organized based on the orientation of the visual stimulus, a cat's neurons exhibit remarkable structure. (See Figure 2.)

Achieving the finest resolution using EM requires imaging very thin slices of neural tissue. One method begins with a block of tissue; after each imaging pass, a

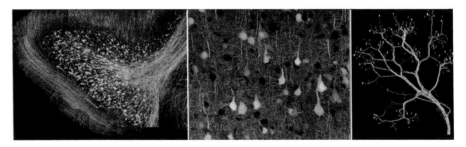

FIGURE 1.
Brainbow images showing individual neurons fluorescing in different colors. By tracking the neurons through stacks of slices, we can follow each neuron's complex branching structure to create the treelike structures in the image on the right.

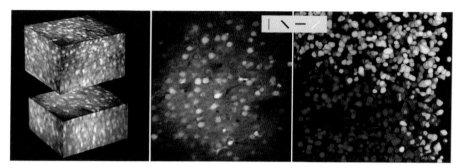

FIGURE 2.

*Neurons in a visual cortex stained in vivo with a calcium-sensitive dye. Left: A 3-D reconstruction
of thousands of neurons in a rat visual cortex, obtained from a stack of images (300 μm on a side).
The neurons are color coded according to the orientation of the visual stimulus that most excited
them. Center: A 2-D image of the plane of section from the left panel. Neurons that responded to
different stimulus orientations (different colors) are arranged seemingly randomly in the cortex.
Inset: Color coding of stimulus orientations. Right: By comparison, the cat visual cortex is
extremely ordered. Neurons that responded preferentially to different stimulus orientations are
segregated with extraordinary precision. This image represents a complete 3-D functional map
of over 1,000 neurons in a 300x300x200 μm volume in the visual cortex [6, 7].*

thin slice is removed (and destroyed) from the block, and then the process is repeated. Researchers in the Lichtman group at Harvard have developed a new device—a
sort of high-tech lathe that they are calling an Automatic Tape-Collecting Lathe
Ultramicrotome (ATLUM)—that can allow efficient nanoscale imaging over large
tissue volumes. (See Figure 3 on the next page.)

The ATLUM [3] automatically sections an embedded block of brain tissue into
thousands of ultrathin sections and collects these on a long carbon-coated tape for
later staining and imaging in a scanning electron microscope (SEM). Because the
process is fully automated, volumes as large as tens of cubic millimeters—large
enough to span entire multi-region neuronal circuits—can be quickly and reliably
reduced to a tape of ultrathin sections. SEM images of these ATLUM-collected sections can attain lateral resolutions of 5 nm or better—sufficient to image individual
synaptic vesicles and to identify and trace all circuit connectivity.

The thin slices are images of one small region at a time. Once a series of individual images is obtained, these images must be stitched together into very large images

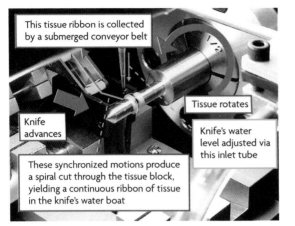

This tissue ribbon is collected by a submerged conveyor belt

Tissue rotates

Knife advances

Knife's water level adjusted via this inlet tube

These synchronized motions produce a spiral cut through the tissue block, yielding a continuous ribbon of tissue in the knife's water boat

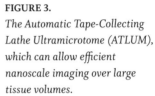

FIGURE 3.

The Automatic Tape-Collecting Lathe Ultramicrotome (ATLUM), which can allow efficient nanoscale imaging over large tissue volumes.

and possibly stacked into volumes. At Microsoft Research, work has proceeded to stitch together and then interactively view images containing billions of pixels.[1] Once these gigapixel-size images are organized into a hierarchical pyramid, the HD View application can stream requested imagery over the Web for viewing.[2] This allows exploration of both large-scale and very fine-scale features. Figure 4 shows a walkthrough of the result.

Once the images are captured and stitched, multiple slices of a sample must be stacked to assemble them into a coherent volume. Perhaps the most difficult task at that point is extracting the individual strands of neurons. Work is under way at Harvard to provide interactive tools to aid in outlining individual "processes" and then tracking them slice to slice to pull out each dendritic and axonal fiber [8, 9]. (See Figure 5.) Synaptic interfaces are perhaps even harder to find automatically; however, advances in both user interfaces and computer vision give hope that the whole process can be made tractable.

Decoding the complete connectome of the human brain is one of the great challenges of the 21st century. Advances at both the biological level and technical level are certain to lead to new successes and discoveries, and they will hopefully help answer fundamental questions about how our brain performs the miracle of thought.

[1] http://research.microsoft.com/en-us/um/redmond/groups/ivm/ICE
[2] http://research.microsoft.com/en-us/um/redmond/groups/ivm/HDView

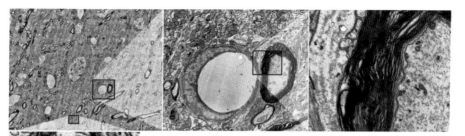

FIGURE 4.

HD View allows interactive exploration of this 2.5-gigapixel image. Left: A slice of neural tissue. The large gray feature in the center is a nucleus of a neuron. Center: A close-up of a capillary and myelinated axon. Right: Close-up myelin layers encircling the cross-section of an axon. Bottom: A zoomed-in view showing tiny vesicles surrounding a synaptic connection between very fine structures.

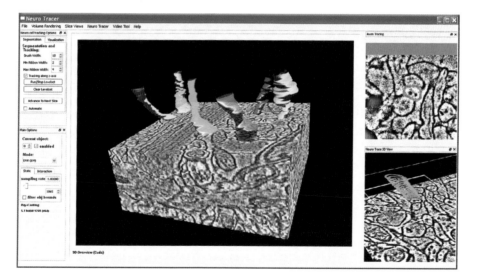

FIGURE 5.

NeuroTrace allows neuroscientists to interactively explore and segment neural processes in high-resolution EM data.

REFERENCES

[1] J. Livet, T. A. Weissman, H. Kang, R. W. Draft, J. Lu, R. A. Bennis, J. R. Sanes, and J. W. Licht-man, "Transgenic strategies for combinatorial expression of fluorescent proteins in the nervous system," *Nature*, vol. 450, pp. 56–62, 2007, doi: 10.1038/nature06293.

[2] S. Hell, "Microscopy and its focal switch," *Nature Methods*, vol. 6, pp. 24–32, 2009, doi: 10.1038/NMeth.1291.

[3] D. Bock, W. C. Lee, A. Kerlin, M. L. Andermann, E. Soucy, S. Yurgenson, and R. C. Reid, "High-throughput serial section electron microscopy in mouse primary visual cortex following in vivo two-photon calcium imaging," *Soc. Neurosci. Abstr.*, vol. 769, no. 12, 2008.

[4] W. Denk and H. Horstmann, "Serial block-face scanning electron microscopy to recon-struct three-dimensional tissue nanostructure," *PLoS Biol.*, vol. 2, p. e329, 2004, doi: 10.1017/S1431927606066268.

[5] K. J. Hayworth, N. Kasthuri, R. Schalek, and J. W. Lichtman, "Automating the Collection of Ultrathin Serial Sections for Large Volume TEM Reconstructions," *Microsc. Microanal.*, vol. 12, pp. 86–87, 2006.

[6] K. Ohki, S. Chung, Y. H. Ch'ng, P. Kara, and R. C. Reid, "Functional imaging with cellular resolu-tion reveals precise microarchitecture in visual cortex," *Nature*, vol. 433, pp. 597–603, 2005, doi:10.1038/nature03274.

[7] K. Ohki, S. Chung, P. Kara, M. Hübener, T. Bonhoeffer, and R. C. Reid, "Highly ordered ar-rangement of single neurons in orientation pinwheels," *Nature*, vol. 442, pp. 925–928, 2006, doi:10.1038/nature05019.

[8] W. Jeong, J. Beyer, M. Hadwiger, A. Vazquez, H. Pfister, and R. Whitaker, "Scalable and Interac-tive Segmentation and Visualization of Neural Processes in EM Datasets," *IEEE Trans. Visual. Comput. Graphics*, Oct. 2009.

[9] A. Vazquez, E. Miller, and H. Pfister, "Multiphase Geometric Couplings for the Segmentation of Neural Processes," *Proceedings of the IEEE Conference on Computer Vision Pattern Recognition (CVPR)*, June 2009.

Toward a Computational Microscope for Neurobiology

ERIC HORVITZ
Microsoft Research

WILLIAM KRISTAN
University of California,
San Diego

A LTHOUGH GREAT STRIDES HAVE BEEN MADE in neurobiology, we do not yet understand how the symphony of communication among neurons leads to rich, competent behaviors in animals. How do local interactions among neurons coalesce into the behavioral dynamics of nervous systems, giving animals their impressive abilities to sense, learn, decide, and act in the world? Many details remain cloaked in mystery. We are excited about the promise of gaining new insights by applying computational methods, in particular machine learning and inference procedures, to generate explanatory models from data about the activities of populations of neurons.

NEW TOOLS FOR NEUROBIOLOGISTS

For most of the history of electrophysiology, neurobiologists have monitored the membrane properties of neurons of vertebrates and invertebrates by using glass micropipettes filled with a conducting solution. Mastering techniques that would impress the most expert of watchmakers, neuroscientists have fabricated glass electrodes with tips that are often less than a micron in diameter, and they have employed special machinery to punch the tips into the cell bodies of single neurons—with the hope that the neurons will function as they normally do within larger assemblies. Such an approach has provided data about the membrane voltages and action potentials of a single cell or just a handful of cells.

However, the relationship between neurobiologists and data about nervous systems is changing. New recording machinery is making data available on the activity of large populations of neurons. Such data makes computational procedures increasingly critical as experimental tools for unlocking new understanding about the connections, architecture, and overall machinery of nervous systems.

New opportunities for experimentation and modeling on a wider scale have become available with the advent of fast optical imaging methods. With this approach, dyes and photomultipliers are used to track calcium levels and membrane potentials of neurons, with high spatial and temporal resolution. These high-fidelity optical recordings allow neurobiologists to examine the simultaneous activity of populations of tens to thousands of neurons. In a relatively short time, data available about the activity of neurons has grown from a trickle of information gleaned via sampling of small numbers of neurons to large-scale observations of neuronal activity.

Spatiotemporal datasets on the behaviors of populations of neurons pose tantalizing inferential challenges and opportunities. The next wave of insights about the neurophysiological basis for cognition will likely come via the application of new kinds of computational lenses that direct an information-theoretic "optics" onto streams of spatiotemporal population data.

We foresee that neurobiologists studying populations of neurons will one day rely on tools that serve as *computational microscopes*—systems that harness machine learning, reasoning, and visualization to help neuroscientists formulate and test hypotheses from data. Inferences derived from the spatiotemporal data streaming from a preparation might even be overlaid on top of traditional optical views during experiments, augmenting those views with annotations that can help with the direction of the investigation.

Intensive computational analyses will serve as the basis for modeling and visualization of the intrinsically high-dimensional population data, where multiple neuronal units interact and contribute to the activity of other neurons and assemblies, and where interactions are potentially context sensitive—circuits and flows might exist dynamically, transiently, and even simultaneously on the same neuronal substrate.

COMPUTATION AND COMPLEXITY

We see numerous opportunities ahead for harnessing fast-paced computations to assist neurobiologists with the science of making inferences from neuron population data. Statistical analyses have already been harnessed in studies of populations of neurons. For example, statistical methods have been used to identify and characterize neuronal activity as trajectories in large dynamical state spaces [1]. We are excited about employing richer machine learning and reasoning to induce explanatory models from case libraries of neuron population data. Computational procedures for induction can assist scientists with teasing insights from raw data on neuronal activity by searching over large sets of alternatives and weighing the plausibility of different explanatory models. The computational methods can be tasked with working at multiple levels of detail, extending upward from circuit-centric exploration of local connectivity and functionality of neurons to potentially valuable higher-level abstractions of neuronal populations—abstractions that may provide us with simplifying representations of the workings of nervous systems.

Beyond generating explanations from observations, inferential models can be harnessed to compute the *expected value of information,* helping neuroscientists to identify the best next test to perform or information to gather, in light of current goals and uncertainties. Computing the value of information can help to direct interventional studies, such as guidance on stimulating specific units, clamping the voltage of particular cells, or performing selective modification of cellular activity via agonist and antagonist pharmacological agents.

We believe that there is promise in both automated and interactive systems, including systems that are used in real-time settings as bench tools. Computational tools might one day even provide real-time guidance for probes and interventions via visualizations and recommendations that are dynamically generated during imaging studies.

Moving beyond the study of specific animal systems, computational tools for analyzing neuron population data will likely be valuable in studies of the construction of nervous systems during embryogenesis, as well as in comparing nervous systems of different species of animals. Such studies can reveal the changes in circuitry and function during development and via the pressures of evolutionary adaptation.

SPECTRUM OF SOPHISTICATION

Neurobiologists study nervous systems of invertebrates and vertebrates across a spectrum of complexity. Human brains are composed of about 100 billion neurons that interact with one another via an estimated 100 trillion synapses. In contrast, the brain of the nematode, *Caenorhabditis elegans (C. elegans),* has just 302 neurons. Such invertebrate nervous systems offer us an opportunity to learn about the principles of neuronal systems, which can be generalized to more complex systems, including our own. For example, *C. elegans* has been a model system for research on the structure of neuronal circuits; great progress has been achieved in mapping the precise connections among its neurons.

Many neurobiologists choose to study simpler nervous systems even if they are motivated by questions about the neurobiological nature of human intelligence. Nervous systems are derived from a family tree of refinements and modifications, so it is likely that key aspects of neuronal information processing have been conserved across brains of a range of complexities. While new abstractions, layers, and interactions may have evolved in more complex nervous systems, brains of different complexities likely rely on a similar neuronal fabric—and there is much that we do not know about that fabric.

In work with our colleagues Ashish Kapoor, Erick Chastain, Johnson Apacible, Daniel Wagenaar, and Paxon Frady, we have been pursuing the use of machine learning, reasoning, and visualization to understand the machinery underlying decision making in *Hirudo,* the European medicinal leech. We have been applying computational analyses to make inferences from optical data about the activity of populations of neurons within the segmental ganglia of *Hirudo.* The ganglia are composed of about 400 neurons, and optical imaging reveals the activity of approximately 200 neurons at a time—all the neurons on one side of the ganglion. Several frames of the optical imaging of *Hirudo* are displayed in Figure 1. The brightness

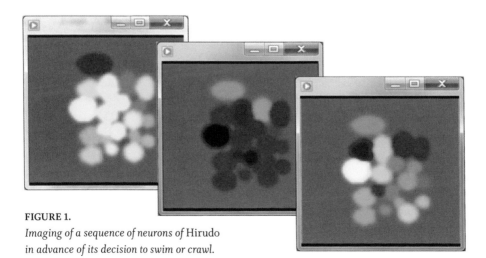

FIGURE 1.
Imaging of a sequence of neurons of Hirudo
in advance of its decision to swim or crawl.

of each of the imaged neurons represents the level of depolarization of the cells, which underlies the production of action potentials.

We are developing analyses and assembling tools in pursuit of our vision of developing computational microscopes for understanding the activity of neuronal populations and their relationship to behavior. In one approach, we generate graphical probabilistic temporal models that can predict the forthcoming behavior of *Hirudo* from a short window of analysis of population data. The models are generated by searching over large spaces of feasible models in which neurons, and abstractions of neurons, serve as random variables and in which temporal and atemporal dependencies are inferred among the variables. The methods can reveal modules of neurons that appear to operate together and that can appear dynamically over the course of activity leading up to decisions by the animal. In complementary work, we are considering the role of neuronal states in defining trajectories through state spaces of a dynamical system.

EMERGENCE OF A COMPUTATIONAL MICROSCOPE

We have started to build interactive viewers and tools that allow scientists to manipulate inferential assumptions and parameters and to inspect implications visually. For example, sliders allow for smooth changes in thresholds for admitting connections among neurons and for probing strengths of relationships and membership in modules. We would love to see a world in which such tools are shared broadly among neuroscientists and are extended with learning, inference, and visualization components developed by the neuroscience community.

Figure 2 on the next page shows a screenshot of a prototype tool we call the MSR Computational Microscope, which was developed by Ashish Kapoor, Erick Chastain, and Eric Horvitz at Microsoft Research as part of a broader collaboration with William Kristan at the University of California, San Diego, and Daniel Wagenaar at California Institute of Technology. The tool allows users to visualize neuronal activity over a period of time and then explore inferences about relationships among neurons in an interactive manner. Users can select from a variety of inferential methods and specify modeling assumptions. They can also mark particular neurons and neuronal subsets as focal points of analyses. The view in Figure 2 shows an analysis of the activity of neurons in the segmental ganglia of *Hirudo*. Inferred informational relationships among cells are displayed via highlighting of neurons and through the generation of arcs among neurons. Such inferences can help to guide exploration and confirmation of physical connections among neurons.

FIGURE 2.

Possible connections and clusters inferred from population data during imaging of Hirudo.

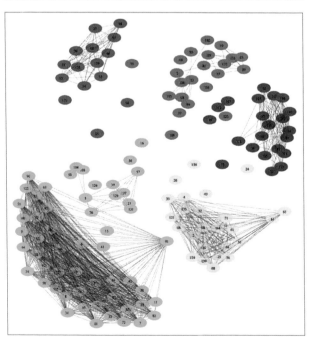

FIGURE 3.

Inferred informational relationships among neurons in a segmental ganglion of Hirudo. *Measures of similarity of the dynamics of neuronal activity over time are displayed via arcs and clusters.*

Figure 3 shows another informational analysis that spatially clusters cells that behave in a similar manner in the ganglia of *Hirudo* over a set of trials. The analysis provides an early vision of how information-theoretic analyses might one day help neurobiologists to discover and probe interactions within and between neuronal subsystems.

We are only at the start of this promising research direction, but we expect to see a blossoming of analyses, tools, and a broader sub-discipline that focuses on the neuroinformatics of populations of neurons. We believe that computational methods will lead us to effective representations and languages for understanding neuronal systems and that they will become essential tools for neurobiologists to gain insight into the myriad mysteries of sensing, learning, and decision making by nervous systems.

REFERENCES

[1] K. L. Briggman, H. D. I. Abarbanel, and W. B. Kristan, Jr., "Optical imaging of neuronal populations during decision-making," *Science*, vol. 307, pp. 896–901, 2005, doi: 10.1126/science.110.

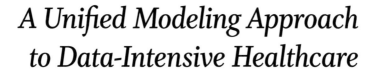

A Unified Modeling Approach to Data-Intensive Healthcare

IAIN BUCHAN
University of Manchester

JOHN WINN
CHRIS BISHOP
Microsoft Research

T HE QUANTITY OF AVAILABLE HEALTHCARE DATA is rising rapidly, far exceeding the capacity to deliver personal or public health benefits from analyzing this data [1]. Three key elements of the rise are electronic health records (EHRs), biotechnologies, and scientific outputs. We discuss these in turn below, leading to our proposal for a unified modeling approach that can take full advantage of a data-intensive environment.

ELECTRONIC HEALTH RECORDS

Healthcare organizations around the world, in both low- and high-resource settings, are deploying EHRs. At the community level, EHRs can be used to manage healthcare services, monitor the public's health, and support research. Furthermore, the social benefits of EHRs may be greater from such population-level uses than from individual care uses.

The use of standard terms and ontologies in EHRs is increasing the structure of healthcare data, but clinical coding behavior introduces new potential biases. For example, the introduction of incentives for primary care professionals to tackle particular conditions may lead to fluctuations in the amount of coding of new cases of those conditions [2]. On the other hand, the falling cost of devices for remote monitoring and near-patient testing is leading to more capture of objective measures in EHRs, which can provide less biased signals but may create the illusion of an increase in disease prevalence simply due to more data becoming available.

Some patients are beginning to access and supplement their own records or edit a parallel health record online [3]. The stewardship of future health records may indeed be more with individuals (patients/citizens/consumers) and communities (families/local populations etc.) than with healthcare organizations. In summary, the use of EHRs is producing more data-intensive healthcare environments in which substantially more data are captured and transferred digitally. Computational thinking and models of healthcare to apply to this wealth of data, however, have scarcely been developed.

BIOTECHNOLOGIES

Biotechnologies have fueled a boom in molecular medical research. Some techniques, such as genome-wide analysis, produce large volumes of data without the sampling bias that a purposive selection of study factors might produce. Such datasets are thus more wide ranging and unselected than conventional experimental measurements. Important biases can still arise from artifacts in the biotechnical processing of samples and data, but these are likely to decrease as the technologies improve. A greater concern is the systematic error that lies outside the data landscape—for example, in a metabolomic analysis that is confounded by not considering the time of day or the elapsed time from the most recent meal to when the sample was taken. The integration of different scales of data, from molecular-level to population-level variables, and different levels of directness of measurement of factors is a grand challenge for data-intensive health science. When realistically complex multi-scale models are available, the next challenge will be to make them accessible to clinicians and patients, who together can evaluate the competing risks of different options for personalizing treatment.

SCIENTIFIC OUTPUTS

The outputs of health science have been growing exponentially [4]. In 2009, a new paper is indexed in PubMed, the health science bibliographic system, on average every 2 minutes. The literature-review approach to managing health knowledge is therefore potentially overloaded. Furthermore, the translation of new knowledge into practice innovation is slow and inconsistent [5]. This adversely affects not only clinicians and patients who are making care decisions but also researchers who are reasoning about patterns and mechanisms. There is a need to combine the mining

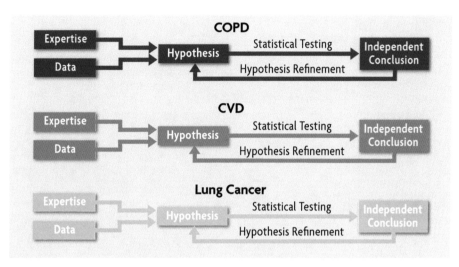

FIGURE 1.

Conventional approaches based on statistical hypothesis testing artificially decompose the healthcare domain into numerous sub-problems. They thereby miss a significant opportunity for statistical "borrowing of strength." Chronic obstructive pulmonary disease (COPD), cardiovascular disease (CVD), and lung cancer can be considered together as a "big three" [6].

of evidence bases with computational models for exploring the burgeoning data from healthcare and research.

Hypothesis-driven research and reductionist approaches to causality have served health science well in identifying the major independent determinants of health and the outcomes of individual healthcare interventions. (See Figure 1.) But they do not reflect the complexity of health. For example, clinical trials exclude as many as 80 percent of the situations in which a drug might be prescribed—for example, when a patient has multiple diseases and takes multiple medications [7]. Consider a newly licensed drug released for general prescription. Clinician X might prescribe the drug while clinician Y does not, which could give rise to natural experiments. In a fully developed data-intensive healthcare system in which the data from those experiments are captured in EHRs, clinical researchers could explore the outcomes of patients on the new drug compared with natural controls, and they could potentially adjust for confounding and modifying factors. However, such adjustments might be extremely complex and beyond the capability of conventional models.

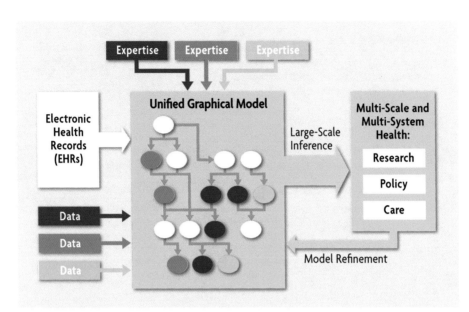

FIGURE 2.

We propose a unified approach to healthcare modeling that exploits the growing statistical resources of electronic health records in addition to the data collected for specific studies.

A UNIFIED APPROACH

We propose a unified modeling approach that can take full advantage of a data-intensive environment without losing the realistic complexity of health. (See Figure 2.) Our approach relies on developments within the machine learning field over the past 10 years, which provide powerful new tools that are well suited to this challenge. Knowledge of outcomes, interventions, and confounding or modifying factors can all be captured and represented through the framework of probabilistic graphical models in which the relevant variables, including observed data, are expressed as a graph [8]. Inferences on this graph can then be performed automatically using a variety of algorithms based on local message passing, such as [9]. Compared with classical approaches to machine learning, this new framework offers a deeper integration of domain knowledge, taken directly from experts or from the literature, with statistical learning. Furthermore, these automatic inference algorithms can scale to datasets of hundreds of millions of records, and new tools such as Infer.NET allow rapid development of solutions within this framework [10]. We illustrate the application of this approach with two scenarios.

In scenario 1, an epidemiologist is investigating the genetic and environmental factors that predispose some children to develop asthma. He runs a cohort study of 1,000 children who have been followed for 10 years, with detailed environmental and physiological measures as well as data on over half a million of the 3 million genetic factors that might vary between individuals. The conventional epidemiology approach might test predefined hypotheses using selected groups of genetic and other factors. A genome-wide scanning approach might also be taken to look for associations between individual genetic factors and simple definitions of health status (e.g., current wheeze vs. no current wheeze at age 5 years). Both of these approaches use relatively simple statistical models. An alternative machine learning approach might start with the epidemiologist constructing a graphical model of the problem space, consulting literature and colleagues to build a graph around the organizing principle—say, "peripheral airways obstruction." This model better reflects the realistic complexity of asthma with a variety of classes of wheeze and other signs and symptoms, and it relates them to known mechanisms. Unsupervised clustering methods are then used to explore how genetic, environmental, and other study factors influence the clustering into different groups of allergic sensitization with respect to skin and blood test results and reports of wheezing. The epidemiologist can relate these patterns to biological pathways, thereby shaping hypotheses to be explored further.

In scenario 2, a clinical team is auditing the care outcomes for patients with chronic angina. Subtly different treatment plans of care are common, such as different levels of investigation and treatment in primary care before referral to specialist care. A typical clinical audit approach might debate the treatment plan, consult literature, examine simple summary statistics, generate some hypotheses, and perhaps test the hypotheses using simple regression models. An alternative machine learning approach might construct a graphical model of the assumed treatment plan, via debate and reference to the literature, and compare this with discovered network topologies in datasets reflecting patient outcomes. Plausible networks might then be used to simulate the potential effects of changes to clinical practice by running scenarios that change edge weights in the underlying graphs. Thus the families of associations in locally relevant data can be combined with evidence from the literature in a scenario-planning activity that involves clinical reasoning and machine learning.

THE FOURTH PARADIGM: HEALTH AVATARS

Unified models clearly have the potential to influence personal health choices, clinical practice, and public health. So is this a paradigm for the future?

The first paradigm of healthcare information might be considered to be the case history plus expert physician, formalized by Hippocrates more than 2,000 years ago and still an important part of clinical practice. In the second paradigm, a medical record is shared among a set of complementary clinicians, each focusing their specialized knowledge on the patient's condition in turn. The third paradigm is evidence-based healthcare that links a network of health professionals with knowledge and patient records in a timely manner. This third paradigm is still in the process of being realized, particularly in regard to capturing the complexities of clinical practice in a digital record and making some aspects of healthcare computable.

We anticipate a fourth paradigm of healthcare information, mirroring that of other disciplines, whereby an individual's health data are aggregated from multiple sources and attached to a unified model of that person's health. The sources can range from body area network sensors to clinical expert oversight and interpretation, with the individual playing a much greater part than at present in building and acting on his or her health information. Incorporating all of this data, the unified model will take on the role of a "health avatar"—the electronic representation of an individual's health as directly measured or inferred by statistical models or clinicians. Clinicians interacting with a patient's avatar can achieve a more integrated view of different specialist treatment plans than they do with care records alone.

The avatar is not only a statistical tool to support diagnosis and treatment, but it is also a communication tool that links the patient and the patient's elected network of clinicians and other trusted caregivers—for what-if treatment discussions, for example. While initially acting as a fairly simple multi-system model, the health avatar could grow in depth and complexity to narrow the gap between avatar and reality. Such an avatar would not involve a molecular-level simulation of a human being (which we view as implausible) but would instead involve a unified statistical model that captures current clinical understanding as it applies to an individual patient.

This paradigm can be extended to communities, where multiple individual avatars interact with a community avatar to provide a unified model of the community's health. Such a community avatar could provide relevant and timely information for use in protecting and improving the health of those in the community. Scarce community resources could be matched more accurately to lifetime healthcare needs, particularly in prevention and early intervention, to reduce the severity and/or duration of illness and to better serve the community as a whole. Clinical, consumer, and public health services could interact more effectively, providing both social benefit and new opportunities for healthcare innovation and enterprise.

CONCLUSION

Data alone cannot lead to data-intensive healthcare. A substantial overhaul of methodology is required to address the real complexity of health, ultimately leading to dramatically improved global public healthcare standards. We believe that machine learning, coupled with a general increase in computational thinking about health, can be instrumental. There is arguably a societal duty to develop computational frameworks for seeking signals in collections of health data if the potential benefit to humanity greatly outweighs the risk. We believe it does.

REFERENCES

[1] J. Powell and I. Buchan, "Electronic health records should support clinical research," *J. Med. Internet Res.*, vol. 7, no. 1, p. e4, Mar. 14, 2005, doi: 10.2196/jmir.7.1.e4.

[2] S. de Lusignan, N. Hague, J. van Vlymen, and P. Kumarapeli, "Routinely-collected general practice data are complex, but with systematic processing can be used for quality improvement and research," *Prim. Care. Inform.*, vol. 14, no. 1, pp. 59–66, 2006.

[3] L. Bos and B. Blobel, Eds., *Medical and Care Compunetics 4*, vol. 127 in Studies in Health Technology and Informatics series. Amsterdam: IOS Press, pp. 311–315.

[4] B. G. Druss and S. C. Marcus, "Growth and decentralization of the medical literature: implications for evidence-based medicine," *J. Med. Libr. Assoc.*, vol. 93, no. 4, pp. 499–501, Oct. 2005, PMID: PMC1250328.

[5] A. Mina, R. Ramlogan, G. Tampubolon, and J. Metcalfe, "Mapping evolutionary trajectories: Applications to the growth and transformation of medical knowledge," *Res. Policy*, vol. 36, no. 5, pp. 789–806, 2007, doi: 10.1016/j.respol.2006.12.007.

[6] M. Gerhardsson de Verdier, "The Big Three Concept - A Way to Tackle the Health Care Crisis?" *Proc. Am. Thorac. Soc.*, vol. 5, pp. 800–805, 2008.

[7] M. Fortin, J. Dionne, G. Pinho, J. Gignac, J. Almirall, and L. Lapointe, "Randomized controlled trials: do they have external validity for patients with multiple comorbidities?" *Ann. Fam. Med.*, vol. 4, no. 2, pp. 104–108, Mar.–Apr. 2006, doi: 10.1370/afm.516.

[8] C. Bishop, *Pattern Recognition and Machine Learning.* Springer, 2006.

[9] J. Winn and C. Bishop, "Variational Message Passing," *J. Mach. Learn. Res.*, vol. 6, pp. 661–694, 2005.

[10] T. Minka, J. Winn, J. Guiver, and A. Kannan, Infer.NET, Microsoft Research Cambridge, http://research.microsoft.com/infernet.

Visualization in Process Algebra Models of Biological Systems

LUCA CARDELLI
Microsoft Research

CORRADO PRIAMI
Microsoft Research -
University of Trento
Centre for Computational
and Systems Biology and
University of Trento

N A RECENT PAPER, NOBEL LAUREATE PAUL NURSE calls for a better understanding of living organisms through "both the development of the appropriate languages to describe information processing in biological systems and the generation of more effective methods to translate biochemical descriptions into the functioning of the logic circuits that underpin biological phenomena." [1]

The language that Nurse wishes to see is a formal language that can be automatically translated into machine executable code and that enables simulation and analysis techniques for proving properties of biological systems. Although there are many approaches to the formal modeling of living systems, only a few provide executable descriptions that highlight the mechanistic steps that make a system move from one state to another [2]. Almost all the techniques related to mathematical modeling abstract from these individual steps to produce global behavior, usually averaged over time.

Computer science provides the key elements to describe mechanistic steps: algorithms and programming languages [3]. Following the metaphor of molecules as processes introduced in [4], process calculi have been identified as a promising tool to model biological systems that are inherently complex, concurrent, and driven by the interactions of their subsystems.

Causality is a key difference between language-based modeling approaches and other techniques. In fact, causality in concurrent languages is strictly related to the notion of concurrency or independence of events, which makes causality substantially different from temporal ordering. An activity A causes an activity B if A is a necessary condition for B to happen and A influences the activity of B—i.e., there is a flow of information from A to B. The second part of the condition defining causality makes clear the distinction between precedence (related only to temporal ordering) and causality (a subset of the temporal ordering in which the flow of information is also considered) [5]. As a consequence, the list of the reactions performed by a system does not provide causal information but only temporal information. It is therefore mandatory to devise new modeling and analysis tools to address causality.

Causality is a key issue in the analysis of complex interacting systems because it helps in dissecting independent components and simplifying models while also allowing us to clearly identify cross-talks between different signaling cascades. Once the experimentalist observes an interesting event in a simulation, it is possible to compact the previous history of the system, exposing only the preceding events that caused the interesting one. This can give precise hints about the causes of a disease, the interaction of a drug with a living system (identifying its efficacy and its side effects), and the regulatory mechanisms of oscillating behaviors.

Causality is a relationship between events, and as such it is most naturally studied within discrete models, which are in turn described via algorithmic modeling languages. Although many modeling languages have been defined in computer science to model concurrent systems, many challenges remain to building algorithmic models for the system-level understanding of biological processes. These challenges include the relationship between low-level local interactions and emergent high-level global behavior; the incomplete knowledge of the systems under investigation; the multi-level and multi-scale representations in time, space, and size; and the causal relations between interactions and the context awareness of the inner components. Therefore, the modeling formalisms that are candidates to propel algorithmic systems biology should be complementary to and interoperable with mathematical modeling. They should address parallelism and complexity, be algorithmic and quantitative, express causality, and be interaction driven, composable, scalable, and modular.

LANGUAGE VISUALIZATION

A fundamental issue in the adoption of formal languages in biology is their usability. A modeling language must be understandable by biologists so they can relate it to their own informal models and to experiments.

One attempt by biologists to connect formal languages and informal descriptions of systems involved the use of a constrained natural language organized in the form of tables that collect all the information related to the structure and dynamic of a system. This narrative representation is informative and structured enough to be compiled into formal description that is amenable to simulation and analysis [6, 7]. Although the narrative modeling style is not yet visual, it is certainly more readable and corresponds better to the intuition of biologists than a formal (programming) language.

The best way to make a language understandable to scientists while also helping to manage complexity is to visualize the language. This is harder than visualizing data or visualizing the results of simulations because a language implicitly describes the full kinetics of a system, including the dynamic relationships between events. Therefore, language visualization must be dynamic, and possibly reactive [8], which means that a scientist should be able to detect and insert events in a running simulation by direct intervention. This requires a one-to-one correspondence between the internal execution of a formal language and its visualization so that the kinetics of the language can be fully reflected in the kinetics of the visualization and vice versa.

This ability to fully match the kinetics of a general (Turing-complete) modeling language to visual representations has been demonstrated, for example, for pi-calculus [9], but many practical challenges remain to adapting such general methods to specific visualization requirements. (See Figure 1 on the next page.) One such requirement, for example, is the visualization and tracking of molecular complexes; to this end, the BlenX language [10] and its support tools permit explicit representation of complexes of biological elements and examination of their evolution in time [11]. (See Figure 2 on page 103.) The graphical representation of complexes is also useful in studying morphogenesis processes to unravel the mechanistic steps of pattern formation. (See Figure 3 on page 104.)

ANALYSIS

Model construction is one step in the scientific cycle, and appropriate modeling languages (along with their execution and visualization capabilities) are important, particularly for modeling complex systems. Ultimately, however, one will want to analyze the model using a large number of techniques. Some of these techniques may be centered on the underlying mathematical framework, such as the analysis of

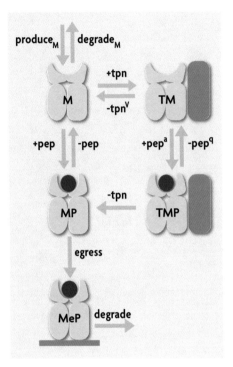

FIGURE 1.

This diagram can be placed in 1:1 correspondence with formal stochastic pi-calculus models [9, 12, 13] so that one can edit either the diagrams or the models. The nodes represent molecular states (the node icons are just for illustration), and the labeled arcs represent interactions with other molecules in the environment. The models use a biochemical variant of pi-calculus with rate weight as superscripts and with +/- for binding and unbinding.

differential equations, Markov chains, or Petri nets generated from the model. Other techniques may be centered on the model description (the language in which the model is written). For example, we may want to know whether two different model descriptions actually represent the same behavior, by some measure of behavior equivalence. This kind of model correspondence can arise, for example, from apparently different biological systems that work by the same fundamental principles. A similar question is whether we can simplify (abstract) a model description and still preserve its behavior, again by some measure of behavior equivalence that may mask some unimportant detail.

Behavioral equivalences are in fact a primary tool in computer science for verifying computing systems. For instance, we can use equivalences to ensure that an implementation is in agreement with a specification, abstracting as much as possible from syntactic descriptions and instead focusing on the semantics (dynamic) of specifications and implementations. So far, biology has focused on syntactic relationships between genes, genomes, and proteins. An entirely new avenue of research is the investigation of the semantic equivalences of biological entities populating complex networks of interactions. This approach could lead to new visions of systems and reinforce the need for computer science to enhance systems biology.

Biology is a data-intensive science. Biological systems are huge collections of in-

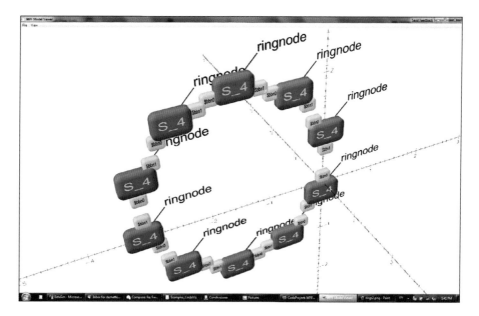

FIGURE 2.

The green S boxes in the diagram represent entities populating the biological system under consideration. The light blue rectangles attached to the green boxes represent the active interfaces/domains available for complexation and decomplexation. The diagram shows how the simulation of the BlenX specification formed a ring complex and provides the position and the connections between boxes for inspection.

teracting components. The last decade of research has contributed to identifying and classifying those components, especially at the molecular level (gene, metabolites, proteins). To make sense of the large amount of data available, we need to implicitly represent them in compact and executable models so that executions can recover the available data as needed. This approach would merge syntax and semantics in unifying representations and would create the need for different ways of storing, retrieving, and comparing data. A model repository that represents the dynamics of biological processes in a compact and mechanistic manner would therefore be extremely valuable and could heighten the understanding of biological data and the basic biological principles governing life. This would facilitate predictions and the optimal design of further experiments to move from data collection to knowledge production.

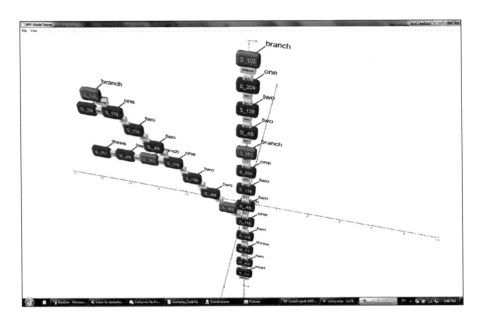

FIGURE 3.

The green, red and blue S boxes in the diagram represent different species populating the biological system under consideration. The light blue rectangles attached to the boxes represent the active interfaces/domains available for complexation and decomplexation. The diagram elucidates how patterns are formed in morphogenesis processes simulated by BlenX specifications.

ANALYSIS VISUALIZATION

Executable models need visualization to make their execution interactive (to dynamically focus on specific features) and reactive (to influence their execution on the fly). Execution is one form of analysis; other analysis methods will need visualization as well. For complex systems, the normal method of "batch" analysis, consisting of running a complex analysis on the model and then mining the output for clues, needs to be replaced with a more interactive, explorative approach.

Model abstraction is an important tool for managing complexity, and we can envision performing this activity interactively—for example, by lumping components together or by hiding components. The notion of lumping will then need an appropriate visualization and an appropriate way of relating the behavior of the original components to the behavior of the lumped components. This doesn't mean visualizing the modeling language, but rather visualizing an abstraction function between models. We therefore suggest visualizing the execution of programs/models in such a way that the output is linked to the source code/model specification and the graphical abstraction performed by the end user is transformed into a formal program/model transformation. The supporting tool would then check which properties the transformation is preserving or not preserving and warn the user accordingly.

All the above reinforces the need for a formal and executable language to model biology as the core feature of an *in silico* laboratory for biologists that could be the next-generation high-throughput tool for biology.

ACKNOWLEDGMENTS

The authors thank Andrew Phillips and Lorenzo Dematté for preparing the figures.

REFERENCES

[1] P. Nurse, "Life, Logic and Information," *Nature*, vol. 454, pp. 424–426, 2008, doi: 10.1038/454424a.

[2] J. Fisher and T. Henzinger, "Executable Cell Biology," *Nature Biotechnology*, vol. 25, pp. 1239–1249, 2007, doi: 10.1038/nbt1356.

[3] C. Priami, "Algorithmic Systems Biology: An opportunity for computer science," *Commun. ACM*, June 2009, doi: 10.1145/1506409.1506427.

[4] A. Regev and E. Shapiro, "Cells as computation," *Nature*, vol. 419, p. 343, 2002, doi: 10.1038/419343a.

[5] P. Degano and C. Priami, "Non-interleaving semantics of mobile processes," *Theor. Comp. Sci.* vol. 216, no. 1–2, pp. 237–270, 1999.

[6] M. L. Guerriero, J. Heath, and C. Priami, "An automated translation from a narrative language for biological modelling into process algebra," *Proc. of CMSB 2007*, LNBI 4695, 2007, pp. 136–151, doi: 10.1007/978-3-540-75140-3_10.

[7] M. L. Guerriero, A. Dudka, N. Underhill-Day, J. Heath, and C. Priami, "Narrative-based computational modelling of the Gp130/JAK/STAT signalling pathway," *BMC Syst. Biol.*, vol. 3, no. 1, p. 40, 2009, doi: 10.1186/1752-0509-3-40.

[8] S. Efroni, D. Harel, and I. R. Cohen, "Reactive Animation: Realistic Modeling of Complex Dynamic Systems," *Computer*, vol. 38, no. 1, pp. 38–47, Jan. 2005, doi: 10.1109/MC.2005.31.

[9] A. Phillips, L. Cardelli, and G. Castagna, "A Graphical Representation for Biological Processes in the Stochastic Pi-calculus," *Trans. Comput. Syst. Biol.*, VII - LNCS 4230, 2006, pp. 123–152, doi: 10.1007/11905455_7.

[10] L. Dematté, C. Priami, and A. Romanel, "The BlenX Language: a tutorial," *Formal Meth. Comput. Syst. Biol.*, LNCS 5016, 2008, pp. 313–365, doi: 10.1145/1506409.1506427.

[11] L. Dematté, C. Priami, and A. Romanel, "The Beta Workbench: a computational tool to study the dynamics of biological systems," *Brief Bioinform*, vol. 9, no. 5, pp. 437–449, 2008, doi: 10.1093/bib/bbn023.

[12] C. Priami, "Stochastic pi-calculus," *Comp. J.*, vol. 38, no. 6, pp. 578–589, 1995, doi: 10.1093/comjnl/38.7.578.

[13] A. Phillips and L. Cardelli, "Efficient, Correct Simulation of Biological Processes in Stochastic Pi-calculus," *Proc. Comput. Meth. Syst. Biol.*, Edinburgh, 2007, pp. 184–199, doi: 10.1007/978-3-540-75140-3_13.

3. SCIENTIFIC INFRASTRUCTURE

Introduction

DARON GREEN | Microsoft Research

W ARNING! The articles in Part 3 of this book use a range of dramatic metaphors, such as "explosion," "tsunami," and even the "big bang," to strikingly illustrate how scientific research will be transformed by the ongoing creation and availability of high volumes of scientific data. Although the imagery may vary, these authors share a common intent by addressing how we must adjust our approach to computational science to handle this new proliferation of data. Their choice of words is motivated by the opportunity for research breakthroughs afforded by these large and rich datasets, but it also implies the magnitude of our culture's loss if our research infrastructure is not up to the task.

Abbott's perspective across all of scientific research challenges us with a fundamental question: whether, in light of the proliferation of data and its increasing availability, the need for sharing and collaboration, and the changing role of computational science, there should be a "new path for science." He takes a pragmatic view of how the scientific community will evolve, and he is skeptical about just how eager researchers will be to embrace techniques such as ontologies and other semantic technologies. While avoiding dire portents, Abbott is nonetheless vivid in characterizing a disconnect between the supply of scientific knowledge and the demands of the private and government sectors.

To bring the issues into focus, Southan and Cameron explore the "tsunami" of data growing in the EMBL-Bank database—a nucleotide sequencing information service. Throughout Part 3 of this book, the field of genetic sequencing serves as a reasonable proxy for a number of scientific domains in which the rate of data production is brisk (in this case, a 200% increase per annum), leading to major challenges in data aggregation, workflow, backup, archiving, quality, and retention, to name just a few areas.

Larus and Gannon inject optimism by noting that the data volumes are tractable through the application of multicore technologies—provided, of course, that we can devise the programming models and abstractions to make this technical innovation effective in general-purpose scientific research applications.

Next, we revisit the metaphor of a calamity induced by a data tidal wave as Gannon and Reed discuss how parallelism and the cloud can help with scalability issues for certain classes of computational problems.

From there, we move to the role of computational workflow tools in helping to orchestrate key tasks in managing the data deluge. Goble and De Roure identify the benefits and issues associated with applying computational workflow to scientific research and collaboration. Ultimately, they argue that workflows illustrate primacy of method as a crucial technology in data-centric research.

Fox and Hendler see "semantic eScience" as vital in helping to interpret interrelationships of complex concepts, terms, and data. After explaining the potential benefits of semantic tools in data-centric research, they explore some of the challenges to their smooth adoption. They note the inadequate participation of the scientific community in developing requirements as well as a lack of coherent discussion about the applicability of Web-based semantic technologies to the scientific process.

Next, Hansen et al. provide a lucid description of the hurdles to visualizing large and complex datasets. They wrestle with the familiar topics of workflow, scalability, application performance, provenance, and user interactions, but from a visualization standpoint. They highlight that current analysis and visualization methods lag far behind our ability to create data, and they conclude that multidisciplinary skills are needed to handle diverse issues such as automatic data interpretation, uncertainty, summary visualizations, verification, and validation.

Completing our journey through these perils and opportunities, Parastatidis considers how we can realize a comprehensive knowledge-based research infrastructure for science. He envisions this happening through a confluence of traditional scientific computing tools, Web-based tools, and select semantic methods.

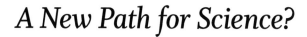

A New Path for Science?

MARK R. ABBOTT
Oregon State University

T HE SCIENTIFIC CHALLENGES of the 21st century will strain the partnerships between government, industry, and academia that have developed and matured over the last century or so. For example, in the United States, beginning with the establishment of the National Science Foundation in 1950, the nation's research university system has blossomed and now dominates the basic research segment. (The applied research segment, which is far larger, is primarily funded and implemented within the private sector.)

One cannot overstate the successes of this system, but it has come to be largely organized around individual science disciplines and rewards individual scientists' efforts through publications and the promotion and tenure process. Moreover, the eternal "restlessness" of the system means that researchers are constantly seeking new ideas and new funding [1, 2]. An unexpected outcome of this system is the growing disconnect between the supply of scientific knowledge and the demand for that knowledge from the private and government sectors [3, 4]. The internal reward structure at universities, as well as the peer review system, favors research projects that are of inherent interest to the scientific community but not necessarily to those outside the academic community.

NEW DRIVERS

It is time to reexamine the basic structures underlying our research enterprise. For example, given the emerging and urgent need for new approaches to climate and energy research in the broad context of sustainability, fundamental research on the global climate system will continue to be necessary, but businesses and policymakers are asking questions that are far more interdisciplinary than in the past. This new approach is more akin to scenario development in support of risk assessment and management than traditional problem solving and the pursuit of knowledge for its own sake.

In climate science, the demand side is focused on feedback between climate change and socioeconomic processes, rare (but high-impact) events, and the development of adaptive policies and management protocols. The science supply side favors studies of the physical and biological aspects of the climate system on a continental or global scale and reducing uncertainties (e.g., [5]). This misalignment between supply and demand hampers society's ability to respond effectively and in a timely manner to the changing climate.

RECENT HISTORY

The information technology (IT) infrastructure of 25 years ago was well suited to the science culture of that era. Data volumes were relatively small, and therefore each data element was precious. IT systems were relatively expensive and were accessible only to experts. The fundamental workflow relied on a data collection system (e.g., a laboratory or a field sensor), transfer into a data storage system, data processing and analysis, visualization, and publication.

Figure 1 shows the architecture of NASA's Earth Observing System Data and Information System (EOSDIS) from the late 1980s. Although many thought that EOSDIS was too ambitious (it planned for 1 terabyte per day of data), the primary argument against it was that it was too centralized for a system that needed to be science driven. EOSDIS was perceived to be a data factory, operating under a set of rigorous requirements with little opportunity for knowledge or technology infusion. Ultimately, the argument was not about centralized versus decentralized but rather who would control the requirements: the science community or the NASA contractor. The underlying architecture, with its well-defined (and relatively modest-sized) data flows and mix of centralized and distributed components, has remained undisturbed, even as the World Wide Web, the Internet, and the volume of online data have grown exponentially.

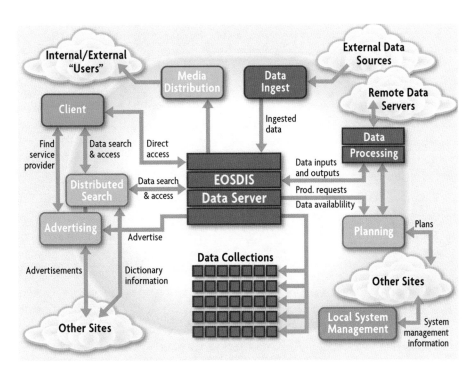

FIGURE 1.

NASA's Earth Observing System Data and Information System (EOSDIS) as planned in 1989.

Today, the suite of national supercomputer centers as well as the notion of "cloud computing" looks much the same as the architecture shown in Figure 1. It doesn't matter whether the network connection is an RS-232 asynchronous connection, a dial-up modem, or a gigabit network, or whether the device on the scientist's desktop is a VT100 graphics terminal or a high-end multicore workstation. Virtualized (but distributed) repositories of data storage and computing capabilities are accessed via network by relatively low-capability devices.

Moore's Law has had 25 years to play out since the design of EOSDIS. Although we generally focus on the increases in capacity and the precipitous decline in the price/performance ratio, the pace of rapid technological innovation has placed enormous pressure on the traditional modes of scientific research. The vast amounts of data have greatly reduced the value of an individual data element, and we are no

---
○
---

longer data-limited but insight-limited. "Data-intensive" should not refer just to the centralized repositories but also to the far greater volumes of data that are network-accessible in offices, labs, and homes and by sensors and portable devices. Thus, data-intensive computing should be considered more than just the ability to store and move larger amounts of data. The complexity of these new datasets as well as the increasing diversity of the data flows is rendering the traditional compute/data-center model obsolete for modern scientific research.

IMPLICATIONS FOR SCIENCE

IT has affected the science community in two ways. First, it has led to the *commoditization* of generic storage and computing. For science tasks that can be accomplished through commodity services, such services are a reasonable option. It will always be more cost effective to use low-profit-margin, high-volume services through centralized mechanisms such as cloud computing. Thus more universities are relying on such services for data backup, e-mail, office productivity applications, and so on.

The second way that IT has affected the science community is through radical *personalization*. With personal access to teraflops of computing and terabytes of storage, scientists can create their own compute clouds. Innovation and new science services will come from the edges of the networks, not the commodity-driven datacenters. Moreover, not just scientists but the vastly larger number of sensors and laboratory instruments will soon be connected to the Internet with their own local computation and storage services. The challenge is to harness the power of this new network of massively distributed knowledge services.

Today, scientific discovery is not accomplished solely through the well-defined, rigorous process of hypothesis testing. The vast volumes of data, the complex and hard-to-discover relationships, the intense and shifting types of collaboration between disciplines, and new types of near-real-time publishing are adding pattern and rule discovery to the scientific method [6]. Especially in the area of climate science and policy, we could see a convergence of this new type of data-intensive research and the new generation of IT capabilities.

The alignment of science supply and demand in the context of continuing scientific uncertainty will depend on seeking out new relationships, overcoming language and cultural barriers to enable collaboration, and merging models and data to evaluate scenarios. This process has far more in common with network gaming than with the traditional scientific method. Capturing the important elements of data preservation, collaboration, provenance, and accountability will require new approaches in the highly distributed, data-intensive research community.

Instead of well-defined data networks and factories coupled with an individually based publishing system that relies on peer review and tenure, this new research enterprise will be more unruly and less predictable, resembling an ecosystem in its approach to knowledge discovery. That is, it will include loose networks of potential services, rapid innovation at the edges, and a much closer partnership between those who create knowledge and those who use it. As with every ecosystem, emergent (and sometimes unpredictable) behavior will be a dominant feature.

Our existing institutions—including federal agencies and research universities—will be challenged by these new structures. Access to data and computation as well as new collaborators will not require the physical structure of a university or millions of dollars in federal grants. Moreover, the rigors of tenure and its strong emphasis on individual achievement in a single scientific discipline may work against these new approaches. We need an organization that integrates natural science with socioeconomic science, balances science with technology, focuses on systems thinking, supports flexible and interdisciplinary approaches to long-term problem solving, integrates knowledge creation and knowledge use, and balances individual and group achievement.

Such a new organization could pioneer integrated approaches to a sustainable future, approaches that are aimed at understanding the variety of possible futures. It would focus on global-scale processes that are manifested on a regional scale with pronounced socioeconomic consequences. Rather than a traditional academic organization with its relatively static set of tenure-track professors, a new organization could take more risks, build and develop new partnerships, and bring in people with the talent needed for particular tasks. Much like in the U.S. television series *Mission Impossible,* we will bring together people from around the world to address specific problems—in this case, climate change issues.

MAKING IT HAPPEN

How can today's IT enable this type of new organization and this new type of science? In the EOSDIS era, it was thought that relational databases would provide the essential services needed to manage the vast volumes of data coming from the EOS satellites. Although database technology provided the baseline services needed for the standard EOS data products, it did not capture the innovation at the edges of the system where science was in control. Today, semantic webs and ontologies are being proposed as a means to enable knowledge discovery and collaboration. However, as with databases, it is likely that the science community will be reluctant to use these inherently complex tools except for the most mundane tasks.

Ultimately, digital technology can provide only relatively sparse descriptions of the richness and complexity of the real world. Moreover, seeking the unusual and unexpected requires creativity and insight—processes that are difficult to represent in a rigid digital framework. On the other hand, simply relying on PageRank[1]-like statistical correlations based on usage will not necessarily lead to detection of the rare and the unexpected. However, new IT tools for the data-intensive world can provide the ability to "filter" these data volumes down to a manageable level as well as provide visualization and presentation services to make it easier to gain creative insights and build collaborations.

The architecture for data-intensive computing should be based on storage, computing, and presentation services at every node of an interconnected network. Providing standard, extensible frameworks that accommodate innovation at the network edges should enable these knowledge "ecosystems" to form and evolve as the needs of climate science and policy change.

REFERENCES

[1] D. S. Greenberg, *Science, Money, and Politics: Political Triumph and Ethical Erosion.* Chicago: University of Chicago Press, 2001.

[2] National Research Council, *Assessing the Impacts of Changes in the Information Technology R&D Ecosystem: Retaining Leadership in an Increasingly Global Environment.* Washington, D.C.: National Academies Press, 2009.

[3] D. Sarewitz and R. A. Pielke, Jr., "The neglected heart of science policy: reconciling supply of and demand for science," *Environ. Sci. Policy,* vol. 10, pp. 5–16, 2007, doi: 10.1016/j.envsci.2006.10.001.

[4] L. Dilling, "Towards science in support of decision making: characterizing the supply of carbon cycle science," *Environ. Sci. Policy,* vol. 10, pp. 48–61, 2007, doi: 10.1016/j.envsci.2006.10.008.

[5] Intergovernmental Panel on Climate Change, *Climate Change 2007: The Physical Science Basis.* New York: Cambridge University Press, 2007.

[6] C. Anderson, "The End of Theory," *Wired,* vol. 16, no. 7, pp. 108–109, 2008.

[1] The algorithm at the heart of Google's search engine.

Beyond the Tsunami: Developing the Infrastructure to Deal with Life Sciences Data

CHRISTOPHER SOUTHAN

GRAHAM CAMERON
EMBL-European Bioinformatics Institute

S CIENTIFIC REVOLUTIONS ARE DIFFICULT TO QUANTIFY, but the rate of data generation in science has increased so profoundly that we can simply examine a single area of the life sciences to appreciate the magnitude of this effect across all of them. Figure 1 on the next page tracks the dramatic increase in the number of individual bases submitted to the European Molecular Biology Laboratory Nucleotide Sequence Database[1] (EMBL-Bank) by the global experimental community. This submission rate is currently growing at 200% per annum.

Custodianship of the data is held by the International Nucleotide Sequence Database Collaboration (INSDC), which consists of the DNA Data Bank of Japan (DDBJ), GenBank in the U.S., and EMBL-Bank in the UK. These three repositories exchange new data on a daily basis. As of May 2009, the totals stood at approximately 250 billion bases in 160 million entries.

A recent submission to EMBL-Bank, accession number FJ982430, illustrates the speed of data generation and the effectiveness of the global bioinformatics infrastructure in responding to a health crisis. It includes the complete H1 subunit sequence of 1,699 bases from the first case of novel H1N1 influenza virus in Denmark. This was submitted on May 4, 2009, within days of

[1] www.ebi.ac.uk/embl

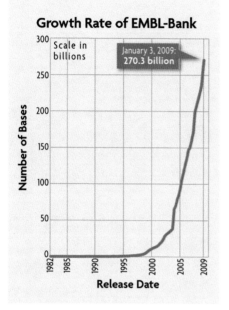

Growth Rate of EMBL-Bank

Scale in billions

January 3, 2009: 270.3 billion

Number of Bases

Release Date

FIGURE 1.

Growth in the number of bases deposited in EMBL-Bank from 1982 to the beginning of 2009.

the infected person being diagnosed. Many more virus subunit sequences have been submitted from the U.S., Italy, Mexico, Canada, Denmark, and Israel since the beginning of the 2009 global H1N1 pandemic.

EMBL-Bank is hosted at the European Bioinformatics Institute (EBI), an academic organization based in Cambridge, UK, that forms part of the European Molecular Biology Laboratory (EMBL). The EBI is a center for both research and services in bioinformatics. It hosts biological data, including nucleic acid, protein sequences, and macromolecular structures. The neighboring Wellcome Trust Sanger Institute generates about 8 percent of the world's sequencing data output. Both of these institutions on the Wellcome Trust Genome campus include scientists who generate data and administer the databases into which it flows, biocurators who provide annotations, bioinformaticians who develop analytical tools, and research groups that seek biological insights and consolidate them through further experimentation. Consequently, it is a community in which issues surrounding computing infrastructure, data storage, and mining are confronted on a daily basis, and in which both local and global collaborative solutions are continually explored.

The collective name for the nucleotide sequencing information service is the European Nucleotide Archive [1]. It includes EMBL-Bank and three other repositories that were set up for new types of data generation: the Trace Archive for trace data from first-generation capillary instruments, the Short Read Archive for data from next-generation sequencing instruments, and a pilot Trace Assembly Archive that stores alignments of sequencing reads with links to finished genomic sequences in EMBL-Bank. Data from all archives are exchanged regularly with the National Center for Biotechnology Information in the U.S. Figure 2 compares the sizes of

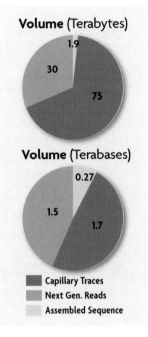

Volume (Terabytes)

1.9

30

75

Volume (Terabases)

0.27

1.5

1.7

- Capillary Traces
- Next Gen. Reads
- Assembled Sequence

FIGURE 2.

The size in data volume and nucleotide numbers of EMBL-Bank, the Trace Archive, and the Short Read Archive as of May 2009.

EMBL-Bank, the Trace Archive, and the Short Read Archive.

THE CHALLENGE OF NEXT-GENERATION SEQUENCING

The introduction in 2005 of so-called next-generation sequencing instruments that are capable of producing millions of DNA sequence reads in a single run has not only led to a huge increase in genetic information but has also placed bioinformatics, and life sciences research in general, at the leading of edge of infrastructure development for the storage, movement, analysis, interpretation, and visualization of petabyte-scale datasets [2]. The Short Read Archive, the European repository for accepting data from these machines, received 30 terabytes (TB) of data in the first six months of operation—equivalent to almost 30% of the entire EMBL-Bank content accumulated over the 28 years since data collection began. The uptake of new instruments and technical developments will not only increase submissions to this archive manyfold within a few years, but it will also prelude the arrival of "next-next-generation" DNA sequencing systems [3].

To meet this demand, the EBI has increased storage from 2,500 TB (2.5 PB) in 2008 to 5,000 TB (5 PB) in 2009—an approximate annual doubling. Even if the capacity keeps pace, bottlenecks might emerge as I/O limitations move to other points in the infrastructure. For example, at this scale, traditional backup becomes impractically slow. Indeed, a hypothetical total data loss at the EBI is estimated to require months of restore time. This means that streamed replication of the original data is becoming a more efficient option, with copies being stored at multiple locations. Another bottleneck example is that technical advances in data transfer speeds now exceed the capacity to write out to disks—about 70 megabits/sec, with no imminent expectation of major performance increases. The problem can be ameliorated by writing to multiple disks, but at a considerable increase in cost.

This inexorable load increase necessitates continual assessment of the balance between submitting derived data to the repositories and storing raw instrument output locally. Scientists at all stages of the process, experimentalists, instrument operators, datacenter administrators, bioinformaticians, and biologists who analyze the results will need to be involved in decisions about storage strategies. For example, in laboratories running high-throughput sequencing instruments, the cost of storing raw data for a particular experiment is already approaching that of repeating the experiment. Researchers may balk at the idea of deleting raw data after processing, but this is a pragmatic option that has to be considered. Less controversial solutions involve a triage of data reduction options between raw output, base calls, sequence reads, assemblies, and genome consensus sequences. An example of such a solution is FASTQ, a text-based format for storing both a nucleotide sequence and its corresponding quality scores, both encoded with a single ASCII character. Developed by the Sanger Institute, it has recently become a standard for storing the output of next-generation sequencing instruments. It can produce a 200-fold reduction in data volume—that is, 99.5% of the raw data can be discarded. Even more compressed sequence data representations are in development.

GENOMES: ROLLING OFF THE PRODUCTION LINE

The production of complete genomes is rapidly advancing our understanding of biology and evolution. The impressive progress is illustrated in Figure 3, which depicts the increase of genome sequencing projects in the Genomes OnLine Database (GOLD).

While the figure was generated based on all global sequencing projects, many of these genomes are available for analysis on the Ensembl Web site hosted jointly by the EBI and the Sanger Institute. The graph shows that, by 2010, well over 5,000 genome projects will have been initiated and more than 1,000 will have produced complete assemblies. A recent significant example is the bovine genome [4], which followed the chicken and will soon be joined by all other major agricultural species. These will not only help advance our understanding of mammalian evolution and domestication, but they will also accelerate genetic improvements for farming and food production.

RESEQUENCING THE HUMAN GENOME: ANOTHER DATA SCALE-UP

Recent genome-wide studies of human genetic variation have advanced our understanding of common human diseases. This has motivated the formation of an international consortium to develop a comprehensive catalogue of sequence variants in

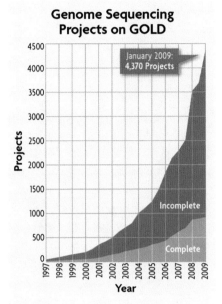

Genome Sequencing Projects on GOLD

January 2009: 4,370 Projects

Incomplete

Complete

Projects

Year

FIGURE 3.

The increase in both initiated and completed genome projects since 1997 in the Genomes OnLine Database (GOLD). Courtesy of GOLD.

multiple human populations. Over the next three years, the Sanger Institute, BGI Shenzhen in China, and the National Human Genome Research Institute's Large-Scale Genome Sequencing Program in the U.S. are planning to sequence a minimum of 1,000 human genomes.

In 2008, the pilot phase of the project generated approximately 1 terabase (trillion bases) of sequence data per month; the number is expected to double in 2009. The total generated will be about 20 terabases. The requirement of about 30 bytes of disk storage per base of sequence can be extrapolated to about 500 TB of data for the entire project. By comparison, the original human genome project took about 10 years to generate about 40 gigabases (billion bases) of DNA sequence. Over the next two years, up to 10 billion bases will be sequenced per day, equating to more than two human genomes (at 2.85 billion per human) every 24 hours. The completed dataset of 6 trillion DNA bases will be 60 times more sequence data than that shown earlier in Figure 1.

THE RAISON D'ÊTRE OF MANAGING DATA: CONVERSION TO NEW KNOWLEDGE

Even before the arrival of the draft human genome in 2001, biological databases were moving from the periphery to the center of modern life sciences research, leading to the problem that the capacity to mine data has fallen behind our ability to generate it. As a result, there is a pressing need for new methods to fully exploit not only genomic data but also other high-throughput result sets deposited in databases. These result sets are also becoming more hypothesis-neutral compared with traditional small-scale, focused experiments. Usage statistics for EBI services, shown in Figure 4 on the next page, show that the biological community, sup-

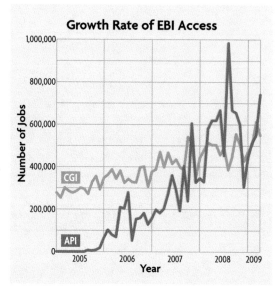

Growth Rate of EBI Access

CGI

API

FIGURE 4.

Web accesses (Common Gateway Interface [CGI]) and Web services usage (application programming interface [API]) recorded on EBI servers from 2005 to 2009.

ported by the bioinformatics specialists they collaborate with, are accessing these resources in increasing numbers.

The Web pages associated with the 63 databases hosted at the EBI now receive over 3.5 million hits per day, representing more than half a million independent users per month. While this does not match the increase in rates of data accumulation, evidence for a strong increase in data mining is provided by the Web services' programmatic access figures, which are approaching 1 million jobs per month. To further facilitate data use, the EBI is developing, using open standards, the EB-eye search system to provide a single entry point. By indexing in various formats (e.g., flat files, XML dumps, and OBO format), the system provides fast access and allows the user to search globally across all EBI databases or individually in selected resources.

EUROPEAN PLANS FOR CONSOLIDATING INFRASTRUCTURE

EBI resources are effectively responding to increasing demand from both the generators and users of data, but increases in scale for the life sciences across the whole of Europe require long-term planning. This is the mission of the ELIXIR project, which aims to ensure a reliable distributed infrastructure to maximize access to biological information that is currently distributed in more than 500 databases throughout Europe. The project addresses not only data management problems but also sustainable funding to maintain the data collections and global collaborations. It is also expected to put in place processes for developing collections for new data types, supporting interoperability of bioinformatics tools, and developing bioinformatics standards and ontologies.

The development of ELIXIR parallels the transition to a new phase in which high-performance, data-intensive computing is becoming essential to progress in the life sciences [5]. By definition, the consequences for research cannot be predicted with certainty. However, some pointers can be given. By mining not only the increasingly comprehensive datasets generated by genome sequencing mentioned above but also transcript data, proteomics information, and structural genomics output, biologists will obtain new insights into the processes of life and their evolution. This will in turn facilitate new predictive power for synthetic biology and systems biology. Beyond its profound impact on the future of academic research, this data-driven progress will also translate to the more applied areas of science—such as pharmaceutical research, biotechnology, medicine, public health, agriculture, and environmental science—to improve the quality of life for everyone.

REFERENCES

[1] G. Cochrane et al., "Petabyte-scale innovations at the European Nucleotide Archive," *Nucleic Acids Res.*, vol. 37, pp. D19–25, Jan. 2009, doi: 10.1093/nar/gkn765.

[2] E. R. Mardis, "The impact of next-generation sequencing technology on genetics," *Trends Genet.*, vol. 24, no. 3, pp. 133–141, Mar. 2008, doi: 10.1016/j.physletb.2003.10.071.

[3] N. Blow, "DNA sequencing: generation next-next," *Nat. Methods*, vol. 5, pp. 267–274, 2008, doi: 10.1038/nmeth0308-267.

[4] Bovine Genome Sequencing and Analysis Consortium, "The genome sequence of taurine cattle: a window to ruminant biology and evolution," *Science*, vol. 324, no. 5926, pp. 522–528, Apr. 24, 2009, doi: 10.1145/1327452.1327492.

[5] G. Bell, T. Hey, and A. Szalay, "Beyond the Data Deluge," *Science*, vol. 323, no. 5919, pp. 1297–1298, Mar. 6, 2009, doi: 10.1126/science.1170411.

Multicore Computing and Scientific Discovery

JAMES LARUS
DENNIS GANNON
Microsoft Research

I N THE PAST HALF CENTURY, parallel computers, parallel computation, and scientific research have grown up together. Scientists and researchers' insatiable need to perform more and larger computations has long exceeded the capabilities of conventional computers. The only approach that has met this need is parallelism—computing more than one operation simultaneously. At one level, parallelism is simple and easy to put into practice. Building a parallel computer by replicating key operating components such as the arithmetic units or even complete processors is not difficult. But it is far more challenging to build a well-balanced machine that is not stymied by internal bottlenecks. In the end, the principal problem has been software, not hardware. Parallel programs are far more difficult to design, write, debug, and tune than sequential software—which itself is still not a mature, reproducible artifact.

THE EVOLUTION OF PARALLEL COMPUTING

The evolution of successive generations of parallel computing hardware has also forced a constant rethinking of parallel algorithms and software. Early machines such as the IBM Stretch, the Cray I, and the Control Data Cyber series all exposed parallelism as vector operations. The Cray II, Encore, Alliant, and many generations of IBM machines were built with multiple processors that shared memory. Because it proved so difficult to increase the number of processors while sharing a single memory, designs evolved further into systems in which no memory was shared and processors shared information by passing messages. Beowulf clusters, consisting of racks of standard PCs connected by Ethernet, emerged as an economical approach to supercomputing. Networks improved in latency and bandwidth, and this form of distributed computing now dominates supercomputers. Other systems, such as the Cray multi-threaded platforms, demonstrated that there were different approaches to addressing shared-memory parallelism. While the scientific computing community has struggled with programming each generation of these exotic machines, the mainstream computing world has been totally satisfied with sequential programming on machines where any parallelism is hidden from the programmer deep in the hardware.

In the past few years, parallel computers have entered mainstream computing with the advent of multicore computers. Previously, most computers were sequential and performed a single operation per time step. Moore's Law drove the improvements in semiconductor technology that doubled the transistors on a chip every two years, which increased the clock speed of computers at a similar rate and also allowed for more sophisticated computer implementations. As a result, computer performance grew at roughly 40% per year from the 1970s, a rate that satisfied most software developers and computer users. This steady improvement ended because increased clock speeds require more power, and at approximately 3 GHz, chips reached the limit of economical cooling. Computer chip manufacturers, such as Intel, AMD, IBM, and Sun, shifted to multicore processors that used each Moore's Law generation of transistors to double the number of independent processors on a chip. Each processor ran no faster than its predecessor, and sometimes even slightly slower, but in aggregate, a multicore processor could perform twice the amount of computation as its predecessor.

PARALLEL PROGRAMMING CHALLENGES

This new computer generation rests on the same problematic foundation of software that the scientific community struggled with in its long experience with parallel computers. Most existing general-purpose software is written for sequential computers and will not run any faster on a multicore computer. Exploiting the potential of these machines requires new, parallel software that can break a task into multiple pieces, solve them more or less independently, and assemble the results into a single answer. Finding better ways to produce parallel software is currently the most pressing problem facing the software development community and is the subject of considerable research and development.

The scientific and engineering communities can both benefit from these urgent efforts and can help inform them. Many parallel programming techniques originated in the scientific community, whose experience has influenced the search for new approaches to programming multicore computers. Future improvements in our ability to program multicore computers will benefit all software developers as the distinction between the leading-edge scientific community and general-purpose computing is erased by the inevitability of parallel computing as the fundamental programming paradigm.

One key problem in parallel programming today is that most of it is conducted at a very low level of abstraction. Programmers must break their code into components that run on specific processors and communicate by writing into shared memory locations or exchanging messages. In many ways, this state of affairs is similar to the early days of computing, when programs were written in assembly languages for a specific computer and had to be rewritten to run on a different machine. In both situations, the problem was not just the lack of reusability of programs, but also that assembly language development was less productive and more error prone than writing programs in higher-level languages.

ADDRESSING THE CHALLENGES

Several lines of research are attempting to raise the level at which parallel programs can be written. The oldest and best-established idea is data parallel programming. In this programming paradigm, an operation or sequence of operations is applied simultaneously to all items in a collection of data. The granularity of the operation can range from adding two numbers in a data parallel addition of two matrices to complex data mining calculations in a map-reduce style computation [1]. The appeal of data parallel computation is that parallelism is mostly hidden from the programmer. Each computation proceeds in isolation from the concurrent computations on other data, and the code specifying the computation is sequential. The developer need not worry about the details of moving data and running computations because they are the responsibility of the runtime system. GPUs (graphics processing units) provide hardware support for this style of programming, and they have recently been extended into GPGPUs (general-purpose GPUs) that perform very high-performance numeric computations.

Unfortunately, data parallelism is not a programming model that works for all types of problems. Some computations require more communication and coordination. For example, protein folding calculates the forces on all atoms in parallel, but local interactions are computed in a manner different from remote interactions. Other examples of computations that are hard to write as data parallel programs include various forms of adaptive mesh refinement that are used in many modern physics simulations in which local structures, such as clumps of matter or cracks in a material structure, need finer spatial resolution than the rest of the system.

A new idea that has recently attracted considerable research attention is transactional memory (TM), a mechanism for coordinating the sharing of data in a multicore computer. Data sharing is a rich source of programming errors because the developer needs to ensure that a processor that changes the value of data has exclusive access to it. If another processor also tries to access the data, one of the two updates can be lost, and if a processor reads the data too early, it might see an inconsistent value. The most common mechanism for preventing this type of error is a lock, which a program uses to prevent more than one processor from accessing a memory location simultaneously. Locks, unfortunately, are low-level mechanisms that are easily and frequently misused in ways that both allow concurrent access and cause deadlocks that freeze program execution.

TM is a higher-level abstraction that allows the developer to identify a group of program statements that should execute atomically—that is, as if no other part of the program is executing at the same time. So instead of having to acquire locks for all the data that the statements might access, the developer shifts the burden to the runtime system and hardware. TM is a promising idea, but many engineering challenges still stand in the way of its widespread use. Currently, TM is expensive to implement without support in the processors, and its usability and utility in large, real-world codes is as yet undemonstrated. If these issues can be resolved, TM promises to make many aspects of multicore programming far easier and less error prone.

Another new idea is the use of functional programming languages. These languages embody a style of programming that mostly prohibits updates to program state. In other words, in these languages a variable can be given an initial value, but that value cannot be changed. Instead, a new variable is created with the new value. This style of programming is well suited to parallel programming because it eliminates the updates that require synchronization between two processors. Parallel, functional programs generally use mutable state only for communication among parallel processors, and they require locks or TM only for this small, distinct part of their data.

Until recently, only the scientific and engineering communities have struggled with the difficulty of using parallel computers for anything other than the most embarrassingly parallel tasks. The advent of multicore processors has changed this situation and has turned parallel programming into a major challenge for all software developers. The new ideas and programming tools developed for mainstream programs will likely also benefit the technical community and provide it with new means to take better advantage of the continually increasing power of multicore processors.

REFERENCES

[1] D. Gannon and D. Reed, "Parallelism and the Cloud," in this volume.

Parallelism and the Cloud

DENNIS GANNON
DAN REED
Microsoft Research

OVER THE PAST DECADE, scientific and engineering research via computing has emerged as the third pillar of the scientific process, complementing theory and experiment. Several national studies have highlighted the importance of computational science as a critical enabler of scientific discovery and national competitiveness in the physical and biological sciences, medicine and healthcare, and design and manufacturing [1-3].

As the term suggests, computational science has historically focused on computation: the creation and execution of mathematical models of natural and artificial processes. Driven by opportunity and necessity, computational science is expanding to encompass both computing and data analysis. Today, a rising tsunami of data threatens to overwhelm us, consuming our attention by its very volume and diversity. Driven by inexpensive, seemingly ubiquitous sensors, broadband networks, and high-capacity storage systems, the tsunami encompasses data from sensors that monitor our planet from deep in the ocean, from land instruments, and from space-based imaging systems. It also includes environmental measurements and healthcare data that quantify biological processes and the effects of surrounding conditions. Simply put, we are moving from data paucity to a data plethora, which is leading to a relative poverty of human attention to any individual datum and is necessitating machine-assisted winnowing.

This ready availability of diverse data is shifting scientific approaches from the traditional, hypothesis-driven scientific method to science based on exploration. Researchers no longer simply ask, "What experiment could I construct to test this hypothesis?" Increasingly, they ask, "What correlations can I glean from extant data?" More tellingly, one wishes to ask, "What insights could I glean if I could fuse data from multiple disciplines and domains?" The challenge is analyzing many petabytes of data on a time scale that is practical in human terms.

The ability to create rich, detailed models of natural and artificial phenomena and to process large volumes of experimental data created by a new generation of scientific instruments that are themselves powered by computing makes computing a universal intellectual amplifier, advancing all of science and engineering and powering the knowledge economy. Cloud computing is the latest technological evolution of computational science, allowing groups to host, process, and analyze large volumes of multidisciplinary data. Consolidating computing and storage in very large datacenters creates economies of scale in facility design and construction, equipment acquisition, and operations and maintenance that are not possible when these elements are distributed. Moreover, consolidation and hosting mitigate many of the sociological and technical barriers that have limited multidisciplinary data sharing and collaboration. Finally, cloud hosting facilitates long-term data preservation—a task that is particularly challenging for universities and government agencies and is critical to our ability to conduct longitudinal experiments.

It is not unreasonable to say that modern datacenters and modern supercomputers are like twins separated at birth. Both are massively parallel in design, and both are organized as a network of communicating computational nodes. The individual nodes of each are based on commodity microprocessors that have multiple cores, large memories, and local disk storage. They both execute applications that are designed to exploit massive amounts of parallelism. Their differences lie in their evolution. Massively parallel supercomputers have been designed to support computation with occasional bursts of input/output and to complete a single massive calculation as fast as possible, one job at a time. In contrast, datacenters direct their power outward to the world and consume vast quantities of input data.

Parallelism can be exploited in cloud computing in two ways. The first is for human access. Cloud applications are designed to be accessed as Web services, so they are organized as two or more layers of processes. One layer provides the service interface to the user's browser or client application. This "Web role" layer accepts users' requests and manages the tasks assigned to the second layer. The second layer of processes, sometimes known as the "worker role" layer, executes the analytical tasks required to satisfy user requests. One Web role and one worker role may be sufficient for a few simultaneous users, but if a cloud application is to be widely used—such as for search, customized maps, social networks, weather services, travel data, or online auctions—it must support thousands of concurrent users.

The second way in which parallelism is exploited involves the nature of the data analysis tasks undertaken by the application. In many large data analysis scenarios, it is not practical to use a single processor or task to scan a massive dataset or data stream to look for a pattern—the overhead and delay are too great. In these cases, one can partition the data across large numbers of processors, each of which can analyze a subset of the data. The results of each "sub-scan" are then combined and returned to the user.

This "map-reduce" pattern is frequently used in datacenter applications and is one in a broad family of parallel data analysis queries used in cloud computing. Web search is the canonical example of this two-phase model. It involves constructing a searchable keyword index of the Web's contents, which entails creating a copy of the Web and sorting the contents via a sequence of map-reduce steps. Three key technologies support this model of parallelism: Google has an internal version [4], Yahoo! has an open source version known as Hadoop, and Microsoft has a map-reduce tool known as DryadLINQ [5]. Dryad is a mechanism to support the execution of distributed collections of tasks that can be configured into an arbitrary directed acyclic graph (DAG). The Language Integrated Query (LINQ) extension to C# allows SQL-like query expressions to be embedded directly in regular programs. The DryadLINQ system can automatically compile these queries into Dryad DAG, which can be executed automatically in the cloud.

Microsoft Windows Azure supports a combination of multi-user scaling and data analysis parallelism. In Azure, applications are designed as stateless "roles" that fetch tasks from queues, execute them, and place new tasks or data into other queues. Map-reduce computations in Azure consist of two pools of worker roles: mappers, which take map tasks off a map queue and push data to the Azure storage, and reducers, which look for reduce tasks that point to data in the storage system that need reducing. Whereas DryadLINQ executes a static DAG, Azure can execute an implicit DAG in which nodes correspond to roles and links correspond to messages in queues. Azure computations can also represent the parallelism generated by very large numbers of concurrent users.

This same type of map-reduce data analysis appears repeatedly in large-scale scientific analyses. For example, consider the task of matching a DNA sample against the thousands of known DNA sequences. This kind of search is an "embarrassingly parallel" task that can easily be sped up if it is partitioned into many independent search tasks over subsets of the data. Similarly, consider the task of searching for patterns in medical data, such as to find anomalies in fMRI scans of brain images, or the task of searching for potential weather anomalies in streams of events from radars.

Finally, another place where parallelism can be exploited in the datacenter is at the hardware level of an individual node. Not only does each node have multiple processors, but each typically has multiple computer cores. For many data analysis tasks, one can exploit massive amounts of parallelism at the instruction level. For example, filtering noise from sensor data may involve invoking a Fast Fourier Transform (FFT) or other spectral methods. These computations can be sped up by using general-purpose graphics processing units (GPGPUs) in each node. Depending on the rate at which a node can access data, this GPGPU-based processing may allow us to decrease the number of nodes required to meet an overall service rate.

The World Wide Web began as a loose federation of simple Web servers that each hosted scientific documents and data of interest to a relatively small community of researchers. As the number of servers grew exponentially and the global Internet matured, Web search transformed what was initially a scientific experiment into a new economic and social force. The effectiveness of search was achievable only because of the available parallelism in massive datacenters. As we enter the period in which all of science is being driven by a data explosion, cloud computing and its inherent ability to exploit parallelism at many levels has become a fundamental new enabling technology to advance human knowledge.

REFERENCES

[1] President's Information Technology Advisory Committee, "Computational Science: Ensuring America's Competitiveness," June 2005, www.nitrd.gov/pitac/reports/20050609_computational/computational.pdf.

[2] D. A. Reed, Ed., "Workshop on The Roadmap for the Revitalization of High-End Computing," June 2003, www.cra.org/reports/supercomputing.pdf.

[3] S. L. Graham, M. Snir, and C. A. Patterson, Eds., Getting Up to Speed: The Future of Supercomputing, Washington, D.C.: National Academies Press, 2004, www.nap.edu/openbook.php?record_id=11148.

[4] J. Dean and S. Ghemawat, "MapReduce: Simplified Data Processing on Large Clusters," OSDI'04: Sixth Symposium on Operating Systems Design and Implementation, San Francisco, CA, Dec. 2004, doi: 10.1145/1327452.1327492.

[5] Y. Yu., M. Isard, D. Fetterly, M. Budiu, Ú. Erlingsson, P. Kumar Gunda, and J. Currey, "DryadLINQ: A System for General-Purpose Distributed Data-Parallel Computing Using a High-Level Language," OSDI'08 Eighth Symposium on Operating Systems Design and Implementation.

The Impact of Workflow Tools on Data-centric Research

CAROLE GOBLE
University of Manchester

DAVID DE ROURE
University of Southampton

W E ARE IN AN ERA OF DATA-CENTRIC SCIENTIFIC RESEARCH, in which hypotheses are not only tested through directed data collection and analysis but also generated by combining and mining the pool of data already available [1-3]. The scientific data landscape we draw upon is expanding rapidly in both scale and diversity. Taking the life sciences as an example, high-throughput gene sequencing platforms are capable of generating terabytes of data in a single experiment, and data volumes are set to increase further with industrial-scale automation. From 2001 to 2009, the number of databases reported in *Nucleic Acids Research* jumped from 218 to 1,170 [4]. Not only are the datasets growing in size and number, but they are only partly coordinated and often incompatible [5], which means that discovery and integration tasks are significant challenges. At the same time, we are drawing on a broader array of data sources: modern biology draws insights from combining different types of "omic" data (proteomic, metabolomic, transcriptomic, genomic) as well as data from other disciplines such as chemistry, clinical medicine, and public health, while systems biology links multi-scale data with multi-scale mathematical models. These data encompass all types: from structured database records to published articles, raw numeric data, images, and descriptive interpretations that use controlled vocabularies.

Data generation on this scale must be matched by scalable processing methods. The preparation, management, and analysis of data are bottlenecks and also beyond the skill of many scientists. Workflows [6] provide (1) a systematic and automated means of conducting analyses across diverse datasets and applications; (2) a way of capturing this process so that results can be reproduced and the method can be reviewed, validated, repeated, and adapted; (3) a visual scripting interface so that computational scientists can create these pipelines without low-level programming concern; and (4) an integration and access platform for the growing pool of independent resource providers so that computational scientists need not specialize in each one. The workflow is thus becoming a paradigm for enabling science on a large scale by managing data preparation and analysis pipelines, as well as the preferred vehicle for computational knowledge extraction.

WORKFLOWS DEFINED

A workflow is a precise description of a scientific procedure—a multi-step process to coordinate multiple tasks, acting like a sophisticated script [7]. Each task represents the execution of a computational process, such as running a program, submitting a query to a database, submitting a job to a compute cloud or grid, or invoking a service over the Web to use a remote resource. Data output from one task is consumed by subsequent tasks according to a predefined graph topology that "orchestrates" the flow of data. Figure 1 presents an example workflow, encoded in the Taverna Workflow Workbench [8], which searches for genes by linking four publicly available data resources distributed in the U.S., Europe, and Japan: BioMart, Entrez, UniProt, and KEGG.

Workflow systems generally have three components: an execution platform, a visual design suite, and a development kit. The platform executes the workflow on behalf of applications and handles common crosscutting concerns, including (1) *invocation* of the service applications and handling the heterogeneity of data types and interfaces on multiple computing platforms; (2) *monitoring and recovery* from failures; (3) *optimization* of memory, storage, and execution, including concurrency and parallelization; (4) *data handling*: mapping, referencing, movement, streaming, and staging; (5) *logging* of processes and data provenance tracking; and (6) *security* and monitoring of access policies. Workflow systems are required to support long-running processes in volatile environments and thus must be robust and capable of fault tolerance and recovery. They also need to evolve continually to harness the growing capabilities of underlying computational and storage

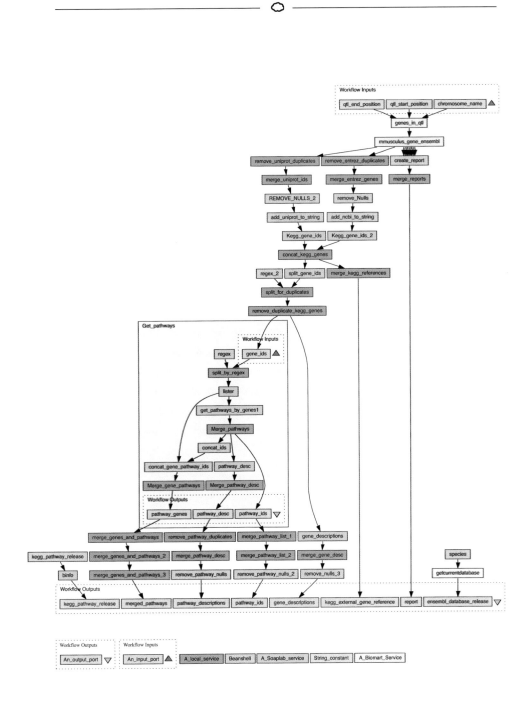

FIGURE 1.

A Taverna workflow that connects several internationally distributed datasets to identify candidate genes that could be implicated in resistance to African trypanosomiasis [11].

resources, delivering greater capacity for analysis.

The design suite provides a visual scripting application for authoring and sharing workflows and preparing the components that are to be incorporated as executable steps. The aim is to shield the author from the complexities of the underlying applications and enable the author to design and understand workflows without recourse to commissioning specialist and specific applications or hiring software engineers. This empowers scientists to build their own pipelines when they need them and how they want them. Finally, the development kit enables developers to extend the capabilities of the system and enables workflows to be embedded into applications, Web portals, or databases. This embedding is transformational: it has the potential to incorporate sophisticated knowledge seamlessly and invisibly into the tools that scientists use routinely.

Each workflow system has its own language, design suite, and software components, and the systems vary in their execution models and the kinds of components they coordinate [9]. Sedna is one of the few to use the industry-standard Business Process Execution Language (BPEL) for scientific workflows [10]. General-purpose open source workflow systems include Taverna,[1] Kepler,[2] Pegasus,[3] and Triana.[4] Other systems, such as the LONI Pipeline[5] for neuroimaging and the commercial Pipeline Pilot[6] for drug discovery, are more geared toward specific applications and are optimized to support specific component libraries. These focus on interoperating applications; other workflow systems target the provisioning of compute cycles or submission of jobs to grids. For example, Pegasus and DAGMan[7] have been used for a series of large-scale eScience experiments such as prediction models in earthquake forecasting using sensor data in the Southern California Earthquake Center (SCEC) CyberShake project.[8]

WORKFLOW USAGE

Workflows liberate scientists from the drudgery of routine data processing so they can concentrate on scientific discovery. They shoulder the burden of routine tasks, they represent the computational protocols needed to undertake data-centric

[1] www.taverna.org.uk
[2] http://kepler-project.org
[3] http://pegasus.isi.edu
[4] www.trianacode.org
[5] http://pipeline.loni.ucla.edu
[6] http://accelrys.com/products/scitegic
[7] www.cs.wisc.edu/condor/dagman
[8] http://epicenter.usc.edu/cmeportal/CyberShake.html

science, and they open up the use of processes and data resources to a much wider group of scientists and scientific application developers.

Workflows are ideal for systematically, accurately, and repeatedly running routine procedures: managing data capture from sensors or instruments; cleaning, normalizing, and validating data; securely and efficiently moving and archiving data; comparing data across repeated runs; and regularly updating data warehouses. For example, the Pan-STARRS[9] astronomical survey uses Microsoft Trident Scientific Workflow Workbench[10] workflows to load and validate telescope detections running at about 30 TB per year. Workflows have also proved useful for maintaining and updating data collections and warehouses by reacting to changes in the underlying datasets. For example, the Nijmegen Medical Centre rebuilt the tGRAP G-protein coupled receptors mutant database using a suite of text-mining Taverna workflows.

At a higher level, a workflow is an explicit, precise, and modular expression of an *in silico* or "dry lab" experimental protocol. Workflows are ideal for gathering and aggregating data from distributed datasets and data-emitting algorithms—a core activity in dataset annotation; data curation; and multi-evidential, comparative science. In Figure 1, disparate datasets are searched to find and aggregate data related to metabolic pathways implicated in resistance to African trypanosomiasis; interlinked datasets are chained together by the dataflow. In this instance, the automated and systematic processing by the workflow overcame the inadequacies of manual data triage—which leads to prematurely excluding data from analysis to cope with the quantity—and delivered new results [11].

Beyond data assembly, workflows codify data mining and knowledge discovery pipelines and parameter sweeps across predictive algorithms. For example, LEAD[11] workflows are driven by external events generated by data mining agents that monitor collections of instruments for significant patterns to trigger a storm prediction analysis; the Jet Propulsion Laboratory uses Taverna workflows for exploring a large space of multiple-parameter configurations of space instruments.

Finally, workflow systems liberate the implicit workflow embedded in an application into an explicit and reusable specification over a common software machinery and shared infrastructure. Expert informaticians use workflow systems directly as means to develop workflows for handling infrastructure; expert

[9] http://pan-starrs.ifa.hawaii.edu
[10] http://research.microsoft.com/en-us/collaboration/tools/trident.aspx
[11] http://portal.leadproject.org

scientific informaticians use them to design and explore new investigative procedures; a larger group of scientists uses precooked workflows with restricted configuration constraints launched from within applications or hidden behind Web portals.

WORKFLOW-ENABLED DATA-CENTRIC SCIENCE

Workflows offer techniques to support the new paradigm of data-centric science. They can be replayed and repeated. Results and secondary data can be computed as needed using the latest sources, providing virtual data (or on-demand) warehouses by effectively providing distributed query processing. *Smart reruns* of workflows automatically deliver new outcomes when fresh primary data and new results become available—and also when new methods become available. The workflows themselves, as first-class citizens in data-centric science, can be generated and transformed dynamically to meet the requirements at hand. In a landscape of data in considerable flux, workflows provide robustness, accountability, and full auditing. By combining workflows and their execution records with published results, we can promote systematic, unbiased, transparent, and comparable research in which outcomes carry the provenance of their derivation. This can potentially accelerate scientific discovery.

To accelerate experimental *design,* workflows can be reconfigured and repurposed as new components or templates. Creating workflows requires expertise that is hard won and often outside the skill set of the researcher. Workflows are often complex and challenging to build because they are essentially forms of programming that require some understanding of the datasets and the tools they manipulate [12]. Hence there is significant benefit in establishing shared collections of workflows that contain standard processing pipelines for immediate reuse or for repurposing in whole or in part. These aggregations of expertise and resources can help propagate techniques and best practices. Specialists can create the application steps, experts can design the workflows and set parameters, and the inexperienced can benefit by using sophisticated protocols.

The myExperiment[12] social Web site has demonstrated that by adopting content-sharing tools for repositories of workflows, we can enable social networking around workflows and provide community support for social tagging, comments, ratings and recommendations, and mixing of new workflows with those previously

---

[12] www.myexperiment.org

deposited [13]. This is made possible by the scale of participation in data-centric science, which can be brought to bear on challenging problems. For example, the environment of workflow execution is in such a state of flux that workflows appear to decay over time, but workflows can be kept current by a combination of expert and community curation.

Workflows enable data-centric science to be a collaborative endeavor on multiple levels. They enable scientists to collaborate over shared data and shared services, and they grant non-developers access to sophisticated code and applications without the need to install and operate them. Consequently, scientists can use the best applications, not just the ones with which they are familiar. Multidisciplinary workflows promote even broader collaboration. In this sense, a workflow system is a framework for reusing a community's tools and datasets that respects the original codes and overcomes diverse coding styles. Initiatives such as the BioCatalogue[13] registry of life science Web services and the component registries deployed at SCEC enable components to be discovered. In addition to the benefits that come from explicit sharing, there is considerable value in the information that may be gathered just through monitoring the use of data sources, services, and methods. This enables automatic monitoring of resources and recommendation of common practice and optimization.

Although the impact of workflow tools on data-centric research is potentially profound—scaling processing to match the scaling of data—many challenges exist over and above the engineering issues inherent in large-scale distributed software [14]. There are a confusing number of workflow platforms with various capabilities and purposes and little compliance with standards. Workflows are often difficult to author, using languages that are at an inappropriate level of abstraction and expecting too much knowledge of the underlying infrastructure. The reusability of a workflow is often confined to the project it was conceived in—or even to its author—and it is inherently only as strong as its components. Although workflows encourage providers to supply clean, robust, and validated data services, component failure is common. If the services or infrastructure decays, so does the workflow. Unfortunately, debugging failing workflows is a crucial but neglected topic. Contemporary workflow platforms fall short of adequately supporting rapid deployment into the user applications that consume them, and legacy application codes need to be integrated and managed.

---

[13] www.biocatalogue.org

————————————————— ◯ —————————————————

CONCLUSION

Workflows affect data-centric research in four ways. First, they shift scientific practice. For example, in a data-driven hypothesis [1], data analysis yields results that are to be tested in the laboratory. Second, they have the potential to empower scientists to be the authors of their own sophisticated data processing pipelines without having to wait for software developers to produce the tools they need. Third, they offer systematic production of data that is comparable and verifiably attributable to its source. Finally, people speak of a data deluge [15], and data-centric science could be characterized as being about the primacy of data as opposed to the primacy of the academic paper or document [16], but it brings with it a method deluge: workflows illustrate *primacy of method* as another crucial paradigm in data-centric research.

REFERENCES

[1] D. B. Kell and S. G. Oliver, "Here is the evidence, now what is the hypothesis? The complementary roles of inductive and hypothesis-driven science in the post-genomic era," *BioEssays*, vol. 26, no. 1, pp. 99–105, 2004, doi: 10.1002/bies.10385.

[2] A. Halevy, P. Norvig, and F. Pereira, "The Unreasonable Effectiveness of Data," *IEEE Intell. Syst.*, vol. 24, no. 2, pp. 8–12. 2009, doi: 10.1109/MIS.2009.36.

[3] C. Anderson, "The End of Theory: The Data Deluge Makes the Scientific Method Obsolete," *Wired*, vol. 16, no. 7, June 23, 2008, www.wired.com/science/discoveries/magazine/16-07/pb_theory.

[4] M. Y. Galperin and G. R. Cochrane, "Nucleic Acids Research annual Database Issue and the NAR online Molecular Biology Database Collection in 2009," *Nucl. Acids Res.*, vol. 37 (Database issue), pp. D1–D4, doi: 10.1093/nar/gkn942.

[5] C. Goble and R. Stevens, "The State of the Nation in Data Integration in Bioinformatics," *J. Biomed. Inform.*, vol. 41, no. 5, pp. 687–693, 2008.

[6] I. J. Taylor, E. Deelman, D. B. Gannon, and M. Shields, Eds., *Workflows for e-Science: Scientific Workflows for Grids.* London: Springer, 2007.

[7] P. Romano, "Automation of in-silico data analysis processes through workflow management systems", *Brief Bioinform*, vol. 9, no. 1, pp. 57–68, Jan. 2008, doi: 10.1093/bib/bbm056.

[8] T. Oinn, M. Greenwood, M. Addis, N. Alpdemir, J. Ferris, K. Glover, C. Goble, A. Goderis, D. Hull, D. Marvin, P. Li, P. Lord, M. Pocock, M. Senger, R. Stevens, A. Wipat, and C. Wroe, "Taverna: lessons in creating a workflow environment for the life sciences," *Concurrency and Computation: Practice and Experience*, vol. 18, no. 10, pp. 1067–1100, 2006, doi: 10.1002/cpe.v18:10.

[9] E. Deelman, D. Gannon, M. Shields, and I. Taylor, "Workflows and e-Science: An overview of workflow system features and capabilities," *Future Gen. Comput. Syst.*, vol. 25, no. 5, pp. 528–540, May 2009, doi: 10.1016/j.future.2008.06.012.

[10] B. Wassermann, W. Emmerich, B. Butchart, N. Cameron, L. Chen, and J. Patel, "Sedna: a BPEL-based environment for visual scientific workflow modelling," in I. J. Taylor, E. Deelman, D. B. Gannon, and M. Shields, Eds., *Workflows for e-Science: Scientific Workflows for Grids.* London: Springer, 2007, pp. 428–449, doi: 10.1.1.103.7892.

[11] P. Fisher, C. Hedeler, K. Wolstencroft, H. Hulme, H. Noyes, S. Kemp, R. Stevens, and A. Brass,

"A Systematic Strategy for Large-Scale Analysis of Genotype-Phenotype Correlations: Identification of candidate genes involved in African Trypanosomiasis," *Nucleic Acids Res.*, vol. 35, no. 16, pp. 5625–5633, 2007, doi: 10.1093/nar/gkm623.

[12] A. Goderis, U. Sattler, P. Lord, and C. Goble, "Seven Bottlenecks to Workflow Reuse and Repurposing in The Semantic Web," *ISWC 2005*, pp. 323–337, doi: 10.1007/11574620_25.

[13] D. De Roure, C. Goble, and R. Stevens, "The Design and Realisation of the myExperiment Virtual Research Environment for Social Sharing of Workflows," *Future Gen. Comput. Syst.*, vol. 25, pp. 561–567, 2009, doi: 10.1016/j.future.2008.06.010.

[14] Y. Gil, E. Deelman, M. Ellisman, T. Fahringer, G. Fox, D. Gannon, C. Goble, M. Livny, L. Moreau, and J. Myers, "Examining the Challenges of Scientific Workflows," *Computer*, vol. 40, pp. 24–32, 2007, doi: 10.1109/MC.2007.421.

[15] G. Bell, T. Hey, and A. Szalay, "Beyond the Data Deluge," *Science*, vol. 323, no. 5919, pp. 1297–1298, Mar. 6, 2009, doi: 10.1126/science.1170411.

[16] G. Erbach, "Data-centric view in e-Science information systems," *Data Sci. J.*, vol. 5, pp. 219–222, 2006, doi: 10.2481/dsj.5.219.

Semantic eScience: Encoding Meaning in Next-Generation Digitally Enhanced Science

PETER FOX
JAMES HENDLER
Rensselaer Polytechnic
Institute

S CIENCE IS BECOMING INCREASINGLY DEPENDENT ON DATA, yet traditional data technologies were not designed for the scale and heterogeneity of data in the modern world. Projects such as the Large Hadron Collider (LHC) and the Australian Square Kilometre Array Pathfinder (ASKAP) will generate petabytes of data that must be analyzed by hundreds of scientists working in multiple countries and speaking many different languages. The digital or electronic facilitation of science, or eScience [1], is now essential and becoming widespread.

Clearly, data-intensive science, one component of eScience, must move beyond data warehouses and closed systems, striving instead to allow access to data to those outside the main project teams, allow for greater integration of sources, and provide interfaces to those who are expert scientists but not experts in data administration and computation. As eScience flourishes and the barriers to free and open access to data are being lowered, other, more challenging, questions are emerging, such as, "How do I use this data that I did not generate?" or "How do I use this data type, which I have never seen, with the data I use every day?" or "What should I do if I really need data from another discipline but I cannot understand its terms?" This list of questions is large and growing as data and information product use increases and as more of science comes to rely on specialized devices.

An important insight into dealing with heterogeneous data is that if you know what the data "means," it will be easier to use. As the volume, complexity, and heterogeneity of data resources grow, scientists increasingly need new capabilities that rely on new "semantic" approaches (e.g., in the form of ontologies—machine encodings of terms, concepts, and relations among them). Semantic technologies are gaining momentum in eScience areas such as solar-terrestrial physics (see Figure 1), ecology,[1] ocean and marine sciences,[2] healthcare, and life sciences,[3] to name but a few. The developers of eScience infrastructures are increasingly in need of semantic-based methodologies, tools, and middleware. They can in turn facilitate scientific knowledge modeling, logic-based hypothesis checking, semantic data integration, application composition, and integrated knowledge discovery and data analysis for different scientific domains and systems noted above, for use by scientists, students, and, increasingly, non-experts.

The influence of the artificial intelligence community and the increasing amount of data available on the Web (which has led many scientists to use the Web as their primary "computer") have led semantic Web researchers to focus both on formal aspects of semantic representation languages and on general-purpose semantic application development. Languages are being standardized, and communities are in turn using those languages to build and use ontologies—specifications of concepts and terms and the relations between them (in the formal, machine-readable sense). All of the capabilities currently needed by eScience—including data integration, fusion, and mining; workflow development, orchestration, and execution; capture of provenance, lineage, and data quality; validation, verification, and trust of data authenticity; and fitness for purpose—need semantic representation and mediation if eScience is to become fully data-intensive.

The need for more semantics in eScience also arises in part from the increasingly distributed and interdisciplinary challenges of modern research. For example, the availability of high spatial-resolution remote sensing data (such as imagery) from satellites for ecosystem science is simultaneously changing the nature of research in other scientific fields, such as environmental science. Yet ground-truthing with *in situ* data creates an immediate data-integration challenge. Questions that arise for researchers who use such data include, "How can 'point' data be reconciled with various satellite data—e.g., swath or gridded—products?" "How is the spatial

---

[1] E.g., the Science Environment for Ecological Knowledge (SEEK) and [2].
[2] E.g., the Marine Metadata Interoperability (MMI) project.
[3] E.g., the Semantic Web Health Care and Life Sciences (HCLS) Interest Group and [3].

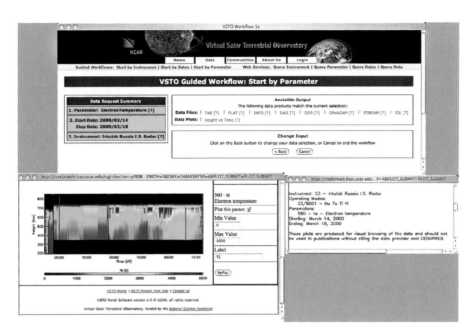

FIGURE 1.

The Virtual Solar-Terrestrial Observatory (VSTO) provides data integration between physical parameters measured by different instruments. VSTO also mediates independent coordinate information to select appropriate plotting types using a semantic eScience approach without the user having to know the underlying representations and structure of the data [4, 5].

registration performed?" "Do these data represent the 'same' thing, at the same vertical (as well as geographic) position or at the same time, and does that matter?" Another scientist, such as a biologist, might need to access the same data from a very different perspective, to ask questions such as, "I found this particular species in an unexpected location. What are the geophysical parameters—temperature, humidity, and so on—for this area, and how has it changed over the last weeks, months, years?" Answers to such questions reside in both the metadata and the data itself. Perhaps more important is the fact that data and information products are increasingly being made available via Web services, so the semantic binding (i.e., the meaning) we seek must shift from being at the data level to being at the Internet/Web service level.

Semantics adds not only well-defined and machine-encoded definitions of vocabularies, concepts, and terms, but it also explains the interrelationships among them (and especially, on the Web, among different vocabularies residing in different documents or repositories) in declarative (stated) and conditional (e.g., rule-based or logic) forms. One of the present challenges around semantic eScience is balancing expressivity (of the semantic representation) with the complexity of defining terms used by scientific experts and implementing the resulting systems. This balance is application dependent, which means there is no one-approach-fits-all solution. In turn, this implies that a peer relationship is required between physical scientists and computer scientists, and between software engineers and data managers and data providers.

The last few years have seen significant development in Web-based (i.e., XML) markup languages, including stabilization and standardization. Retrospective data and their accompanying catalogs are now provided as Web services, and real-time and near-real-time data are becoming standardized as sensor Web services are emerging. This means that diverse datasets are now widely available. Clearinghouses for such service registries, including the Earth Observing System Clearinghouse (ECHO) and the Global Earth Observation System of Systems (GEOSS) for Earth science, are becoming populated, and these complement comprehensive inventory catalogs such as NASA's Global Change Master Directory (GCMD). However, these registries remain largely limited to syntax-only representations of the services and underlying data. Intensive human effort—to match inputs, outputs, and preconditions as well as the meaning of methods for the services—is required to utilize them.

Project and community work to develop data models to improve lower-level interoperability is also increasing. These models expose domain vocabularies, which is helpful for immediate domains of interest but not necessarily for crosscutting areas such as Earth science data records and collections. As noted in reports from the international level to the agency level, data from new missions, together with data from existing agency sources, are increasingly being used synergistically with other observing and modeling sources. As these data sources are made available as services, the need for interoperability among differing vocabularies, services, and method representations remains, and the limitations of syntax-only (or lightweight semantics, such as coverage) become clear. Further, as demand for information products (representations of the data beyond pure science use) increases, the need for non-specialist access to information services based on science data is rapidly increasing. This need is not being met in most application areas.

Those involved in extant efforts (noted earlier, such as solar-terrestrial physics, ecology, ocean and marine sciences, healthcare, and life sciences) have made the case for interoperability that moves away from reliance on agreements at the data-element, or syntactic, level toward a higher scientific, or semantic, level. Results from such research projects have demonstrated these types of data integration capabilities in interdisciplinary and cross-instrument measurement use. Now that syntax-only interoperability is no longer state-of-the-art, the next logical step is to use the semantics to begin to enable a similar level of semantic support at the data-as-a-service level.

Despite this increasing awareness of the importance of semantics to data-intensive eScience, participation from the scientific community to develop the particular requirements from specific science areas has been inadequate. Scientific researchers are growing ever more dependent on the Web for their data needs, but to date they have not yet created a coherent agenda for exploring the emerging trends being enabled by semantic technologies and for interacting with Semantic Web researchers. To help create such an agenda, we need to develop a multi-disciplinary field of *semantic eScience* that fosters the growth and development of data-intensive scientific applications based on semantic methodologies and technologies, as well as related knowledge-based approaches. To this end, we issue a four-point call to action:

- Researchers in science must work with colleagues in computer science and informatics to develop field-specific requirements and to implement and evaluate the languages, tools, and applications being developed for semantic eScience.

- Scientific and professional societies must provide the settings in which the needed rich interplay between science requirements and informatics capabilities can be realized, and they must acknowledge the importance of this work in career advancement via citation-like metrics.

- Funding agencies must increasingly target the building of communities of practice, with emphasis on the types of interdisciplinary teams of researchers and practitioners that are needed to advance and sustain semantic eScience efforts.

- All parties—scientists, societies, and funders—must play a role in creating governance around controlled vocabularies, taxonomies, and ontologies that can be used in scientific applications to ensure the currency and evolution of knowledge encoded in semantics.

Although early efforts are under way in all four areas, much more must be done. The very nature of dealing with the increasing complexity of modern science demands it.

REFERENCES

[1] T. Hey and A. E. Trefethen, "Cyberinfrastructure for e-Science," *Science,* vol. 308, no. 5723, May 2005, pp. 817–821, doi: 10.1126/science.1110410.

[2] J. Madin, S. Bowers, M. Schildhauer, S. Krivov, D. Pennington, and F. Villa, "An Ontology for Describing and Synthesizing Ecological Observation Data," *Ecol. Inf.,* vol. 2, no. 3, pp. 279–296, 2007, doi: 10.1016/j.ecoinf.2007.05.004.

[3] E. Neumann, "A Life Science Semantic Web: Are We There Yet?" *Sci. STKE,* p. 22, 2005, doi: 10.1126/stke.2832005pe22.

[4] P. Fox, D. McGuinness, L. Cinquini, P. West, J. Garcia, and J. Benedict, "Ontology-supported scientific data frameworks: The virtual solar-terrestrial observatory experience," *Comput. Geosci.,* vol. 35, no. 4, pp. 724–738, 2009, doi: 10.1.1.141.1827.

[5] D. McGuinness, P. Fox, L. Cinquini, P. West, J. Garcia, J. L. Benedict, and D. Middleton, "The Virtual Solar-Terrestrial Observatory: A Deployed Semantic Web Application Case Study for Scientific Research," *AI Mag.,* vol. 29, no. 1 , pp. 65–76, 2007, doi: 10.1145/1317353.1317355.

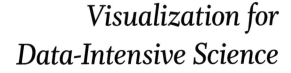

Visualization for Data-Intensive Science

CHARLES HANSEN
CHRIS R. JOHNSON
VALERIO PASCUCCI
CLAUDIO T. SILVA
University of Utah

S INCE THE ADVENT OF COMPUTING, the world has experienced an information "big bang": an explosion of data. The amount of information being created is increasing at an exponential rate. Since 2003, digital information has accounted for 90 percent of all information produced [1], vastly exceeding the amount of information on paper and on film. One of the greatest scientific and engineering challenges of the 21st century will be to understand and make effective use of this growing body of information. Visual data analysis, facilitated by interactive interfaces, enables the detection and validation of expected results while also enabling unexpected discoveries in science. It allows for the validation of new theoretical models, provides comparison between models and datasets, enables quantitative and qualitative querying, improves interpretation of data, and facilitates decision making. Scientists can use visual data analysis systems to explore "what if" scenarios, define hypotheses, and examine data using multiple perspectives and assumptions. They can identify connections among large numbers of attributes and quantitatively assess the reliability of hypotheses. In essence, visual data analysis is an integral part of scientific discovery and is far from a solved problem. Many avenues for future research remain open. In this article, we describe visual data analysis topics that will receive attention in the next decade [2, 3].

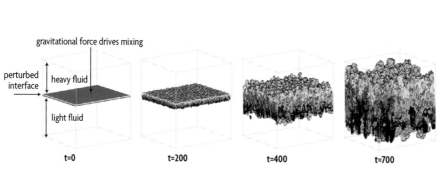

gravitational force drives mixing

perturbed interface

heavy fluid

light fluid

t=0   t=200   t=400   t=700

FIGURE 1.

Interactive visualization of four timesteps of the 1152³ simulation of a Rayleigh-Taylor instability. Gravity drives the mixing of a heavy fluid on top of a lighter one. Two envelope surfaces capture the mixing region.

VISUS: PROGRESSIVE STREAMING FOR SCALABLE DATA EXPLORATION

In recent years, computational scientists with access to the world's largest super-computers have successfully simulated a number of natural and man-made phenomena with unprecedented levels of detail. Such simulations routinely produce massive amounts of data. For example, hydrodynamic instability simulations performed at Lawrence Livermore National Laboratory (LLNL) in early 2002 produced several tens of terabytes of data, as shown in Figure 1. This data must be visualized and analyzed to verify and validate the underlying model, understand the phenomenon in detail, and develop new insights into its fundamental physics. Therefore, both visualization and data analysis algorithms require new, advanced designs that enable high performance when dealing with large amounts of data.

Data-streaming techniques and out-of-core computing specifically address the issues of algorithm redesign and data layout restructuring, which are necessary to enable scalable processing of massive amounts of data. For example, space-filling curves have been used to develop a static indexing scheme called ViSUS,[1] which produces a data layout that enables the hierarchical traversal of *n*-dimensional regular grids. Three features make this approach particularly attractive: (1) the order of the data is independent of the parameters of the physical hardware (a cache-oblivious approach), (2) conversion from Z-order used in classical database approaches is achieved using a simple sequence of bit-string manipulations, and (3) it does not introduce any data replication. This approach has

---

[1] www.pascucci.org/visus

FIGURE 2.

Scalability of the ViSUS infrastructure, which is used for visualization in a variety of applications (such as medical imaging, subsurface modeling, climate modeling, microscopy, satellite imaging, digital photography, and large-scale scientific simulations) and with a wide range of devices (from the iPhone to the powerwall).

been used for direct streaming and real-time monitoring of large-scale simulations during execution [4].

Figure 2 shows the ViSUS streaming infrastructure streaming LLNL simulation codes and visualizing them in real time on the Blue Gene/L installation at the Supercomputing 2004 exhibit (where Blue Gene/L was introduced as the new fastest supercomputer in the world). The extreme scalability of this approach allows the use of the same code base for a large set of applications while exploiting a wide range of devices, from large powerwall displays to workstations, laptop computers, and handheld devices such as the iPhone.

Generalization of this class of techniques to the case of unstructured meshes remains a major problem. More generally, the fast evolution and growing diversity of hardware pose a major challenge in the design of software infrastructures that are intrinsically scalable and adaptable to a variety of computing resources and running conditions. This poses theoretical and practical questions that future researchers in visualization and analysis for data-intensive applications will need to address.

VISTRAILS: PROVENANCE AND DATA EXPLORATION

Data exploration is an inherently creative process that requires the researcher to locate relevant data, visualize the data and discover relationships, collaborate with peers while exploring solutions, and disseminate results. Given the volume of data and complexity of analyses that are common in scientific exploration, new tools are needed and existing tools should be extended to better support creativity.

The ability to systematically capture provenance is a key requirement for these tools. The provenance (also referred to as the audit trail, lineage, or pedigree) of a data product contains information about the process and data used to derive the data product. The importance of keeping provenance for data products is well recognized in the scientific community [5, 6]. It provides important documentation that is key to preserving the data, determining its quality and authorship, and reproducing and validating the results. The availability of provenance also supports reflective reasoning, allowing users to store temporary results, make inferences from stored knowledge, and follow chains of reasoning backward and forward.

VisTrails[2] is an open source system that we designed to support exploratory computational tasks such as visualization, data mining, and integration. VisTrails provides a comprehensive provenance management infrastructure and can be easily combined with existing tools and libraries. A new concept we introduced with VisTrails is the notion of *provenance of workflow evolution* [7]. In contrast to previous workflow and visualization systems, which maintain provenance only for derived data products, VisTrails treats the workflows (or pipelines) as first-class data items and keeps their provenance. VisTrails is an extensible system. Like workflow systems, it allows pipelines to be created that combine multiple libraries. In addition, the VisTrails provenance infrastructure can be integrated with interactive tools, which cannot be easily wrapped in a workflow system [8].

Figure 3 shows an example of an exploratory visualization using VisTrails. In the center, the visual trail, or *vistrail,* captures all modifications that users apply to the visualizations. Each node in the vistrail tree corresponds to a pipeline, and the edges between two nodes correspond to changes applied to transform the parent pipeline into the child (e.g., through the addition of a module or a change to a parameter value). The tree-based representation allows a scientist to return to a previous version in an intuitive way, undo bad changes, compare workflows, and be reminded of the actions that led to a particular result.

Ad hoc approaches to data exploration, which are widely used in the scientific community, have serious limitations. In particular, scientists and engineers need

---

[2] http://vistrails.sci.utah.edu

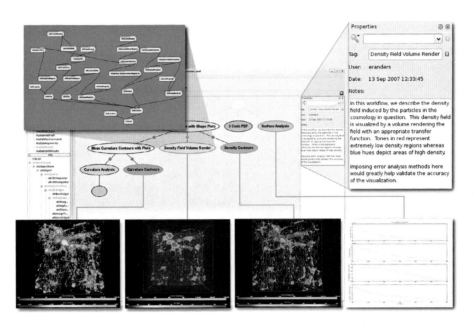

FIGURE 3.

An example of an exploratory visualization for studying celestial structures derived from cosmological simulations using VisTrails. Complete provenance of the exploration process is displayed as a "vistrail." Detailed metadata are also stored, including free-text notes made by the scientist, the date and time the workflow was created or modified, optional descriptive tags, and the name of the person who created it.

to expend substantial effort managing data (e.g., scripts that encode computational tasks, raw data, data products, images, and notes) and need to record provenance so that basic questions can be answered, such as: Who created the data product and when? When was it modified, and by whom? What process was used to create it? Were two data products derived from the same raw data? This process is not only time consuming but error prone. The absence of provenance makes it hard (and sometimes impossible) to reproduce and share results, solve problems collaboratively, validate results with different input data, understand the process used to solve a particular problem, and reuse the knowledge involved in the data analysis process. It also greatly limits the longevity of the data product. Without precise and sufficient information about how it was generated, its value is greatly diminished. Visualization systems aimed at the scientific domain need to provide a flexible

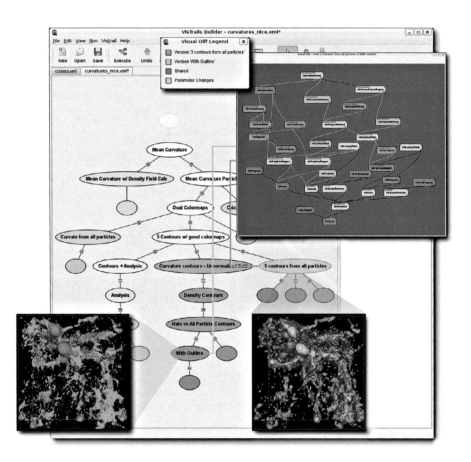

FIGURE 4.

Representing provenance as a series of actions that modify a pipeline makes visualizing the differences between two workflows possible. The difference between two workflows is represented in a meaningful way, as an aggregation of the two. This is both informative and intuitive, reducing the time it takes to understand how two workflows are functionally different.

framework that not only enables scientists to perform complex analyses over large datasets but also captures detailed provenance of the analysis process.

Figure 4 shows ParaView[3] (a data analysis and visualization tool for extreme-

[3] www.paraview.org

ly large datasets) and the VisTrails Provenance Explorer transparently capturing a complete exploration process. The provenance capture mechanism was implemented by inserting monitoring code in ParaView's undo/redo mechanism, which captures changes to the underlying pipeline specification. Essentially, the action on top of the undo stack is added to the vistrail in the appropriate place, and undo is reinterpreted to mean "move up the version tree." Note that the change-based representation is both simple and compact—it uses substantially less space than the alternative approach of storing multiple instances, or versions, of the state.

FLOW VISUALIZATION TECHNIQUES

A precise qualitative and quantitative assessment of three-dimensional transient flow phenomena is required in a broad range of scientific, engineering, and medical applications. Fortunately, in many cases the analysis of a 3-D vector field can be reduced to the investigation of the two-dimensional structures produced by its interaction with the boundary of the object under consideration. Typical examples of such analysis for fluid flows include airfoils and reactors in aeronautics, engine walls and exhaust pipes in the automotive industry, and rotor blades in turbomachinery.

Other applications in biomedicine focus on the interplay between bioelectric fields and the surface of an organ. In each case, numerical simulations of increasing size and sophistication are becoming instrumental in helping scientists and engineers reach a deeper understanding of the flow properties that are relevant to their task. The scientific visualization community has concentrated a significant part of its research efforts on the design of visualization methods that convey local and global structures that occur at various spatial and temporal scales in transient flow simulations. In particular, emphasis has been placed on the interactivity of the corresponding visual analysis, which has been identified as a critical aspect of the effectiveness of the proposed algorithms.

A recent trend in flow visualization research is to use GPUs to compute image space methods to tackle the computational complexity of visualization techniques that support flows defined over curved surfaces. The key feature of this approach is the ability to efficiently produce a dense texture representation of the flow without explicitly computing a surface parameterization. This is achieved by projecting onto the image plane the flow corresponding to the visible part of the surface, allowing subsequent texture generation in the image space through backward integration and iterative blending. Although the use of partial surface parameterization obtained by projection results in an impressive performance gain, texture patterns

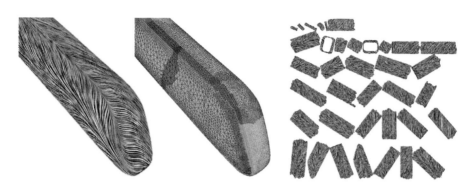

FIGURE 5.
Simulation of a high-speed ICE train. Left: The GPUFLIC result. Middle: Patch configurations. Right: Charts in texture space.

stretching beyond the visible part of the self-occluded surface become incoherent due to the lack of full surface parameterization.

To address this problem, we have introduced a novel scheme that fully supports the creation of high-quality texture-based visualizations of flows defined over arbitrary curved surfaces [9]. Called Flow Charts, our scheme addresses the issue mentioned previously by segmenting the surface into overlapping patches, which are then individually parameterized into charts and packed in the texture domain. The overlapped region provides each local chart with a smooth representation of its direct vicinity in the flow domain as well as with the inter-chart adjacency information, both of which are required for accurate and non-disrupted particle advection. The vector field and the patch adjacency relation are naturally represented as textures, enabling efficient GPU implementation of state-of-the-art flow texture synthesis algorithms such as GPUFLIC and UFAC.

Figure 5 shows the result of a simulation of a high-speed German Intercity-Express (ICE) train traveling at a velocity of about 250 km/h with wind blowing from the side at an incidence angle of 30 degrees. The wind causes vortices to form on the lee side of the train, creating a drop in pressure that adversely affects the train's ability to stay on the track. These flow structures induce separation and attachment flow patterns on the train surface. They can be clearly seen in the proposed images close to the salient edges of the geometry.

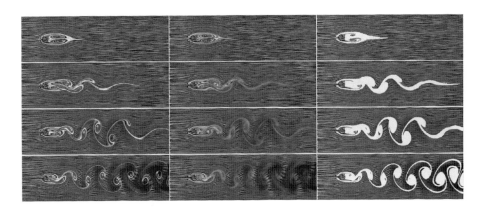

FIGURE 6.

Visualization of the Karman dataset using dye advection. Left column: Physically based dye advection. Middle column: Texture advection method. Right column: Level-set method. The time sequence is from top to bottom.

The effectiveness of a physically based formulation can be seen with the Karman dataset (Figure 6), a numerical simulation of the classical Von Kármán vortex street phenomenon, in which a repeating pattern of swirling vortices is caused by the separation of flow passing over a circular-shaped obstacle. The visualization of dye advection is overlaid on dense texture visualization that shows instantaneous flow structures generated by GPUFLIC. The patterns generated by the texture-advection method are hazy due to numerical diffusion and loss of mass. In a level-set method, intricate structures are lost because of the binary dye/background threshold. Thanks to the physically based formulation [10], the visualization is capable of accurately conveying detailed structures not shown using the traditional texture-advection method.

FUTURE DATA-INTENSIVE VISUALIZATION CHALLENGES

Fundamental advances in visualization techniques and systems must be made to extract meaning from large and complex datasets derived from experiments and from upcoming petascale and exascale simulation systems. Effective data analysis and visualization tools in support of predictive simulations and scientific knowledge discovery must be based on strong algorithmic and mathematical foundations and must allow scientists to reliably characterize salient features in their data. New mathematical methods in areas such as topology, high-order tensor analysis, and statistics will constitute the core of feature extraction and uncertainty modeling using formal definition of complex shapes, patterns, and space-time distributions. Topological methods are becoming increasingly important in the development of advanced data analysis because of their expressive power in describing complex shapes at multiple scales. The recent introduction of robust combinatorial techniques for topological analysis has enabled the use of topology—not only for presentation of known phenomena but for the detection and quantification of new features of fundamental scientific interest.

Our current data-analysis capabilities lag far behind our ability to produce simulation data or record observational data. New visual data analysis techniques will need to dynamically consider high-dimensional probability distributions of quantities of interest. This will require new contributions from mathematics, probability, and statistics. The scaling of simulations to ever-finer granularity and timesteps brings new challenges in visualizing the data that is generated. It will be crucial to develop smart, semi-automated visualization algorithms and methodologies to help filter the data or present "summary visualizations" to enable scientists to begin analyzing the immense datasets using a more top-down methodological path. The ability to fully quantify uncertainty in high-performance computational simulations will provide new capabilities for verification and validation of simulation codes. Hence, uncertainty representation and quantification, uncertainty propagation, and uncertainty visualization techniques need to be developed to provide scientists with credible and verifiable visualizations.

New approaches to visual data analysis and knowledge discovery are needed to enable researchers to gain insight into this emerging form of scientific data. Such approaches must take into account the multi-model nature of the data; provide the means for scientists to easily transition views from global to local model data; allow blending of traditional scientific visualization and information visualization; perform hypothesis testing, verification, and validation; and address the challenges posed by the use of vastly different grid types and by the various elements of the multi-model code. Tools that leverage semantic information and hide details of dataset formats will be critical to enabling visualization and analysis experts to concentrate on the design of these approaches rather than becoming mired in the trivialities of particular data representations [11].

ACKNOWLEDGMENTS

Publication is based, in part, on work supported by DOE: VACET, DOE SDM, DOE C-SAFE Alliance Center, the National Science Foundation (grants IIS-0746500, CNS-0751152, IIS-0713637, OCE-0424602, IIS-0534628, CNS-0514485, IIS-0513692, CNS-0524096, CCF-0401498, OISE-0405402, CNS-0615194, CNS-0551724, CCF-0541113, IIS-0513212, and CCF-0528201), IBM Faculty Awards (2005, 2006, and 2007), NIH NCRR Grant No. 5P41RR012553-10 and Award Number KUS-C1-016-04, made by King Abdullah University of Science and Technology (KAUST). The authors would like to thank Juliana Freire and the VisTrails team for help with the third section of this article.

REFERENCES

[1] C. R. Johnson, R. Moorhead, T. Munzner, H. Pfister, P. Rheingans, and T. S. Yoo, Eds., *NIH-NSF Visualization Research Challenges Report,* IEEE Press, ISBN 0-7695-2733-7, 2006, http://vgtc.org/wpmu/techcom/national-initiatives/nihnsf-visualization-research-challenges-report-january-2006, doi: 10.1109/MCG.2006.44.

[2] NSF Blue Ribbon Panel Report on Simulation-Based Engineering Science (J. T. Oden, T. Belytschko, J. Fish, T. Hughes, C. R. Johnson, D. Keyes, A. Laub, L. Petzold, D. Srolovitz, and S. Yip), "Simulation-Based Engineering Science," 2006, www.nd.edu/~dddas/References/SBES_Final_Report.pdf.

[3] NIH-NSF Visualization Research Challenges, http://erie.nlm.nih.gov/evc/meetings/vrc2004.

[4] V. Pascucci, D. E. Laney, R. J. Frank, F. Gygi, G. Scorzelli, L. Linsen, and B. Hamann, "Real-time monitoring of large scientific simulations," *SAC,* pp. 194–198, ACM, 2003, doi: 10.1.1.66.9717.

[5] S. B. Davidson and J. Freire, "Provenance and scientific workflows: challenges and opportunities," *Proc. ACM SIGMOD,* pp. 1345–1350, 2008, doi: 10.1.1.140.3264.

[6] J. Freire, D. Koop, E. Santos, and C. Silva, "Provenance for computational tasks: A survey," *Comput. Sci. Eng,* vol. 10, no. 3, pp. 11–21, 2008, doi: 10.1109/MCSE.2008.79.

[7] J. Freire, C. T. Silva, S. P. Callahan, E. Santos, C. E. Scheidegger, and H. T. Vo, "Managing rapidly-evolving scientific workflows," International Provenance and Annotation Workshop (IPAW), LNCS 4145, pp. 10–18, 2006, doi: 10.1.1.117.5530.

[8] C. Silva, J. Freire, and S. P. Callahan, "Provenance for visualizations: Reproducibility and beyond," *IEEE Comput. Sci. Eng.,* 2007, doi: 10.1109/MCSE.2007.106.

[9] G.-S. Li, X. Tricoche, D. Weiskopf, and C. Hansen, "Flow charts: Visualization of vector fields on arbitrary surfaces," *IEEE Trans. Visual. Comput. Graphics,* vol. 14, no. 5, pp. 1067–1080, 2008, doi: 10.1109/TVCG.2008.58.

[10] G.-S. Li, C. Hansen, and X. Tricoche, "Physically-based dye advection for flow visualization. *Comp. Graphics Forum J.,* vol. 27, no. 3, pp. 727–735, 2008, doi: 10.1111/j.1467-8659.2008.01201.x.

[11] "Visualization and Knowledge Discovery: Report from the DOE/ASCR Workshop on Visual Analysis and Data Exploration at Extreme Scale," C. R. Johnson, R. Ross, S. Ahern, J. Ahrens, W. Bethel, K. L. Ma, M. Papka, J. van Rosendale, H. W. Shen, and J. Thomas, www.sci.utah.edu/vaw2007/DOE-Visualization-Report-2007.pdf, 2007.

A Platform for All That We Know: Creating a Knowledge-Driven Research Infrastructure

SAVAS PARASTATIDIS
Microsoft Research

COMPUTER SYSTEMS HAVE BECOME A VITAL PART of the modern research environment, supporting all aspects of the research lifecycle [1]. The community uses the terms "eScience" and "eResearch" to highlight the important role of computer technology in the ways we undertake research, collaborate, share data and documents, submit funding applications, use devices to automatically and accurately collect data from experiments, deploy new generations of microscopes and telescopes to increase the quality of the acquired imagery, and archive everything along the way for provenance and long-term preservation [2, 3].

However, the same technological advances in data capture, generation, and sharing and the automation enabled by computers have resulted in an unprecedented explosion in data—a situation that applies not only to research but to every aspect of our digital lives. This data deluge, especially in the scientific domain, has brought new research infrastructure challenges, as highlighted by Jim Gray and Alex Szalay [4]. The processing, data transfer, and storage demands are far greater today than just a few years ago. It is no surprise that we are talking about the emergence of a new research methodology—the "fourth paradigm"—in science.

Through the use of technology and automation, we are trying to keep up with the challenges of the data deluge. The emergence of the Web as an application, data sharing, and collaboration platform has broken many barriers in the way research is undertaken and disseminated. The emerging cloud computing infrastructures (e.g., Amazon's[1]) and the new generation of data-intensive computing platforms (e.g., DISC,[2] Google's MapReduce,[3] Hadoop,[4] and Dryad[5]) are geared toward managing and processing large amounts of data. Amazon is even offering a "sneakernet"[6]-like service[7] to address the problem of transferring large amounts of data into its cloud. Companies such as Google, Yahoo!, and Microsoft are demonstrating that it is possible to aggregate huge amounts of data from around the Web and store, manage, and index it and then build engaging user experiences around it.

The primary focus of the current technologies addresses only the first part of the data-information-knowledge-wisdom spectrum.[8] Computers have become efficient at storing, managing, indexing, and computing (research) data. They are even able to represent and process some of the information hidden behind the symbols used to encode that data. Nevertheless, we are still a long way from having computer systems that can automatically discover, acquire, organize, analyze, correlate, interpret, infer, and reason over information that's on the Internet, that's hidden on researchers' hard drives, or that exists only in our brains. We do not yet have an infrastructure capable of managing and processing knowledge on a global scale, one that can act as the foundation for a generation of knowledge-driven services and applications.

So, if the fourth paradigm is about data and information, it is not unreasonable to foresee a future, not far away, where we begin thinking about the challenges of managing knowledge and machine-based understanding on a very large scale. We researchers will probably be the first to face this challenge.

[1] http://aws.amazon.com
[2] www.pdl.cmu.edu/DISC
[3] http://labs.google.com/papers/mapreduce.html
[4] http://hadoop.apache.org
[5] http://research.microsoft.com/en-us/projects/dryad
[6] http://en.wikipedia.org/wiki/Sneakernet
[7] http://aws.amazon.com/importexport
[8] http://en.wikipedia.org/wiki/DIKW

KNOWLEDGE-ORIENTED RESEARCH INFRASTRUCTURES

The work by the Semantic Web[9] community has resulted in a number of technologies to help with data modeling, information representation, and the interexchange of semantics, always within the context of a particular application domain. Given the formal foundations of some of these technologies (e.g., the Web Ontology Language, or OWL), it has been possible to introduce reasoning capabilities, at least for some specific bounded domains (e.g., BioMoby[10]).

Moving forward, the work of the Semantic Web community will continue to play a significant role in the interoperable exchange of information and knowledge. More importantly, as representation technologies such as RDF (Resource Description Framework), OWL, and microformats become widely accepted, the focus will transition to the computational aspects of semantic understanding and knowledge. The challenge we will face is the automation of the aggregation and combination of huge amounts of semantically rich information and, very crucially, the processes by which that information is generated and analyzed. Today, we must start thinking about the technologies we'll need in order to semantically describe, analyze, and combine the information and the algorithms used to produce it or consume it, and to do so on a global scale. If today's cloud computing services focus on offering a scalable platform for computing, tomorrow's services will be built around the management of knowledge and reasoning over it.

We are already seeing some attempts to infer knowledge based on the world's information. Services such as OpenCyc,[11] Freebase,[12] Powerset,[13] True Knowledge,[14] and Wolfram|Alpha[15] demonstrate how facts can be recorded in such a way that they can be combined and made available as answers to a user's questions. Wolfram|Alpha, in particular, has made use of domain experts to encode the computational aspects of processing the data and information that they have aggregated from around the Web and annotated. It demonstrates how a consumer-oriented service can be built on top of a computational infrastructure in combination with natural language processing. It is likely that many similar services will emerge in the near future, initially targeting specialized technical/academic communities

---

[9] http://en.wikipedia.org/wiki/Semantic_Web
[10] www.biomoby.org
[11] www.opencyc.org
[12] www.freebase.com
[13] www.powerset.com
[14] www.trueknowledge.com
[15] www.wolframalpha.com

and later expanding to all domains of interest. As with other service-oriented applications on the Web, the incorporation of computational knowledge services for scientists will be an important aspect of any research cyberinfrastructure.

The myGrid[16] and myExperiment[17] projects demonstrate the benefits of capturing and then sharing, in a semantically rich way, the definitions of workflows in science. Such workflows effectively document the process by which research-related information is produced and the steps taken toward reaching (or unsuccessfully trying to reach) a conclusion. Imagine the possibilities of expanding this idea to all aspects of our interaction with information. Today, for example, when someone enters "GDP of Brazil vs. Japan" as a query in Wolfram|Alpha, the engine knows how to interpret the input and produce a comparison graph of the GDP (gross domestic product) of the two countries. If the query is "Ford," the engine makes an assumption about its interpretation but also provides alternatives (e.g., "person" if the intended meaning might be Henry Ford or Gerald Rudolph Ford, Jr., vs. "business entity" if the intended meaning might be the Ford Motor Company). The context within which specific information is to be interpreted is important in determining what computational work will be performed. The same ideas could be implemented as part of a global research infrastructure, where Wolfram|Alpha could be one of the many available interoperable services that work together to support researchers.

The research community would indeed benefit greatly from a global infrastructure whose focus is on knowledge sharing and in which all applications and services are built with knowledge exchange and processing at their core. This is not to suggest that there should be yet another attempt to unify and centrally manage all knowledge representation. Scientists will always be better at representing and reasoning over their own domain. However, a research infrastructure should accommodate all domains and provide the necessary glue for information to be cross-linked, correlated, and discovered in a semantically rich manner.

Such an infrastructure must provide the right set of services to not only allow access to semantically rich information but also expose computational services that operate on the world's knowledge. Researchers would be able to ask questions related to their domain of expertise, and a sea of knowledge would immediately be accessible to them. The processes of acquiring and sharing knowledge would be automated, and associated tools (e.g., a word processor that records an author's intended

---

[16] www.mygrid.org.uk
[17] www.myexperiment.org

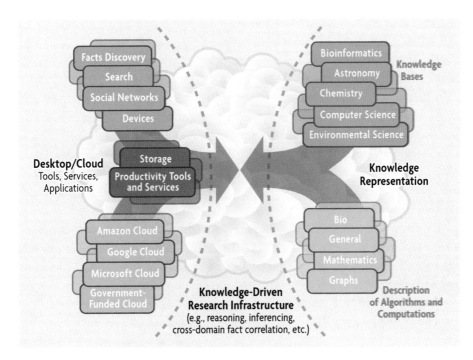

FIGURE 1.

High-level view of a research infrastructure that brings together knowledge bases and computational services.

use of a term[18]) would make it even easier to analyze, do research, and publish results. Natural language processing will aid in the interaction with the knowledge-based ecosystem of information, tools, and services, as shown in Figure 1.

Note that this proposed research infrastructure would not attempt to realize artificial intelligence (AI)—despite the fact that many of the technologies from the Semantic Computing[19] community (from data modeling and knowledge representation to natural language processing and reasoning) have emerged from work in

---

[18] http://ucsdbiolit.codeplex.com

[19] A distinction is assumed between the general approach of computing based on semantic technologies (machine learning, neural networks, ontologies, inference, etc.) and the Semantic Web as described in [5] and [6], which refers to a specific ecosystem of technologies, such as RDF and OWL. The Semantic Web technologies are considered to be just some of the many tools at our disposal when building semantics-based and knowledge-based solutions.

the AI field over the decades. The primary focus of the proposed cyberinfrastructure is automated knowledge management rather than intelligence.

MASHING UP KNOWLEDGE

Interdisciplinary research has gained a lot of momentum, especially as the result of eScience and cyberinfrastructure activities. Technology has played an enabling role by primarily supporting collaboration, sharing of information, and data management within the context of a research project. In the future, researchers should not have to think about how their questions, assumptions, theories, experiments, or data correlate with existing knowledge across disciplines in one scientific domain or even across domains.

The process of combining information from existing scientific knowledge generated by different researchers at different times and in different locations, including the specific methodologies that were followed to produce conclusions, should be automatic and implicitly supported by the research infrastructure.[20] For example, it should be trivial for a young Ph.D. researcher in chemistry to pose work items to a computer as natural language statements like "Locate 100,000 molecules that are similar to the known HIV protease inhibitors, then compute their electronic properties and dock them into viral escape mutants." This illustrates the use of natural language processing and also the need for researchers to agree on vocabularies for capturing knowledge—something already occurring in many scientific domains through the use of Semantic Web technologies. Furthermore, the example illustrates the need to be able to capture the computational aspects of how existing knowledge is processed and how new facts are generated.

The research community has already started working on bringing the existing building blocks together to realize a future in which machines can further assist researchers in managing and processing knowledge. As an example, the oreChem[21] project aims to automate the process by which chemistry-related knowledge captured in publications is extracted and represented in machine-processable formats, such as the Chemistry Markup Language (CML). Through the use of chemistry-related ontologies, researchers will be able to declaratively describe the computations they would like to perform over the body of machine-processable knowledge.

---

[20] Assuming that open access to research information has become a reality.
[21] http://research.microsoft.com/orechem

While projects such as oreChem do not attempt to realize a large-scale infrastructure for computable scientific knowledge, they do represent the first investigations toward such a vision. Going forward, the boundaries of domains will become less rigid so that cross-discipline knowledge (computational) mashups can become an important aspect of any semantics-enabled, knowledge-driven research infrastructure. The ability to cross-reference and cross-correlate information, facts, assumptions, and methodologies from different research domains on a global scale will be a great enabler for our future researchers.

A CALL TO ACTION

Today, platforms that offer implementations of the MapReduce computational pattern (e.g., Hadoop and Dryad) make it easy for developers to perform data-intensive computations at scale. In the future, it will be very important to develop equivalent platforms and patterns to support knowledge-related actions such as aggregation, acquisition, inference, reasoning, and information interpretation. We should aim to provide scientists with a cyberinfrastructure on top of which it should be easy to build a large-scale application capable of exploiting the world's computer-represented scientific knowledge.

The interoperable exchange of information, whether representing facts or processes, is vital to successfully sharing knowledge. Communities need to come together—and many of them are already doing so—in order to agree on vocabularies for capturing facts and information specific to their domains of expertise. Research infrastructures of the future will create the necessary links across such vocabularies so that information can be interlinked as part of a global network of facts and processes, as per Tim Berners-Lee's vision for the Semantic Web.

The future research infrastructures, which will be knowledge driven, will look more like Vannevar Bush's memex than today's data-driven computing machines. As Bush said, "Wholly new forms of encyclopedias will appear, ready made with a mesh of associative trails running through them, ready to be dropped into the memex and there amplified." [7] We are not far from that vision today.

ACKNOWLEDGMENTS

The author would like to thank Peter Murray Rust (University of Cambridge) for his explanation of the oreChem project, Evelyne Viegas (Microsoft Research) for insightful discussions and great ideas over the years on all things related to Semantic Computing, and Tony Hey for his continuous support, encouragement, and trust.

REFERENCES

[1] L. Dirks and T. Hey, "The Coming Revolution in Scholarly Communications & Cyberinfrastructure," *CT Watch Q.*, vol. 3, no. 3, 2007.

[2] National Science Foundation, "Cyberinfrastructure Vision for 21st Century Discovery," March 2007.

[3] J. Taylor (n.d.), "UK eScience Programme," retrieved from www.e-science.clrc.ac.uk.

[4] J. Gray and A. Szalay, "eScience - A Transformed Scientific Method," Presentation to the Computer Science and Technology Board of the National Research Council, Jan. 11, 2007, retrieved from http://research.microsoft.com/en-us/um/people/gray/talks/NRC-CSTB_eScience.ppt. (Edited transcript in this volume.)

[5] T. Berners-Lee, J. A. Hendler, and O. Lasilla, "The Semantic Web," *Scientific American,* vol. 284, no. 5, pp. 35–43, May 2001, www.sciam.com/article.cfm?id=the-semantic-web.

[6] N. Shadbolt, W. Hall, and T. Berners-Lee, "The Semantic Web Revisited," *IEEE Intell. Syst.,* vol. 21, no. 3, pp. 96–101, 2006, doi: 10.1109/MIS.2006.62.

[7] V. Bush, "As We May Think," *The Atlantic,* July 1945, doi: 10.3998/3336451.0001.101.

4. SCHOLARLY COMMUNICATION

Introduction

LEE DIRKS | Microsoft Research

J IM GRAY'S PASSION FOR eSCIENCE WAS ADMIRED BY MANY, but few were aware of his deep desire to apply computing to increase the productivity of scholars and accelerate the pace of discovery and innovation for scientific researchers. Several authors in Part 4 of this book knew and worked with Jim. All of the authors not only share his vision but are actively endeavoring to make it a reality.

Lynch introduces how the Fourth Paradigm applies to the field of scholarly communication. His article is organized around a central question: what are the effects of data-intensive science on the scientific record? He goes on to ask: what has become of the scholarly record—an ever-changing, ever-evolving set of data, publications, and related supporting materials of staggering volume? In this new world, not only does the individual scientist benefit (as the end user), but through data-intensive computing we can expect more cross-domain ventures that accelerate discovery, highlight new connections, and suggest unforeseen links that will speed science forward.

Ginsparg delves into the nuts and bolts of the rapid transformation of scholarly publications. He references key examples of cutting-edge work and promising breakthroughs across multiple disciplines. In the process, he notes the siloed nature of the sciences and encourages us to learn from one another and adopt best practices across discipline boundaries. He also provides a helpful roadmap that outlines an ideal route to a vision he shared with Jim Gray of "community-driven scientific knowledge curation and creation."

Van de Sompel and Lagoze stress that academics have yet to realize the full potential benefits of technology for scholarly communication. The authors make a crucial point that the hardest issues are social or dependent on humans, which means they cannot be easily resolved by new applications and additional silicon. They call for the development of open standards and interoperability protocols to help mitigate this situation.

The issues of sharing scientific data at an international level are addressed by Fitzgerald, Fitzgerald, and Pappalardo. Scientists sometimes encounter the greatest constraints at the national or regional level, which prevent them from participating in the global scientific endeavor. Citing a specific example, the authors appeal for coordination beyond the scientific community and recommend that policymakers work to avoid introducing impediments into the system.

Wilbanks puts a fine point on a common theme throughout this section: in many ways, scientists are often unwittingly responsible for holding back science. Even though, as professionals, we envision, instrument, and execute on innovative scientific endeavors, we do not always actually adopt or fully realize the systems we have put in place. As an amalgamated population of forward-thinking researchers, we often live behind the computational curve. He notes that it is crucial for connectivity to span all scientific fields and for multidisciplinary work and cooperation across domains, in turn, to fuel revolutionary advancements.

Hannay closes the section by highlighting the interconnectedness of our networked world despite lingering social barriers between various scientific fields. He notes that science's gradual shift from a cottage enterprise to a large-scale industry is part of the evolution of how we conduct science. He provides intriguing examples from around the world of research that can point a way to the future of Web-based communication, and he declares that we are living in an awkward age immediately prior to the advent of semantic reality and interconnectedness.

Research is evolving from small, autonomous scholarly guilds to larger, more enlightened, and more interconnected communities of scientists who are increasingly interdependent upon one another to move forward. In undertaking this great endeavor together—as Jim envisioned—we will see science, via computation, advance further and faster than ever before.

Jim Gray's Fourth Paradigm and the Construction of the Scientific Record

CLIFFORD LYNCH
Coalition for Networked
Information

N THE LATTER PART OF HIS CAREER, Jim Gray led the thinking of a group of scholars who saw the emergence of what they characterized as a fourth paradigm of scientific research. In this essay, I will focus narrowly on the implications of this fourth paradigm, which I will refer to as "data-intensive science" [1], for the nature of scientific communication and the scientific record.

Gray's paradigm joins the classic pair of opposed but mutually supporting scientific paradigms: theory and experimentation. The third paradigm—that of large-scale computational simulation—emerged through the work of John von Neumann and others in the mid-20th century. In a certain sense, Gray's fourth paradigm provides an integrating framework that allows the first three to interact and reinforce each other, much like the traditional scientific cycle in which theory offered predictions that could be experimentally tested, and these experiments identified phenomena that required theoretical explanation. The contributions of simulation to scientific progress, while enormous, fell short of their initial promise (for example, in long-term weather prediction) in part because of the extreme sensitivity of complex systems to initial conditions and chaotic behaviors [2]; this is one example in which simulation, theory, and experiment in the context of massive amounts of data must all work together.

To understand the effects of data-intensive science on the

scientific record,[1] it is first necessary to review the nature of that record, what it is intended to accomplish, and where it has and hasn't succeeded in meeting the needs of the various paradigms and the evolution of science.

To a first approximation, we can think of the modern scientific record, dating from the 17th century and closely tied to the rise of both science and scholarly societies, as comprising an aggregation of independent scientific journals and conference presentations and proceedings, plus the underlying data and other evidence to support the published findings. This record is stored in a highly distributed and, in some parts, highly redundant fashion across a range of libraries, archives, and museums around the globe. The data and evidentiary components have expanded over time: written observational records too voluminous to appear in journals have been stored in scientific archives, and physical evidence held in natural history museums is now joined by a vast array of digital datasets, databases, and data archives of various types, as well as pre-digital observational records (such as photographs) and new collections of biological materials. While scientific monographs and some specialized materials such as patents have long been a limited but important part of the record, "gray literature," notably technical reports and preprints, have assumed greater importance in the 20th century. In recent years, we have seen an explosion of Web sites, blogs, video clips, and other materials (generally quite apart from the traditional publishing process) become a significant part of this record, although the boundaries of these materials and various problems related to their persistent identification, archiving and continued accessibility, vetting, and similar properties have been highly controversial.

The scientific record is intended to do a number of things. First and foremost, it is intended to *communicate* findings, hypotheses, and insights from one person to another, across space and across time. It is intended to organize: to establish common nomenclature and terminology, to connect related work, and to develop disciplines. It is a vehicle for *building up communities* and for a form of large-scale *collaboration* across space and time. It is a means of documenting, managing, and often, ultimately, resolving controversies and disagreements. It can be used to establish *precedence* for ideas and results, and also (through citation and bibliometrics) to offer evidence for the quality and significance of scientific work. The scientific record is intended to be trustworthy, in several senses. In the small and in the near

---

[1] For brevity and clearest focus, I've limited the discussion here to science. But just as it's clear that eScience is only a special case of eResearch and data-intensive science is a form of data-intensive scholarship, many of the points here should apply, with some adaptation, to the humanities and the social sciences.

term, pre-publication peer review, editorial and authorial reputation, and transparency in reporting results are intended to ensure confidence in the correctness of individual articles. In the broader sense, across spans of time and aggregated collections of materials, findings are validated and errors or deliberate falsifications, particularly important ones, are usually identified and corrected by the community through post-publication discussion or formal review, reproduction, reuse and extension of results, and the placement of an individual publication's results in the broader context of scientific knowledge.

A very central idea that is related simultaneously to trustworthiness and to the ideas of collaboration and building upon the work of others is that of *reproducibility* of scientific results. While this is an ideal that has often been given only reluctant practical support by some scientists who are intent on protecting what they view as proprietary methods, data, or research leads, it is nonetheless what fundamentally distinguishes science from practices such as alchemy. The scientific record—not necessarily a single, self-contained article but a collection of literature and data within the aggregate record, or an article and all of its implicit and explicit "links" in today's terminology—should make enough data available, and contain enough information about methods and practices, that another scientist could reproduce the same results starting from the same data. Indeed, he or she should be able to do additional work that helps to place the initial results in better context, to perturb assumptions and analytic methods, and to see where these changes lead. It is worth noting that the ideal of reproducibility for sophisticated experimental science often becomes problematic over long periods of time: reproducing experimental work may require a considerable amount of tacit knowledge that was part of common scientific practice and the technology base at the time the experiment was first carried out but that may be challenging and time consuming to reproduce many decades later.

How well did the scientific record work during the long dominance of the first two scientific paradigms? In general, pretty well, I believe. The record (and the institutions that created, supported, and curated it) had to evolve in response to two major challenges. The first was mainly in regard to experimental science: as experiments became more complicated, sophisticated, and technologically mediated, and as data became more extensive and less comprehensively reproduced as part of scientific publications, the linkages between evidence and writings became more complex and elusive. In particular, as extended computation (especially mechanically or electromechanically assisted computation carried out by groups of human "computers") was applied to data, difficulties in reproducibility began to extend far beyond access to data and understanding of methods. The affordances of a scholarly record based on print and physical artifacts offered little relief here; the best that could be done was to develop organized systems of data archives and set some expectations about data deposit or obligations to make data available.

The second evolutionary challenge was the sheer scale of the scientific enterprise. The literature became huge; disciplines and sub-specialties branched and branched again. Tools and practices had to be developed to help manage this scale—specialized journals, citations, indices, review journals and bibliographies, managed vocabularies, and taxonomies in various areas of science. Yet again, given the affordances of the print-based system, all of these innovations seemed to be too little too late, and scale remained a persistent and continually overwhelming problem for scientists.

The introduction of the third paradigm in the middle of the 20th century, along with the simultaneous growth in computational technologies supporting experimental and theoretical sciences, intensified the pressure on the traditional scientific record. Not only did the underlying data continue to grow, but the output of simulations and experiments became large and complex datasets that could only be summarized, rather than fully documented, in traditional publications. Worst of all, software-based computation for simulation and other purposes became an integral part of the question of experimental reproducibility.[2] It's important to recognize how long it really took to reach the point when computer hardware was reasonably trustworthy in carrying out large-scale floating-point computations.[3] (Even today, we are very limited in our ability to produce provably correct large-scale software; we rely on the slow growth of confidence through long and widespread use, preferably in a range of different hardware and platform environments. Documenting complex software configurations as part of the provenance of the products of data-intensive science remains a key research challenge in data curation and scientific workflow structuring.) The better news was that computational technologies began to help with the management of the enormous and growing body of sci-

[2] Actually, the ability to comprehend and reproduce extensive computations became a real issue for theoretical science as well; the 1976 proof of the four-color theorem in graph theory involved exhaustive computer analysis of a very large number of special cases and caused considerable controversy within the mathematical community about whether such a proof was really fully valid. A more recent example would be the proposed proof of the Kepler Conjecture by Thomas Hales.

[3] The IEEE floating-point standard dates back to only 1985. I can personally recall incidents with major mainframe computers back in the 1970s and 1980s in which shipped products had to be revised in the field after significant errors were uncovered in their hardware and/or microcode that could produce incorrect computational results.

entific literature as many of the organizational tools migrated to online databases and information retrieval systems starting in the 1970s and became ubiquitous and broadly affordable by the mid-1990s.

With the arrival of the data-intensive computing paradigm, the scientific record and the supporting system of communication and publication have reached a Janus moment where we are looking both backward and forward. It has become clear that data and software must be integral parts of the record—a set of first-class objects that require systematic management and curation in their own right. We see this reflected in the emphasis on data curation and reuse in the various cyberinfrastructure and eScience programs [3-6]. These datasets and other materials will be interwoven in a complex variety of ways [7] with scientific papers, now finally authored in digital form and beginning to make serious structural use of the new affordances of the digital environment, and at long last bidding a slow farewell to the initial model of electronic scientific journals, which applied digital storage and delivery technologies to articles that were essentially images of printed pages. We will also see tools such as video recordings used to supplement traditional descriptions of experimental methods, and the inclusion of various kinds of two- or three-dimensional visualizations. At some level, one can imagine this as the perfecting of the traditional scientific paper genre, with the capabilities of modern information technology meeting the needs of the four paradigms. The paper becomes a window for a scientist to not only actively understand a scientific result, but also reproduce it or extend it.

However, two other developments are taking hold with unprecedented scale and scope. The first is the development of reference data collections, often independent of specific scientific research even though a great deal of research depends on these collections and many papers make reference to data in these collections. Many of these are created by robotic instrumentation (synoptic sky surveys, large-scale sequencing of microbial populations, combinatorial chemistry); some also introduce human editorial and curatorial work to represent the best current state of knowledge about complex systems (the annotated genome of a given species, a collection of signaling pathways, etc.) and may cite results in the traditional scientific literature to justify or support assertions in the database. These reference collections are an integral part of the scientific record, of course, although we are still struggling with how best to manage issues such as versioning and the fixity of these resources. These data collections are used in very different ways than traditional papers; most often, they are computed upon rather than simply read.

As these reference collections are updated, the updates may trigger new computations, the results of which may lead to new or reassessed scientific results. More and more, at least some kinds of contributions to these reference data collections will be recognized as significant scholarly contributions in their own right. One might think of this as scientists learning to more comprehensively understand the range of opportunities and idioms for contributing to the scholarly record in an era of data and computationally intensive science.

Finally, the scientific record itself is becoming a major object of ongoing computation—a central reference data collection—at least to the extent to which copyright and technical barriers can be overcome to permit this [8]. Data and text mining, inferencing, integration among structured data collections and papers written in human languages (perhaps augmented with semantic markup to help computationally identify references to particular kinds of objects—such as genes, stars, species, chemical compounds, or places, along with their associated properties—with a higher degree of accuracy than would be possible with heuristic textual analysis algorithms), information retrieval, filtering, and clustering all help to address the problems of the ever-growing scale of the scientific record and the ever-increasing scarcity of human attention. They also help exploit the new technologies of data-intensive science to more effectively extract results and hypotheses from the record. We will see very interesting developments, I believe, as researchers use these tools to view the "public" record of science through the lens of various collections of proprietary knowledge (unreleased results, information held by industry for commercial advantage, or even government intelligence).

In the era of data-intensive computing, we are seeing people engage the scientific record in two ways. *In the small,* one or a few articles at a time, human beings read papers as they have for centuries, but with computational tools that allow them to move beyond the paper to engage the underlying science and data much more effectively and to move from paper to paper, or between paper and reference data collection, with great ease, precision, and flexibility. Further, these encounters will integrate with collaborative environments and with tools for annotation, authoring, simulation, and analysis. But now we are also seeing scholars engage the scientific record *in the large,* as a corpus of text and a collection of interlinked data resources, through the use of a wide range of new computational tools. This engagement will identify papers of interest; suggest hypotheses that might be tested through combinations of theoretical, experimental, and simulation investigations; or at times directly produce new data or results. As the balance of engagement in the large and in the small shifts (today, it is still predominantly in the small, I believe), we will see this change many aspects of scientific culture and scientific publishing practice, probably including views on open access to the scientific literature, the application of various kinds of markup and the choice of authoring tools for scientific papers, and disciplinary norms about data curation, data sharing, and overall data lifecycle. Further, I believe that in the practice of data-intensive science, one set of data will, over time, figure more prominently, persistently, and ubiquitously in scientific work: the scientific record itself.

ACKNOWLEDGMENTS

My thanks to the participants at the April 24, 2009, Buckland-Lynch-Larsen "Friday Seminar" on information access at the University of California, Berkeley, School of Information for a very helpful discussion on a draft of this material.

REFERENCES

[1] G. Bell, T. Hey, and A. Szalay, "Beyond the Data Deluge," *Science*, vol. 323, pp. 1297–1298, Mar. 6, 2009, doi: 10.1126/science.1170411.

[2] Freeman Dyson's 2008 Einstein lecture, "Birds and Frogs," *Notices Am. Math. Soc.*, vol. 56, no. 2, pp. 212–224, Feb. 2009, www.ams.org/notices/200902/rtx090200212p.pdf.

[3] National Science Board, "Long-Lived Digital Data Collections: Enabling Research and Education in the 21st Century," National Science Foundation, 2005, www.nsf.gov/pubs/2005/nsb0540/start.jsp.

[4] Association of Research Libraries, "To Stand the Test of Time: Long-term Stewardship of Digital Data Sets in Science and Engineering," Association of Research Libraries, 2006. www.arl.org/pp/access/nsfworkshop.shtml.

[5] Various reports available from the National Science Foundation Office of Cyberinfrastructure, www.nsf.gov/dir/index.jsp?org=OCI, including the Cyberinfrastructure Vision document and the Atkins report.

[6] L. Lyon, "Dealing with Data: Roles, Rights, Responsibilities and Relationships," (consultancy report), UKOLN and the Joint Information Systems Committee (JISC), 2006, www.jisc.ac.uk/whatwedo/programmes/programme_digital_repositories/project_dealing_with_data.aspx.

[7] C. A. Lynch, "The Shape of the Scientific Article in the Developing Cyberinfrastructure," *CT Watch*, vol. 3, no. 3, pp. 5–11, Aug. 2007, www.ctwatch.org/quarterly/articles/2007/08/the-shape-of-the-scientific-article-in-the-developing-cyberinfrastructure.

[8] C. A. Lynch, "Open Computation: Beyond Human-Reader-Centric Views of Scholarly Literatures," in Neil Jacobs, Ed., *Open Access: Key Strategic, Technical and Economic Aspects.* Oxford: Chandos Publishing, 2006, pp. 185–193, www.cni.org/staff/cliffpubs//OpenComputation.pdf.

Text in a Data-centric World

PAUL GINSPARG
Cornell University

FIRST MET JIM GRAY WHEN HE WAS THE MODERATOR of the database subject area of arXiv, part of the expansion into computer science that arXiv initiated in 1998. Soon afterward, he was instrumental in facilitating the full-text harvest of arXiv by large-scale search engines, beginning with Google and followed by Microsoft and Yahoo!—previous robotic crawls of arXiv being overly restricted in the 1990s due to their flooding of the servers with requests. Jim understood the increasing role of text as a form of data, and the need for text to be ingestible and treatable like any other computable object. In 2005, he was involved in both arXiv and PubMed Central and expressed to me his mystification that while the two repositories served similar roles, they seemed to operate in parallel universes, not connecting in any substantive way. His vision was of a world of scholarly resources—text, databases, and any other associated materials—that were seamlessly navigable and interoperable.

Many of the key open questions regarding the technological transformation of scholarly infrastructure were raised well over a decade ago, including the long-term financial model for implementing quality control, the architecture of the article of the future, and how all of the pieces will merge into an interoperable whole. While answers have remained elusive, there is reason to expect significant near-term progress on at least the latter two questions. In [1], I described how the range of possibilities for large and comprehensive full-text aggregations were just starting to be probed and offered the PubMed Central database as an exemplar of a forward-looking approach. Its full-text XML documents are parsed to permit multiple "related material views" for a given article, with links to genomic, nucleotide, inheritance, gene expression, protein, chemical, taxonomic, and other related databases. This methodology is now beginning to spread, along with more general forms of semantic enhancement: facilitating automated discovery and reasoning, providing links to related documents and data, providing access to actionable data within articles, and permitting integration of data between articles.

A recent example of semantic enhancement by a publisher is the Royal Society of Chemistry's journal *Molecular BioSystems*.[1] Its enhanced HTML highlights terms in the text that are listed in chemical terminology databases and links them to the external database entries. Similarly, it highlights and links terms from gene, sequence, and cell ontologies. This textual markup is implemented by editors with subject-matter expertise, assisted by automated text-mining tools. An example of a fully automated tool for annotation of scientific terms is EMBL Germany's Reflect,[2] which operates as an external service on any Web page or as a browser plug-in. It tags gene, protein, and small molecule names, and the tagged items are linked to the relevant sequence, structure, or interaction databases.

In a further thought experiment, Shotton et al. [2] marked up an article by hand using off-the-shelf technologies to demonstrate a variety of possible semantic enhancements—essentially a minimal set that would likely become commonplace in the near future. In addition to semantic markup of textual terms and live linkages of DOIs and other URLs where feasible, they implemented a reorderable reference list, a document summary including document statistics, a tag cloud of technical terms, tag trees of marked-up named entities grouped by semantic type, citation analysis (within each article), a "Citations in Context" tooltip indicating the type of citation (background, intellectual precedent, refutation, and so on), downloadable spreadsheets for tables and figures, interactive figures, and data fusion with results from other research articles and with contextual online maps. (See Figure 1.) They emphasize the future importance of domain-specific structured digital abstracts— namely, machine-readable metadata that summarize key data and conclusions of articles, including a list of named entities in the article with precise database iden-

---

[1] www.rsc.org/Publishing/Journals/mb
[2] http://reflect.ws, winner of the recent Elsevier Grand Challenge (www.elseviergrandchallenge.com).

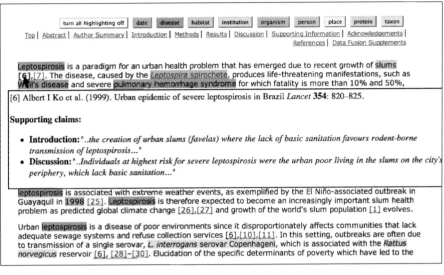

FIGURE 1.

A screenshot of "Exemplar Semantic Enhancements" from http://imageweb.zoo.ox.ac.uk/pub/ 2008/plospaper/latest, as described in [2]. Different semantic classes of terms are linked and can be optionally highlighted using the buttons in the top row. Hovering the mouse pointer over an in-text reference citation displays a box containing key supporting statements or figures from the cited document.

tifiers, a list of the main results described via controlled vocabulary, and a description, using standard evidence codes, of the methodology employed. The use of controlled vocabularies in this structured summary will enable not only new metrics for article relatedness but also new forms of automated reasoning.

Currently, recognition of named entities (e.g., gene names) in unstructured text is relatively straightforward, but reliable extraction of relationships expressed in conventional text is significantly more difficult. The next generation of automated knowledge extraction and processing tools, operating on structured abstracts and semantically enhanced text, will bring us that much closer to direct searching and browsing of "knowledge"—i.e., via synthesized concepts and their relationships. Further enhancements will include citation network analysis, automated image analysis, more generalized data mashups, and prekeyed or configurable algorithms that provide new types of semantic lenses through which to view the text, data, and images. All of these features can also be federated into hub environments where users can annotate articles and related information, discover hidden associations, and share new results.

In the near term, semantic text enhancement will be performed by a combination of semi-supervised tools used by authors,[3] tools used by editors, and automated tools applied to both new and archival publications. Many legacy authors will be unwilling to spend time enhancing their documents, especially if much additional effort is required. Certainly many publishers will provide the markup as a value-added component of the publication process—i.e., as part of their financial model. The beneficial effects of this enhancement, visible to all readers, will create pressure in the open sector for equally powerful tools, perhaps after only a small time lag as each new feature is developed. It is more natural to incorporate the semantics from the outset rather than trying to layer it on afterwards—and in either case, PDF will not provide a convenient transport format. With the correct document format, tools, and incentives, authors may ultimately provide much of the structural and semantic metadata during the course of article writing, with marginal additional effort.

In the longer term, there remains the question of where the semantic markup should be hosted, just as with other data published to the Web: Should publishers host datasets relevant to their own publications, or should there be independent SourceForge-like data repositories? And how should the markup be stored: as triple-stores internal to the document or as external attachments specifying relationships and dependencies? As knowledge progresses, there will be new linkages, new things to annotate, and existing annotations that may lead to changed resources or data. Should it be possible to peel these back and view the document in the context of any previous time frame?

To avoid excessive one-off customization, the interactions between documents and data and the fusion of different data sources will require a generic, interoperable semantic layer over the databases. Such structures will also make the data more accessible to generic search engines, via keyword searches and natural-language queries. Having the data accessible in this way should encourage more database maintainers to provide local semantic interfaces, thereby increasing integration into the global data network and amplifying the community benefits of open access to text and data. Tim Berners-Lee[4] has actively promoted the notion of linked data

---

[3] For example, Pablo Fernicola's "Article Authoring Add-in for Microsoft Office Word 2007," www.microsoft.com/downloads/details.aspx?familyid=09c55527-0759-4d6d-ae02-51e90131997e.

[4] www.w3.org/DesignIssues/LinkedData.html

for all such purposes, not just by academics or for large and commonly used data-bases. Every user makes a small contribution to the overall structure by linking an object to a URI, which can be dereferenced to find links to more useful data. Such an articulated semantic structure facilitates simpler algorithms acting on World Wide Web text and data and is more feasible in the near term than building a layer of complex artificial intelligence to interpret free-form human ideas using some probabilistic approach.

New forms of interaction with the data layer are also embedded in discussions of Wolfram|Alpha,[5] a new resource (made publicly available only after this writing) that uses substantial personnel resources to curate many thousands of data feeds into a format suitable for manipulation by a Mathematica algorithmic and visualization engine. Supplemented by a front end that interprets semi-natural-language queries, this system and its likely competition will dramatically raise user expectations for new forms of synthesized information that is available directly via generic search en-gines. These applications will develop that much more quickly over data repositories whose semantic layer is curated locally rather than requiring centralized curation.

Much of the recent progress in integrating data with text via semantic enhance-ment, as described above, has been with application to the life sciences literature. In principle, text mining and natural-language processing tools that recognize relevant entities and automatically link to domain-specific ontologies have natural analogs in all fields—for example, astronomical objects and experiments in astron-omy; mathematical terms and theorems in mathematics; physical objects, termi-nology, and experiments in physics; and chemical structures and experiments in chemistry. While data-intensive science is certainly the norm in astrophysics, the pieces of the data network for astrophysics do not currently mesh nearly as well as in the life sciences. Most paradoxically, although the physics community was ahead in many of these digital developments going back to the early 1990s (including the development of the World Wide Web itself at CERN, a high-energy physics lab) and in providing open access to its literature, there is currently no coordinated effort to develop semantic structures for most areas of physics. One obstacle is that in many distributed fields of physics, such as condensed-matter physics, there are no dominant laboratories with prominent associated libraries to establish and main-tain global resources.

<hr>

[5] www.wolframalpha.com, based on a private demonstration on April 23, 2009, and a public presentation on April 28, 2009, http://cyber.law.harvard.edu/events/2009/04/wolfram.

In the biological and life sciences, it's also possible that text will decrease in value over the next decade compared with the semantic services that direct researchers to actionable data, help interpret information, and extract knowledge [3]. In most scientific fields, however, the result of research is more than an impartial set of database entries. The scientific article will retain its essential role of using carefully selected data to persuade readers of the truth of its author's hypotheses. Database entries will serve a parallel role of providing access to complete and impartial datasets, both for further exploration and for automated data mining. There are also important differences among areas of science in the role played by data. As one prominent physicist-turned-biologist commented to me recently, "There are no fundamental organizing principles in biology"[6]—suggesting that some fields may always be intrinsically more data driven than theory driven. Science plays different roles within our popular and political culture and hence benefits from differing levels of support. In genomics, for example, we saw the early development of GenBank, its adoption as a government-run resource, and the consequent growth of related databases within the National Library of Medicine, all heavily used.

It has also been suggested that massive data mining, and its attendant ability to tease out and predict trends, could ultimately replace more traditional components of the scientific method [4]. This viewpoint, however, confuses the goals of fundamental theory and phenomenological modeling. Science aims to produce far more than a simple mechanical prediction of correlations; instead, its goal is to employ those regularities extracted from data to construct a unified means of understanding them *a priori*. Predictivity of a theory is thus primarily crucial as a validator of its conceptual content, although it can, of course, have great practical utility as well.

So we should neither overestimate the role of data nor underestimate that of text, and all scientists should track the semantic enhancement of text and related data-driven developments in the biological and life sciences with great interest— and perhaps with envy. Before too long, some archetypal problem might emerge in the physical sciences[7] that formerly required many weeks of complex query traversals of databases, manually maintained browser tabs, impromptu data analysis scripts, and all the rest of the things we do on a daily basis. For example, a future researcher with seamless semantic access to a federation of databases—including band structure properties and calculations, nuclear magnetic resonance (NMR)

[6] Wally Gilbert, dinner on April 27, 2009. His comment may have been intended in a more limited context than implied here.

[7] As emphasized to me by John Wilbanks in a discussion on May 1, 2009.

and X-ray scattering measurements, and mechanical and other properties—might instantly find a small modification to a recently fabricated material to make it the most efficient photovoltaic ever conceived. Possibilities for such progress in finding new sources of energy or forestalling long-term climate change may already be going unnoticed in today's unintegrated text/database world. If classes of such problems emerge and an immediate solution can be found via automated tools acting directly on a semantic layer that provides the communication channels between open text and databases, then other research communities will be bootstrapped into the future, benefiting from the new possibilities for community-driven scientific knowledge curation and creation embodied in the Fourth Paradigm.

REFERENCES

[1] P. Ginsparg, "Next-Generation Implications of Open Access," www.ctwatch.org/quarterly/articles/2007/08/next-generation-implications-of-open-access, accessed Aug. 2007.

[2] D. Shotton, K. Portwin, G. Klyne, and A. Miles, "Adventures in Semantic Publishing: Exemplar Semantic Enhancements of a Research Article," *PLoS Comput. Biol.*, vol. 5, no. 4, p. e1000361, 2009, doi: 10.1371/journal.pcbi.1000361.

[3] P. Bourne, "Will a Biological Database Be Different from a Biological Journal?" *PLoS Comput. Biol.*, vol. 1, no. 3, p. e34, 2005, doi: 10.1371/journal.pcbi.0010034. This article was intentionally provocative.

[4] C. Anderson, "The End of Theory: The Data Deluge Makes the Scientific Method Obsolete," *Wired*, June 2008, www.wired.com/science/discoveries/magazine/16-07/pb_theory. This article was also intentionally provocative.

All Aboard: Toward a Machine-Friendly Scholarly Communication System

HERBERT
VAN DE SOMPEL
Los Alamos National
Laboratory

CARL LAGOZE
Cornell University

*"The current scholarly communication system
is nothing but a scanned copy of the paper-based system."*

THIS SENTENCE, WHICH WE USED for effect in numerous conference presentations and eventually fully articulated in a 2004 paper [1], is still by and large true. Although scholarly publishers have adopted new technologies that have made access to scholarly materials significantly easier (such as the Web and PDF documents), these changes have not realized the full potential of the new digital and networked reality. In particular, they do not address three shortcomings of the prevailing scholarly communication system:

- Systemic issues, particularly the unbreakable tie in the publication system between the act of making a scholarly claim and the peer-review process

- Economic strains that are manifested in the "serials crisis," which places tremendous burdens on libraries

- Technical aspects that present barriers to an interoperable information infrastructure

We share these concerns about the state of scholarly communication with many others worldwide. Almost a decade ago, we collaborated with members of that global community to begin the Open Archives Initiative (OAI), which had a significant impact on the direction and pace of the Open Access movement. The OAI Protocol for Metadata Harvesting (OAI-PMH) and the concurrent OpenURL effort reflected our initial focus on the process-related aspects of scholarly communication. Other members of the community focused on the scholarly content itself. For example, Peter Murray-Rust addressed the flattening of structured, machine-actionable information (such as tabular data and data points underlying graphs) into plain text suited only for human consumption [2].

A decade after our initial work in this area, we are delighted to observe the rapid changes that are occurring in various dimensions of scholarly communication. We will touch upon three areas of change that we feel are significant enough to indicate a fundamental shift.

AUGMENTING THE SCHOLARLY RECORD WITH A MACHINE-ACTIONABLE SUBSTRATE

One motivation for machine readability is the flood of literature that makes it impossible for researchers to keep up with relevant scholarship [3]. Agents that *read* and *filter* on scholars' behalf can offer a solution to this problem. The need for such a mechanism is heightened by the fact that researchers increasingly need to absorb and process literature across disciplines, connecting the dots and combining existing disparate findings to arrive at new insights. This is a major issue in life sciences fields that are characterized by many interconnected disciplines (such as genetics, molecular biology, biochemistry, pharmaceutical chemistry, and organic chemistry). For example, the lack of uniformly structured data across related biomedical domains is cited as a significant barrier to translational research—the transfer of discoveries in basic biological and medical research to application in patient care at the clinical level [4].

Recently, we have witnessed a significant push toward a machine-actionable representation of the knowledge embedded in the life sciences literature, which supports reasoning across disciplinary boundaries. Advanced text analysis techniques are being used to extract entities and entity relations from the existing literature, and shared ontologies have been introduced to achieve uniform knowledge representation. This approach has already led to new discoveries based on information embedded in literature that was previously readable only by humans. Other disciplines have engaged in similar activities, and some initiatives are allowing scholars to start publishing entity and entity-relation information at the time of an article's publication, to avoid the post-processing that is current practice [5].

The launch of the international Concept Web Alliance, whose aim is to provide a global interdisciplinary platform to *discuss, design, and potentially certify solutions for the interoperability and usability of massive, dispersed, and complex data,* indicates that the trend toward a machine-actionable substrate is being taken seriously by both academia and the scholarly information industry. The establishment of a machine-actionable representation of scholarly knowledge can help scholars and learners deal with information abundance. It can allow for new discoveries to be made by reasoning over a body of established knowledge, and it can increase the speed of discovery by helping scholars to avoid redundant research and by revealing promising avenues for new research.

INTEGRATION OF DATASETS INTO THE SCHOLARLY RECORD

Even though data have always been a crucial ingredient in scientific explorations, until recently they were not treated as first-class objects in scholarly communication, as were the research papers that reported on findings extracted from the data. This is rapidly and fundamentally changing. The scientific community is actively discussing and exploring implementation of all core functions of scholarly communication—*registration, certification, awareness, archiving, and rewarding* [1]—for datasets.

For example, the Data Pyramid proposed in [6] clearly indicates how attention to trust *(certification)* and digital preservation *(archiving)* for datasets becomes vital as their application reaches beyond personal use and into the realms of disciplinary communities and society at large. The international efforts aimed at enabling the sharing of research data [7] reflect recognition of the need for an infrastructure to facilitate discovery of shared datasets *(awareness)*. And efforts aimed at defining a standard citation format for datasets [8] take for granted that they are primary scholarly artifacts. These efforts are motivated in part by the belief that researchers should gain credit (be *rewarded*) for the datasets they have compiled and shared. Less than a decade or so ago, these functions of scholarly communication largely applied only to the scholarly literature.

EXPOSURE OF PROCESS AND ITS INTEGRATION INTO THE SCHOLARLY RECORD

Certain aspects of the scholarly communication process have been exposed for a long time. Citations made in publications indicate the use of prior knowledge to generate new insights. In this manner, the scholarly citation graph reveals aspects of scholarly dynamics and is thus actively used as a research focus to detect connections between disciplines and for trend analysis and prediction. However, interpretation of the scholarly citation graph is often error prone due to imperfect manual or automatic citation extraction approaches and challenging author disambiguation issues. The coverage of citation graph data is also partial (top-ranked journals only or specific disciplines only), and unfortunately the most representative graph (Thomson Reuters) is proprietary.

The citation graph problem is indicative of a broader problem: there is no unambiguous, recorded, and visible trace of the evolution of a scholarly asset through the system, nor is there information about the nature of the evolution. The problem is that relationships, which are known at the moment a scholarly asset goes through a step in a value chain, are lost the moment immediately after, in many cases forever. The actual dynamics of scholarship—the interaction/connection between assets, authors, readers, quality assessments about assets, scholarly research areas, and so on—are extremely hard to recover after the fact. Therefore, it is necessary to establish a layer underlying scholarly communication—a grid for scholarly communication that records and exposes such dynamics, relationships, and interactions.

A solution to this problem is emerging through a number of innovative initiatives that make it possible to publish information about the scholarly process in machine-readable form to the Web, preferably at the moment that events of the above-described type happen and hence, when all required information is available.

Specific to the citation graph case, the Web-oriented citation approach explored by the CLADDIER project demonstrates a mechanism for encoding an accurate, crawlable citation graph on the Web. Several initiatives are aimed at introducing author identifiers [9] that could help establish a less ambiguous citation graph. A graph augmented with citation semantics, such as that proposed by the Citation Typing Ontology effort, would also reveal why an artifact is being cited—an important bit of information that has remained elusive until now [10].

Moving beyond citation data, other efforts to expose the scholarly process include projects that aim to share scholarly usage data (the process of paying attention to scholarly information), such as COUNTER, MESUR, and the bX scholarly recommender service. Collectively, these projects illustrate the broad applicability of this type of process-related information for the purpose of collection development, computation of novel metrics to assess the impact of scholarly artifacts [11], analysis of current research trends [12], and recommender systems. As a result of this work, several projects in Europe are pursuing technical solutions for sharing detailed usage data on the Web.

Another example of process capture is the successful myExperiment effort, which provides a social portal for sharing computational workflow descriptions. Similar efforts in the chemistry community allow the publication and sharing of laboratory notebook information on the Web [13].

We find these efforts particularly inspiring because they allow us to imagine a next logical step, which would be the sharing of provenance data. Provenance data reveal the history of inputs and processing steps involved in the execution of workflows and are a critical aspect of scientific information, both to establish trust in the veracity of the data and to support the reproducibility demanded of all experimental science. Recent work in the computer science community [14] has yielded systems capable of maintaining detailed provenance information within a single environment. We feel that provenance information that describes and interlinks workflows, datasets, and processes is a new kind of process-type metadata that has a key role in network-based and data-intensive science—similar in importance to descriptive metadata, citation data, and usage data in article-based scholarship. Hence, it seems logical that eventually provenance information will be exposed so it can be leveraged by a variety of tools for discovery, analysis, and impact assessment of some core products of new scholarship: workflows, datasets, and processes.

LOOKING FORWARD

As described above, the scholarly record will emerge as the result of the intertwining of traditional and new scholarly artifacts, the development of a machine-actionable scholarly knowledge substrate, and the exposure of meta-information about the scholarly process. These facilities will achieve their full potential only if they are grounded in an appropriate and interoperable cyberinfrastructure that is based on the Web and its associated standards. The Web will not only contribute to the sustainability of the scholarly process, but it will also integrate scholarly debate seamlessly with the broader human debate that takes place on the Web.

We have recently seen an increased Web orientation in the development of approaches to scholarly interoperability. This includes the exploration or active use of uniform resource identifiers (URIs), more specifically HTTP URIs, for the identification of scholarly artifacts, concepts, researchers, and institutions, as well as the use of the XML, RDF, RDFS, OWL, RSS, and Atom formats to support the representation and communication of scholarly information and knowledge. These foundational technologies are increasingly being augmented with community-specific and community-driven yet compliant specializations. Overall, a picture is beginning to emerge in which all constituents of the new scholarly record (both human and machine-readable) are published on the Web, in a manner that complies with general Web standards and community-specific specializations of those standards. Once published on the Web, they can be accessed, gathered, and mined by both human and machine agents.

Our own work on the OAI Object Reuse & Exchange (OAI-ORE) specifications [15], which define an approach to identifying and describing eScience assets that are aggregations of multiple resources, is an illustration of this emerging Web-centric cyberinfrastructure approach. It builds on core Web technologies and also adheres to the guidelines of the Linked Data effort, which is rapidly emerging as the most widespread manifestation of years of Semantic Web work.

When describing this trend toward the use of common Web approaches for scholarly purposes, we are reminded of Jim Gray, who insisted throughout the preliminary discussions leading to the OAI-ORE work that any solution should leverage common feed technologies—RSS or Atom. Jim was right in indicating that many special-purpose components of the cyberinfrastructure need to be developed to meet the requirements of scholarly communication, and in recognizing that others are readily available as a result of general Web standardization activities.

As we look into the short-term future, we are reminded of one of Jim Gray's well-known quotes: "May all your problems be technical." With this ironic comment, Jim was indicating that behind even the most difficult technical problems lies an even more fundamental problem: assuring the integration of the cyberinfrastructure into human workflows and practices. Without such integration, even the best cyberinfrastructure will fail to gain widespread use. Fortunately, there are indications that we have learned this lesson from experience through the years with other large-scale infrastructure projects such as the Digital Libraries Initiatives. The Sustainable Digital Data Preservation and Access Network Partners (DataNet) program funded by the Office of Cyberinfrastructure at the U.S. National Science Foundation (NSF) has recently awarded funding for two 10-year projects that focus on cyberinfrastructure as a sociotechnical problem—one that requires both knowledge of technology and understanding of how the technology integrates into the communities of use. We believe that this wider focus will be one of the most important factors in changing the nature of scholarship and the ways that it is communicated over the coming decade.

We are confident that the combination of the continued evolution of the

Web, new technologies that leverage its core principles, and an understanding of the way people use technology will serve as the foundation of a fundamentally rethought scholarly communication system that will be friendly to both humans and machines. With the emergence of that system, we will happily refrain from using our once-beloved scanned copy metaphor.

REFERENCES

[1] H. Van de Sompel, S. Payette, J. Erickson, C. Lagoze, and S. Warner, "Rethinking Scholarly Communication: Building the System that Scholars Deserve," *D-Lib Mag.,* vol. 10, no. 9, 2004, www.dlib.org/dlib/september04/vandesompel/09vandesompel.html.

[2] P. Murray-Rust and H. S. Rzepa, "The Next Big Thing: From Hypermedia to Datuments," *J. Digit. Inf.,* vol. 5, no. 1, 2004.

[3] C. L. Palmer, M. H. Cragin, and T. P. Hogan, "Weak information work in scientific discovery," *Inf. Process. Manage.,* vol. 43, no. 3., pp. 808–820, 2007, doi: 10.1016/j.ipm.2006.06.003.

[4] A. Ruttenberg, T. Clark, W. Bug, M. Samwald, O. Bodenreider, H. Chen, D. Doherty, K. Forsberg, Y. Gao, V. Kashyap, J. Kinoshita, J. Luciano, M. S. Marshall, C. Ogbuji, J. Rees, S. Stephens, G. T. Wong, E. Wu, D. Zaccagnini, T. Hongsermeier, E. Neumann, I. Herman, and K. H. Cheung, "Advancing translational research with the Semantic Web," *BMC Bioinf.,* vol. 8, suppl. 3, p. S2, 2007, doi: 10.1186/1471-2105-8-S3-S2.

[5] D. Shotton, K. Portwin, G. Klyne, and A. Miles, "Adventures in Semantic Publishing: Exemplar Semantic Enhancements of a Research Article," *PLoS Comput. Biol.,* vol. 5, no. 4, p. e1000361, 2009, doi: 10.1371/journal.pcbi.1000361.

[6] F. Berman, "Got data?: a guide to data preservation in the information age," *Commun. ACM,* vol. 51, no. 12, pp. 50–56, 2008, doi: 10.1145/1409360.1409376.

[7] R. Ruusalepp, "Infrastructure Planning and Data Curation: A Comparative Study of International Approaches to Enabling the Sharing of Research Data," JISC, Nov. 30, 2008, www.dcc.ac.uk/docs/publications/reports/Data_Sharing_Report.pdf.

[8] M. Altman and G. King, "A Proposed Standard for the Scholarly Citation of Quantitative Data," *D-Lib Magazine,* vol. 13, no. 3/4, 2007.

[9] M. Enserink, "Science Publishing: Are You Ready to Become a Number?" *Science,* vol. 323, no. 5922, 2009, doi: 10.1126/science.323.5922.1662.

[10] N. Kaplan, "The norm of citation behavior," *Am. Documentation,* vol. 16. pp. 179–184, 1965.

[11] J. Bollen, H. Van de Sompel, A. Hagberg, and R. Chute, "A Principal Component Analysis of 39 Scientific Impact Measures," *PLoS ONE,* vol. 4, no. 6, p. e6022, 2009, doi: 10.1371/journal.pone.0006022.

[12] J. Bollen, H. Van de Sompel, A. Hagberg, L. Bettencourt, R. Chute, and L. Balakireva, "Clickstream Data Yields High-Resolution Maps of Science," *PLoS ONE,* vol. 4, no. 3, p. e4803, 2009, doi: 10.1371/journal.pone.0004803.

[13] S. J. Coles, J. G. Frey, M. B. Hursthouse, M. E. Light, A. J. Milsted, L. A. Carr, D. De Roure, C. J. Gutteridge, H. R. Mills, K. E. Meacham, M. Surridge, E. Lyon, R. Heery, M. Duke, and M. Day, "An e-science environment for service crystallography from submission to dissemination," *J. Chem. Inf. Model.,* vol. 46, no. 3, 2006, doi: 10.1021/ci050362w.

[14] R. Bose and J. Frew, "Lineage retrieval for scientific data processing: a survey," *ACM Comput. Surv. (CSUR),* vol. 37, no. 1, pp. 1–28, 2005, doi: 10.1145/1057977.1057978.

[15] H. Van de Sompel, C. Lagoze, C. E. Nelson, S. Warner, R. Sanderson, and P. Johnston, "Adding eScience Publications to the Data Web," *Proc. Linked Data on the Web 2009,* Madrid.

The Future of Data Policy

ANNE FITZGERALD
BRIAN FITZGERALD
KYLIE PAPPALARDO
Queensland University
of Technology

ADVANCES IN INFORMATION AND COMMUNICATION technologies have brought about an information revolution, leading to fundamental changes in the way that information is collected or generated, shared, and distributed [1, 2]. The importance of establishing systems in which research findings can be readily made available to and used by other researchers has long been recognized in international scientific collaborations. Acknowledgment of the need for data access and sharing is most evident in the framework documents underpinning many of the large-scale observational projects that generate vast amounts of data about the Earth, water, the marine environment, and the atmosphere.

For more than 50 years, the foundational documents of major collaborative scientific projects have typically included as a key principle a commitment to ensuring that research outputs will be openly and freely available. While these agreements are often entered into at the international level (whether between governments or their representatives in international organizations), individual researchers and research projects typically operate locally, within a national jurisdiction. If the data access principles adopted by international scientific collaborations are to be effectively implemented, they must be supported by the national policies and laws in place in the countries in which participating researchers are operating. Failure to establish a bridge between, on the one hand, data access principles enunciated at the international level and, on the other hand, the policies and laws at the national level means that the benefits flowing from data sharing are at risk of being thwarted by domestic objectives [3].

The need for coherence among data sharing principles adopted by international science collaborations and the policy and legal frameworks in place in the national jurisdictions where researchers operate is highlighted by the Global Earth Observation System of Systems[1] (GEOSS) initiated in 2005 by the Group on Earth Observations (GEO) [1, p. 125]. GEOSS seeks to connect the producers of environmental data and decision-support tools with the end users of these products, with the aim of enhancing the relevance of Earth observations to global issues. The end result will be a global public infrastructure that generates comprehensive, near-real-time environmental data, information, and analyses for a wide range of users.

The vision for GEOSS is as a "system of systems," built on existing observational systems and incorporating new systems for Earth observation and modeling that are offered as GEOSS components. This emerging public infrastructure links a diverse and growing array of instruments and systems for monitoring and forecasting changes in the global environment. This system of systems supports policymakers, resource managers, science researchers, and many other experts and decision makers.

INTERNATIONAL POLICIES

One of GEO's earliest actions was to explicitly acknowledge the importance of data sharing in achieving its vision and to agree on a strategic set of data sharing principles for GEOSS [4]:

- There will be full and open exchange of data, metadata and products shared within GEOSS, recognizing relevant international instruments, and national policies and legislation.

- All shared data, metadata, and products will be made available with minimum time delay and at minimum cost.

- All shared data, metadata, and products free of charge or no more than cost of reproduction will be encouraged for research and education.

[1] www.earthobservations.org/index.html

These principles, though significant, are not strictly new. A number of other international policy statements promote public availability and open exchange of data, including the Bermuda Principles (1996) and the Berlin Declaration on Open Access to Knowledge in the Sciences and Humanities (2003) [5].

The Bermuda Principles were developed by scientists involved in the International Human Genome Sequencing Consortium and their funding agencies and represented an agreement among researchers about the need to establish a basis for the rapid and open sharing of prepublication data on gene sequences [6]. The Bermuda Principles required automatic release of sequence assemblies larger than 1 KB and immediate publication of finished annotated sequences. They sought to make the entire gene sequence freely available to the public for research and development in order to maximize benefits to society.

The Berlin Declaration had the goal of supporting the open access paradigm via the Internet and promoting the Internet as a fundamental instrument for a global scientific knowledge base. It defined "open access contribution" to include scientific research results, raw data, and metadata, and it required open access contributions to be deposited in an online repository and made available under a "free, irrevocable, worldwide, right of access to, and a license to copy, use, distribute, transmit and display the work publicly and to make and distribute derivative works, in any digital medium for any responsible purpose, subject to proper attribution of authorship." [7]

In fact, the GEOSS principles map closely to the data sharing principles espoused in the Antarctic Treaty, signed almost 50 years earlier in Washington, D.C., in 1959, which has received sustained attention in Australia, particularly in relation to marine data research.[2] Article III of the Antarctic Treaty states:

> 1. In order to promote international cooperation in scientific investigation in Antarctica, as provided for in Article II of the present Treaty, the Contracting Parties agree that, to the greatest extent feasible and practicable: … (c) scientific observations and results from Antarctica shall be exchanged and made freely available. [8]

The data sharing principles stated in the Antarctic Treaty, the GEOSS 10-Year Implementation Plan, the Bermuda Principles, and the Berlin Declaration, among

---

[2] Other international treaties with such provisions include the UN Convention on the Law of the Sea, the Ozone Protocol, the Convention on Biodiversity, and the Aarhus Convention.

others, are widely acknowledged to be not only beneficial but crucial to information flows and the availability of data. However, problems arise because, in the absence of a clear policy and legislative framework at the national level, other considerations can operate to frustrate the effective implementation of the data sharing objectives that are central to international science collaborations [5, 9]. Experience has shown that without an unambiguous statement of data access policy and a supporting legislative framework, good intentions are too easily frustrated in practice.

NATIONAL FRAMEWORKS

The key strategy in ensuring that international policies requiring "full and open exchange of data" are effectively acted on in practice lies in the development of a coherent policy and legal framework at a national level. (See Figure 1.) The national framework must support the international principles for data access and sharing but also be clear and practical enough for researchers to follow at a research project level. While national frameworks for data sharing are well established in the United States and Europe, this is not the case in many other jurisdictions (including Australia). Kim Finney of the Antarctic Data Centre has drawn attention to the difficulties in implementing Article III(1)(c) of the Antarctic Treaty in the absence of established data access policies in signatories to the treaty. She points out that being able to achieve the goal set out in the treaty requires a genuine willingness on the part of scientists to make their data available to other researchers. This willingness is lacking, despite the treaty's clear intention that Antarctic science data be "exchanged and made freely available." Finney argues that there is a strong need for a data access policy in Antarctic member states, because without such a policy, the level of conformance with the aspirations set out in the Antarctic Treaty is patchy at best [10] [1, pp. 77–78].

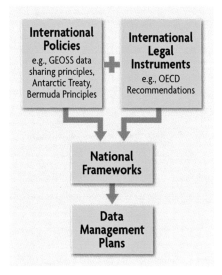

FIGURE 1.

A regulatory framework for data-sharing arrangements.

In the U.S., the Office of Management and Budget (OMB) Circular A-130 establishes the data access and reuse policy framework for the executive branch departments and agencies of the U.S. federal government [11] [1, pp. 174–175]. As well as acknowledging that government information is a valuable public resource and that the nation stands to benefit from the dissemination of government information, OMB Circular A-130 requires that improperly restrictive practices be avoided. Additionally, Circular A-16, entitled "Coordination of Geographic Information and Related Spatial Data Activities," provides that U.S. federal agencies have a responsibility to "[c]ollect, maintain, disseminate, and preserve spatial information such that the resulting data, information, or products can be readily shared with other federal agencies and non-federal users, and promote data integration between all sources." [12] [1, pp. 181–183]

In Europe, the policy framework consists of the broad-reaching Directive on the Re-use of Public Sector Information (2003) (the PSI Directive) [13], as well as the specific directive establishing an Infrastructure for Spatial Information (2007) (the INSPIRE Directive) [14] and the Directive on Public Access to Environmental Information (2003) [15], which obliges public authorities to provide timely access to environmental information.

In negotiating the PSI Directive, the European Parliament and Council of the European Union recognized that the public sector is the largest producer of information in Europe and that substantial social and economic benefits stood to be gained if this information were available for access and reuse. However, European content firms engaging in the aggregation of information resources into value-added information products would be at a competitive disadvantage if they did not have clear policies or uniform practices to guide them in relation to access to and reuse of public sector information. The lack of harmonization of policies and practices regarding public sector information was seen as a barrier to the development of digital products and services based on information obtained from different countries [1, pp. 137–138]. In response, the PSI Directive establishes a framework of rules governing the reuse of existing documents held by the public sector bodies of EU member states. Furthermore, the INSPIRE Directive establishes EU policy and principles relating to spatial data held by or on behalf of public authorities and to the use of spatial data by public authorities in the performance of their public tasks.

Unlike the U.S. and Europe, however, Australia does not currently have a national policy framework addressing access to and use of data. In particular, the current situation with respect to public sector information (PSI) access and reuse is fragmented and lacks a coherent policy foundation, whether viewed in terms of interactions within or among the different levels of government at the local, state/ territory, and federal levels or between the government, academic, and private sectors.[3] In 2008, the "Venturous Australia" report of the Review of the National Innovation System recommended (in Recommendation 7.7) that Australia establish a National Information Strategy to optimize the flow of information in the Australian economy [16]. However, just how a National Information Strategy could be established remains unclear.

A starting point for countries like Australia that have yet to establish national frameworks for the sharing of research outputs has been provided by the Organisation for Economic Co-operation and Development (OECD). At the Seoul Ministerial Meeting on the Future of the Internet Economy in 2008, the OECD Ministers endorsed statements of principle on access to research data produced as a result of public funding and on access to public sector information. These documents establish principles to guide availability of research data, including openness, transparency, legal conformity, interoperability, quality, efficiency, accountability, and sustainability, similar to the principles expressed in the GEOSS statement. The openness principle in the OECD Council's Recommendation on Access to Research Data from Public Funding (2006) states:

A) Openness
Openness means access on equal terms for the international research community at the lowest possible cost, preferably at no more than the marginal cost of dissemination. Open access to research data from public funding should be easy, timely, user-friendly and preferably Internet-based. [17]

OECD Recommendations are OECD legal instruments that describe standards or objectives that OECD member countries (such as Australia) are expected to implement, although they are not legally binding. However, through long-standing practice of member countries, a Recommendation is considered to have great moral force [2, p. 11]. In Australia, the Prime Minister's Science, Engineering and Innovation Council (PMSEIC) Data for Science Working Group, in its 2006 report "From Data to Wisdom: Pathways to Successful Data Management for Australian Science," recommended that OECD guidelines be taken into account in the development of a strategic framework for management of research data in Australia [18].

The development of a national framework for data management based on

---

[3] There has been little policy advancement in Australia on the matter of access to government information since the Office of Spatial Data Management's Policy on Spatial Data Access and Pricing in 2001.

principles promoting data access and sharing (such as the OECD Recommendation) would help to incorporate international policy statements and protocols such as the Antarctic Treaty and the GEOSS Principles into domestic law. This would provide stronger guidance (if not a requirement) for researchers to consider and, where practicable, incorporate these data sharing principles into their research project data management plans [5, 9].

CONCLUSION

Establishing data sharing arrangements for complex, international eResearch collaborations requires appropriate national policy and legal frameworks and data management practices. While international science collaborations typically express a commitment to data access and sharing, in the absence of a supporting national policy and legal framework and good data management practices, such objectives are at risk of not being implemented. Many complications are inherent in eResearch science collaborations, particularly where they involve researchers operating in distributed locations. Technology has rendered physical boundaries irrelevant, but legal jurisdictional boundaries remain. If research data is to flow as intended, it will be necessary to ensure that national policies and laws support the data access systems that have long been regarded as central to international science collaborations. In developing policies, laws, and practices at the national level, guidance can be found in the OECD's statements on access to publicly funded research data, the U.S. OMB's Circular A-130, and various EU directives.

It is crucial that countries take responsibility for promoting policy goals for access and reuse of data at all three levels in order to facilitate information flows. It is only by having the proper frameworks in place that we can be sure to keep afloat in the data deluge.

REFERENCES

[1] A. Fitzgerald, "A review of the literature on the legal aspects of open access policy, practices and licensing in Australia and selected jurisdictions," July 2009, Cooperative Research Centre for Spatial Information and Queensland University of Technology, www.aupsi.org.

[2] Submission of the Intellectual Property: Knowledge, Culture and Economy (IP: KCE) Research Program, Queensland University of Technology, to the Digital Economy Future Directions paper, Australian Government, prepared by B. Fitzgerald, A. Fitzgerald, J. Coates, and K. Pappalardo, Mar. 4, 2009, p. 2, www.dbcde.gov.au/digital_economy/digital_economy_consultation/submissions (under "Queensland University of Technology QUT Law Faculty").

[3] B. Fitzgerald, Ed., *Legal Framework for e-Research: Realising the Potential.* Sydney University Press, 2008, http://eprints.qut.edu.au/14439.

[4] Group on Earth Observations (GEO), "GEOSS 10-Year Implementation Plan," adopted Feb. 16,

2005, p. 4, www.earthobservations.org/docs/10-Year%20Implementation%20Plan.pdf.

[5] A. Fitzgerald and K. Pappalardo, "Building the Infrastructure for Data Access and Reuse in Collaborative Research: An Analysis of the Legal Context," OAK Law Project and Legal Framework for e-Research Project, 2007, http://eprints.qut.edu.au/8865.

[6] Bermuda Principles, 1996, www.ornl.gov/sci/techresources/Human_Genome/research/bermuda.shtml, accessed on June 10, 2009.

[7] Berlin Declaration on Open Access to Knowledge in the Sciences and Humanities (2003), http://oa.mpg.de/openaccess-berlin/berlindeclaration.html, accessed on June 10, 2009.

[8] The Antarctic Treaty (1959), signed in Washington, D.C., Dec. 1, 1959; entry into force for Australia and generally: June 23, 1961, [1961] ATS 12 (Australian Treaty Series, 1961, no. 12), www.austlii.edu.au/cgi-bin/sinodisp/au/other/dfat/treaties/1961/12.html?query=antarctic, accessed June 5, 2009.

[9] A. Fitzgerald, K. Pappalardo, and A. Austin, "Practical Data Management: A Legal and Policy Guide," OAK Law Project and Legal Framework for e-Research Project, 2008, http://eprints.qut.edu.au/14923.

[10] Scientific Committee on Antarctic Research (SCAR) Data and Information Strategy 2008–2013, Joint Committee on Antarctic Data Management (JCADM) and Standing Committee on Antarctic Geographic Information (SC-AGI), authored by K. Finney, Australian Antarctic Data Centre, Australian Antarctic Division (revised May 2008), p. 40, www.jcadm.scar.org/fileadmin/filesystem/jcadm_group/Strategy/SCAR_DIM_StrategyV2-CSKf_final.pdf.

[11] Office of Management and Budget Circular A-130 on Management of Federal Information Resources (OMB Circular A-130), 2000, www.whitehouse.gov/omb/circulars/a130/a130trans4.html.

[12] Office of Management and Budget Circular A-16 on the Coordination of Geographic Information and Related Spatial Data Activities (OMB Circular A-16), issued Jan. 16, 1953, revised 1967, 1990, 2002, Sec. 8, www.whitehouse.gov/omb/circulars_a016_rev/#8.

[13] European Parliament and Council of the European Union, Directive 2003/98/EC of the European Parliament and of the Council of 17 November 2003 on the re-use of the public sector information, 2003, OJ L 345/90, http://eur-lex.europa.eu/LexUriServ/LexUriServ.do?uri=CELEX:32003L0098:EN:HTML.

[14] European Parliament and Council of the European Union, Directive 2007/2/EC of the European Parliament and of the Council of 14 March 2007 establishing an infrastructure for spatial information, 2007, OJ L 108/1, Apr. 25, 2007, http://eur-lex.europa.eu/LexUriServ/LexUriServ.do?uri=OJ:L:2007:108:0001:01:EN:HTML.

[15] European Parliament and Council of the European Union, Directive 2003/4/EC of the European Parliament and of the Council of 28 January 2003 on public access to environmental information and Repealing Council Directive 90/313/EEC OJL 041, Feb. 14, 2003, pp. 0026–0032, http://eur-lex.europa.eu/LexUriServ/LexUriServ.do?uri=CELEX:32003L0004:EN:HTML.

[16] Cutler & Company, "Venturous Australia: Building Strength in Innovation," Review of the National Innovation System, p. 95, 2008, www.innovation.gov.au/innovationreview/Pages/home.aspx.

[17] OECD, "Recommendation of the Council concerning Access to Research Data from Public Funding," C(2006)184, Dec. 14, 2006, http://webdomino1.oecd.org/horizontal/oecdacts.nsf/Display/3A5FB1397B5ADFB7C12572980053C9D3?OpenDocument, accessed on June 5, 2009. Note that these have also been published in "OECD Principles and Guidelines for Access to Research Data from Public Funding," 2007.

[18] Prime Minister's Science, Engineering and Innovation Council (PMSEIC) Working Group on Data for Science, "From Data to Wisdom: Pathways to Successful Data Management for Australian Science," Recommendation 9, p. 12, Dec. 2006, www.dest.gov.au/sectors/science_innovation/publications_resources/profiles/Presentation_Data_for_Science.htm.

I Have Seen the Paradigm Shift, and It Is Us

JOHN WILBANKS
Creative Commons

TEND TO GET NERVOUS WHEN I HEAR TALK OF PARADIGM SHIFTS. The term itself has been debased through inaccurate popular use—even turning into a joke on *The Simpsons*—but its original role in Thomas Kuhn's *Structure of Scientific Revolutions* [1] is worth revisiting as we examine the idea of a Fourth Paradigm and its impact on scholarly communication [2].

Kuhn's model describes a world of science in which a set of ideas becomes dominant and entrenched, creating a worldview (the infamous "paradigm") that itself gains strength and power. This set of ideas becomes powerful because it represents a plausible explanation for observed phenomena. Thus we get the luminiferous aether, the miasma theory of infectious disease, and the idea that the sun revolves around the Earth. The set of ideas, the worldview, the paradigm, gains strength through incrementalism. Each individual scientist tends to work in a manner that adds, bit by bit, to the paradigm. The individual who can make a big addition to the worldview gains authority, research contracts, awards and prizes, and seats on boards of directors.

All involved gain an investment in the set of ideas that goes beyond the ideas themselves. Industries and governments (and the people who work in them) build businesses and policies that depend on the worldview. This adds a layer of defense—an immune system of sorts—that protects the worldview against attack.

Naysayers are marginalized. New ideas lie fallow, unfunded, and unstaffed. Fear, uncertainty, and doubt color perceptions of new ideas, methods, models, and approaches that challenge the established paradigm.

Yet worldviews fall and paradigms shatter when they stop explaining the observed phenomena or when an experiment conclusively proves the paradigm wrong. The aether was conclusively disproven after hundreds of years of incrementalism. As was miasma, as was geocentrism. The time for a shift comes when the old ways of explaining things simply can no longer match the new realities.

This strikes me as being the idea behind Jim Gray's argument about the fourth data paradigm [3] and the framing of the "data deluge"—that our capacity to measure, store, analyze, and visualize data is the new reality to which science must adapt. Data is at the heart of this new paradigm, and it sits alongside empiricism, theory, and simulation, which together form the continuum we think of as the modern scientific method.

But I come to celebrate the first three paradigms, not to bury them. Empiricism and theory got us a long way, from a view of the world that had the sun revolving around the Earth to quantum physics. Simulation is at the core of so much contemporary science, from anthropological re-creations of ancient Rome to weather prediction. The accuracy of simulations and predictions represents the white-hot center of policy debates about economics and climate change. And it's vital to note that empiricism and theory are essential to a good simulation. I can encode a lovely simulation on my screen in which there is no theory of gravity, but if I attempt to drive my car off a cliff, empiricism is going to bite my backside on the way down.

Thus, this is actually not a paradigm shift in the Kuhnian sense. Data is not sweeping away the old reality. Data is simply placing a set of burdens on the methodologies and social habits we use to deal with and communicate our empiricism and our theory, on the robustness and complexity of our simulations, and on the way we expose, transmit, and integrate our knowledge.

What needs to change is our paradigm of ourselves as scientists—not the old paradigms of discovery. When we started to realize that stuff was made of atoms, that we were made of genes, that the Earth revolved around the sun, those were paradigm shifts in the Kuhnian sense. What we're talking about here cuts across those classes of shift. Data-intensive science, if done right, will mean more paradigm shifts of scientific theory, happening faster, because we can rapidly assess our worldview against the "objective reality" we can so powerfully measure.

The data deluge strategy might be better informed by networks than by Kuhnian dynamics. Networks have a capacity to scale that is useful in our management of the data overload—they can convert massive amounts of information into a good thing so the information is no longer a "problem" that must be "solved." And there is a lesson in the way networks are designed that can help us in exploring the data deluge: if we are to manage the data deluge, we need an open strategy that follows the network experience.

By this I mean the "end-to-end," layer-by-layer, designed information technology and communications networks that are composed of no more than a stack of protocols. The Internet and the Web have been built from documents that propose standard methods for transferring information, describing how to display that information, and assigning names to computers and documents. Because we all agree to use those methods, because those methods can be used by anyone without asking for permission, the network emerges and scales.

In this view, data is not a "fourth paradigm" but a "fourth network layer" (atop Ethernet, TCP/IP, and the Web [4]) that interoperates, top to bottom, with the other layers. I believe this view captures the nature of the scientific method a little better than the concept of the paradigm shift, with its destructive nature. Data is the result of incremental advances in empiricism-serving technology. It informs theory, it drives and validates simulations, and it is served best by two-way, standard communication with those layers of the knowledge network.

To state it baldly, the paradigm that needs destruction is the idea that we as scientists exist as un-networked individuals. Now, if this metaphor is acceptable, it holds two lessons for us as we contemplate network design for scholarly communication at the data-intensive layer.

The first lesson, captured perfectly by David Isenberg, is that the Internet "derives its disruptive quality from a very special property: IT IS PUBLIC." [5] It's public in several ways. The standard specifications that define the Internet are themselves open and public—free to read, download, copy, and make derivatives from. They're open in a copyright sense. Those specifications can be adopted by anyone who wants to make improvements and extensions, but their value comes from the fact that a lot of people use them, not because of private improvements. As Isenberg notes, this allows a set of "miracles" to emerge: the network grows without a master, lets us innovate without asking for permission, and grows and discovers markets (think e-mail, instant messaging, social networks, and even pornography). Changing the public nature of the Internet threatens its very existence. This is not intuitive to those of us raised in a world of rivalrous economic goods and traditional economic theory. It makes no sense that Wikipedia exists, let alone that it kicks Encyclopedia Britannica to the curb.

As Galileo might have said, however, "And yet it moves." [6] Wikipedia does exist, and the network—a consensual hallucination defined by a set of dry requests for comments—carries Skype video calls for free between me and my family in Brazil. It is an engine for innovation the likes of which we have never seen. And from the network, we can draw the lesson that new layers of the network related to data should encode the idea of publicness—of standards that allow us to work together openly and transfer the network effects we know so well from the giant collection of documents that is the Web to the giant collections of data we can so easily compile.

The second lesson comes from another open world, that of open source software. Software built on the model of distributed, small contributions joined together through technical and legal standardization was another theoretical impossibility subjected to a true Kuhnian paradigm shift by the reality of the Internet. The ubiquitous ability to communicate, combined with the low cost of acquiring programming tools and the visionary application of public copyright licenses, had the strangest impact: it created software that worked, and scaled. The key lesson is that we can harness the power of millions of minds if we standardize, and the products can in many cases outperform those built in traditional, centralized environments. (A good example is the Apache Web server, which has been the most popular Web server software on the Internet since 1996.)

Creative Commons applied these lessons to licensing and created a set of standard licenses for cultural works. These have in turn exploded to cover hundreds of millions of digital objects on the network. Open licensing turns out to have remarkable benefits—it allows for the kind of interoperability (and near-zero transaction costs) that we know from technical networks to occur on a massive scale for rights associated with digital objects such as songs and photographs—and scientific information.

Incentives are the confounding part of all of this to traditional economic theory. Again, this is a place where a Kuhnian paradigm shift is indeed happening—the old theory could not contemplate a world in which people did work for free, but the new reality proves that it happens. Eben Moglen provocatively wrote in 1999 that collaboration on the Internet is akin to electrical induction—an emergent property of the network unrelated to the incentives of any individual contributor. We should not ask why there is an incentive for collaborative software development any more than we ask why electrons move in a current across a wire. We should instead ask, what is the resistance in the wire, or in the network, to the emergent property? Moglen's Metaphorical Corollaries to Faraday's Law and Ohm's Law[1] still resonate 10 years on.

There is a lot of resistance in the network to a data-intensive layer. And it's actually not based nearly as much on intellectual property issues as it was on software (although the field strength of copyright in resisting the transformation of peer-reviewed literature is very strong and is actively preventing the "Web revolution" in that realm of scholarly communication). With data, problems are caused by copyright,[2] but resistance also comes from many other sources: it's hard to annotate and reuse data, it's hard to send massive data files around, it's hard to combine data that was not generated for recombination, and on and on. Thus, to those who didn't generate it, data has a very short half-life. This resistance originates with the paradigm of ourselves as individual scientists, not the paradigms of empiricism, theory, or simulation.

I therefore propose that our focus be Moglen-inspired and that we resist the resistance. We need investment in annotation and curation, in capacity to store and render data, and in shared visualization and analytics. We need open standards for sharing and exposing data. We need the RFCs (Requests for Comments) of the data layer. And, above all, we need to teach scientists and scholars to work in this new layer of data. As long as we practice a micro-specialization guild culture of training, the social structure of science will continue to provide significant resistance to the data layer.

We need to think of ourselves as connected nodes that need to pass data, test theories, access each others' simulations. And given that every graph about data collection capacity is screaming up exponentially, we need scale in our capacity to use that data, and we need it badly. We need to network ourselves and our knowledge. Nothing else we have designed to date as humans has proven to scale as fast as an open network.

Like all metaphors, the network one has its limits. Networking knowledge is harder than networking documents. Emergent collaboration in software is easier

---

[1] "Moglen's Metaphorical Corollary to Faraday's Law says that if you wrap the Internet around every person on the planet and spin the planet, software flows in the network. It's an emergent property of connected human minds that they create things for one another's pleasure and to conquer their uneasy sense of being too alone. The only question to ask is, what's the resistance of the network? Moglen's Metaphorical Corollary to Ohm's Law states that the resistance of the network is directly proportional to the field strength of the 'intellectual property' system." [7]

[2] Data receives wildly different copyright treatment across the world, which causes confusion and makes international licensing schemes complex and difficult. [8]

because the tools are cheap and ubiquitous—that's not the case in high-throughput physics or molecular biology. Some of the things that make the Web great don't work so well for science and scholarship because the concept of agreement-based ratings find you only the stuff that represents a boring consensus and not the interesting stuff along the edges.

But there is precious little in terms of alternatives to the network approach. The data deluge is real, and it's not slowing down. We can measure more, faster, than ever before. We can do so in massively parallel fashion. And our brain capacity is pretty well frozen at one brain per person. We have to work together if we're going to keep up, and networks are the best collaborative tool we've ever built as a culture. And that means we need to make our data approach just as open as the protocols that connect computers and documents. It's the only way we can get the level of scale that we need.

There is another nice benefit to this open approach. We have our worldviews and paradigms, our opinions and our arguments. It's our nature to think we're right. But we might be wrong, and we are most definitely not completely right. Encoding our current worldviews in an open system would mean that those who come along later can build on top of us, just as we build on empiricism and theory and simulation, whereas encoding ourselves in a closed system would mean that what we build will have to be destroyed to be improved. An open data layer to the network would be a fine gift to the scientists who follow us into the next paradigm—a grace note of good design that will be remembered as a building block for the next evolution of the scientific method.

REFERENCES

[1] T. S. Kuhn, *The Structure of Scientific Revolutions*. Chicago: University of Chicago Press, 1996.
[2] G. Bell, T. Hey, and A. Szalay, "Beyond the Data Deluge," *Science*, vol. 323, pp. 1297–1298, Mar. 6, 2009, doi: 10.1126/science.1170411.
[3] J. Gray and A. Szalay, "eScience - A Transformed Scientific Method," presentation to the Computer Science and Technology Board of the National Research Council, Mountain View, CA, Jan. 11, 2007. (Edited transcript in this volume.)
[4] Joi Ito, keynote presentation at ETech, San Jose, CA, Mar. 11, 2009.
[5] "Broadband without Internet ain't worth squat," by David Isenberg, keynote address delivered at Broadband Properties Summit, accessed on Apr. 30, 2009, at http://isen.com/blog/2009/04/broadband-without-internet-ain-worth.html.
[6] Wikipedia, http://en.wikipedia.org/wiki/E_pur_si_muove, accessed on Apr. 30, 2009.
[7] E. Moglen, "Anarchism Triumphant: Free Software and the Death of Copyright," *First Monday*, vol. 4, no. 8, Aug. 1999, http://emoglen.law.columbia.edu/my_pubs/nospeech.html.
[8] Science Commons Protocol on Open Access Data, http://sciencecommons.org/projects/publishing/open-access-data-protocol.

From Web 2.0 to the Global Database

TIMO HANNAY
Nature Publishing Group

O NE OF THE MOST ARTICULATE OF WEB COMMENTATORS, Clay Shirky, put it best. During his "Lessons from Napster" talk at the O'Reilly Peer-to-Peer Conference in 2001, he invited his audience to consider the infamous prediction of IBM's creator, Thomas Watson, that the world market for computers would plateau at somewhere around five [1]. No doubt some of the people listening that day were themselves carrying more than that number of computers on their laps or their wrists and in their pockets or their bags. And that was even before considering all the other computers about them in the room—inside the projector, the sound system, the air conditioners, and so on. But only when the giggling subsided did he land his killer blow. "We now know that that number was wrong," said Shirky. "He overestimated by four." Cue waves of hilarity from the assembled throng.

Shirky's point, of course, was that the defining characteristic of the Web age is not so much the ubiquity of computing devices (transformational though that is) but rather their interconnectedness. We are rapidly reaching a time when any device not connected to the Internet will hardly seem like a computer at all. The network, as they say, is the computer.

This fact—together with the related observation that the dominant computing platform of our time is not Unix or Windows or

Mac OS, but rather the Web itself—led Tim O'Reilly to develop a vision for what he once called an "Internet operating system" [2], which subsequently evolved into a meme now known around the world as "Web 2.0" [3].

Wrapped in that pithy (and now, unfortunately, overexploited) phrase are two important concepts. First, Web 2.0 acted as a reminder that, despite the dot-com crash of 2001, the Web was—and still is—changing the world in profound ways. Second, it incorporated a series of best-practice themes (or "design patterns and business models") for maximizing and capturing this potential. These themes included:

- Network effects and "architectures of participation"

- The Long Tail

- Software as a service

- Peer-to-peer technologies

- Trust systems and emergent data

- Open APIs and mashups

- AJAX

- Tagging and folksonomies

- "Data as the new 'Intel Inside'"

The first of these has widely become seen as the most significant. The Web is more powerful than the platforms that preceded it because it is an open network and lends itself particularly well to applications that enable collaboration. As a result, the most successful Web applications use the network on which they are built to produce their own network effects, sometimes creating apparently unstoppable momentum. This is how a whole new economy can arise in the form of eBay. And how tiny craigslist and Wikipedia can take on the might of mainstream media and reference publishing, and how Google can produce excellent search results by surreptitiously recruiting every creator of a Web link to its cause.

If the Web 2.0 vision emphasizes the global, collaborative nature of this new medium, how is it being put to use in perhaps the most global and collaborative of all human endeavors, scientific research? Perhaps ironically, especially given the origins of the Web at CERN [4], scientists have been relatively slow to embrace approaches that fully exploit the Web, at least in their professional lives. Blogging, for example, has not taken off in the same way that it has among technologists, political pundits, economists, or even mathematicians. Furthermore, collaborative environments such as OpenWetWare[1] and Nature Network[2] have yet to achieve anything like mainstream status among researchers. Physicists long ago learned to share their findings with one another using the arXiv preprint server,[3] but only because it replicated habits that they had previously pursued by post and then e-mail. Life and Earth scientists, in contrast, have been slower to adopt similar services, such as Nature Precedings.[4]

This is because the barriers to full-scale adoption are not only (or even mainly) technical, but also psychological and social. Old habits die hard, and incentive systems originally created to encourage information sharing through scientific journals can now have the perverse effect of discouraging similar activities by other routes.

Yet even if these new approaches are growing more slowly than some of us would wish, they are still growing. And though the timing of change is difficult to predict, the long-term trends in scientific research are unmistakable: greater specialization, more immediate and open information sharing, a reduction in the size of the "minimum publishable unit," productivity measures that look beyond journal publication records, a blurring of the boundaries between journals and databases, and reinventions of the roles of publishers and editors. Most important of all—and arising from this gradual but inevitable embrace of information technology—we will see an increase in the rate at which new discoveries are made and put to use. Laboratories of the future will indeed hum to the tune of a genuinely new kind of computationally driven, interconnected, Web-enabled science.

Look, for example, at chemistry. That granddaddy of all collaborative sites, Wikipedia,[5] now contains a great deal of high-quality scientific information, much of it provided by scientists themselves. This includes rich, well-organized, and interlinked information about many thousands of chemical compounds. Meanwhile, more specialized resources from both public and private initiatives—notably PubChem[6] and ChemSpider[7]—are growing in content, contributions, and usage

[1] http://openwetware.org
[2] http://network.nature.com
[3] www.arxiv.org
[4] http://precedings.nature.com
[5] http://wikipedia.org
[6] http://pubchem.ncbi.nlm.nih.gov
[7] www.chemspider.com

despite the fact that chemistry has historically been a rather proprietary domain. (Or perhaps in part because of it, but that is a different essay.)

And speaking of proprietary domains, consider drug discovery. InnoCentive,[8] a company spun off from Eli Lilly, has blazed a trail with a model of open, Web-enabled innovation that involves organizations reaching outside their walls to solve research-related challenges. Several other pharmaceutical companies that I have spoken with in recent months have also begun to embrace similar approaches, not principally as acts of goodwill but in order to further their corporate aims, both scientific and commercial.

In industry and academia alike, one of the most important forces driving the adoption of technologically enabled collaboration is sheer necessity. Gone are the days when a lone researcher could make a meaningful contribution to, say, molecular biology without access to the data, skills, or analyses of others. As a result, over the last couple of decades many fields of research, especially in biology, have evolved from a "cottage industry" model (one small research team in a single location doing everything from collecting the data to writing the paper) into a more "industrial" one (large, distributed teams of specialists collaborating across time and space toward a common end).

In the process, they are gathering vast quantities of data, with each stage in the progression being accompanied by volume increases that are not linear but exponential. The sequencing of genes, for example, has long since given way to whole genomes, and now to entire species [5] and ecosystems [6]. Similarly, one-dimensional protein-sequence data has given way to three-dimensional protein structures, and more recently to high-dimensional protein interaction datasets.

This brings changes that are not just quantitative but also qualitative. Chris Anderson has been criticized for his *Wired* article claiming that the accumulation and analysis of such vast quantities of data spells the end of science as we know it [7], but he is surely correct in his milder (but still very significant) claim that there comes a point in this process when "more is different." Just as an information retrieval algorithm like Google's PageRank [8] required the Web to reach a certain scale before it could function at all, so new approaches to scientific discovery will be enabled by the sheer scale of the datasets we are accumulating.

But realizing this value will not be easy. Everyone concerned, not least researchers and publishers, will need to work hard to make the data more useful. This will

---

[8] www.innocentive.com

involve a range of approaches, from the relatively formal, such as well-defined standard data formats and globally agreed identifiers and ontologies, to looser ones, like free-text tags [9] and HTML microformats [10]. These, alongside automated approaches such as text mining [11], will help to give each piece of information context with respect to all the others. It will also enable two hitherto largely separate domains—the textual, semi-structured world of journals and the numeric, highly structured world of databases—to come together into one integrated whole. As the information held in journals becomes more structured, as that held in many databases becomes more curated, and as these two domains establish richer mutual links, the distinction between them might one day become so fuzzy as to be meaningless.

Improved data structures and richer annotations will be achieved in large part by starting at the source: the laboratory. In certain projects and fields, we already see reagents, experiments, and datasets being organized and managed by sophisticated laboratory information systems. Increasingly, we will also see the researchers' notes move from paper to screen in the form of electronic laboratory notebooks, enabling them to better integrate with the rest of the information being generated. In areas of clinical significance, these will also link to biopsy and patient information. And so, from lab bench to research paper to clinic, from one finding to another, we will join the dots as we explore terra incognita, mapping out detailed relationships where before we had only a few crude lines on an otherwise blank chart.

Scientific knowledge—indeed, all of human knowledge—is fundamentally connected [12], and the associations are every bit as enlightening as the facts themselves. So even as the quantity of data astonishingly balloons before us, we must not overlook an even more significant development that demands our recognition and support: that the information itself is also becoming more interconnected. One link, tag, or ID at a time, the world's data are being joined together into a single seething mass that will give us not just one global computer, but also one global database. As befits this role, it will be vast, messy, inconsistent, and confusing. But it will also be of immeasurable value—and a lasting testament to our species and our age.

REFERENCES

[1] C. Shirky, "Lessons from Napster," talk delivered at the O'Reilly Peer-to-Peer Conference, Feb. 15, 2001, www.openp2p.com/pub/a/p2p/2001/02/15/lessons.html.

[2] T. O'Reilly, "Inventing the Future," 2002, www.oreillynet.com/pub/a/network/2002/04/09/future.html.

[3] T. O'Reilly, "What Is Web 2.0," 2005, www.oreillynet.com/pub/a/oreilly/tim/news/2005/09/30/what-is-web-20.html.

[4] T. Berners-Lee, *Weaving the Web*. San Francisco: HarperOne, 1999.

[5] "International Consortium Announces the 1000 Genomes Project," www.genome.gov/26524516.

[6] J. C. Venter et al., "Environmental genome shotgun sequencing of the Sargasso Sea," *Science*, vol. 304, pp. 66–74, 2004, doi:10.1126/science.1093857.

[7] C. Anderson, "The End of Theory: The Data Deluge Makes the Scientific Method Obsolete," *Wired*, June 2008, www.wired.com/science/discoveries/magazine/16-07/pb_theory.

[8] S. Brin and L. Page, "The Anatomy of a Large-Scale Hypertextual Web Search Engine," 1998, http://ilpubs.stanford.edu:8090/361.

[9] http://en.wikipedia.org/wiki/Tag_(metadata)

[10] http://en.wikipedia.org/wiki/Microformat

[11] http://en.wikipedia.org/wiki/Text_mining

[12] E. O. Wilson, *Consilience: The Unity of Knowledge*. New York: Knopf, 1998.

The Way Forward

CRAIG MUNDIE | Microsoft

T HE MULTI-DISCIPLINARY NATURE OF THE ARTICLES collected in this book offers a unique perspective on data-driven scientific discovery—and a glimpse into an exciting future.

As we move into the second decade of the 21st century, we face an extraordinary range of challenges—healthcare, education, energy and the environment, digital access, cyber-security and privacy, public safety, and more. But along with the other contributors to this book, I believe these challenges can be transformed into opportunities with the help of radical new developments in science and technology.

As Jim Gray observed, the first, second, and third paradigms of science—empirical, analytical, and simulation—have successfully carried us to this point in history. Moreover, there is no doubt that if we rely on existing paradigms and technologies, we will continue to make incremental progress. But if we are to achieve *dramatic* breakthroughs, new approaches will be required. We need to embrace the next, fourth paradigm of science.

Jim's vision of this paradigm called for a new scientific methodology focused on the power of *data-intensive science*. Today, that vision is becoming reality. Computing technology, with its pervasive connectivity via the Internet, already underpins almost all scientific study. We are amassing previously unimaginable amounts of data in digital form—data that will help bring about a profound transformation of scientific research and insight. At the same time, computing is on the cusp of a wave of disruptive technological advances—such as multicore architecture, client-plus-cloud computing, natural user interfaces, and quantum computing—that promises to revolutionize scientific discovery.

Data-intensive science promises breakthroughs across a broad spectrum. As the Earth becomes increasingly instrumented with low-cost, high-bandwidth sensors, we will gain a better understanding of our environment via a virtual, distributed whole-Earth "macroscope." Similarly, the night sky is being brought closer with high-bandwidth, widely available data-visualization systems. This virtuous circle of computing technology and data access will help educate the public about our planet and the Universe at large—making us all participants in the experience of science and raising awareness of its immense benefit to everyone.

In healthcare, a shift to data-driven medicine will have an equally transformative impact. The ability to compute genomics and proteomics will become feasible on a personal scale, fundamentally changing how medicine is practiced. Medical data will be readily available in real time—tracked, benchmarked, and analyzed against our unique characteristics, ensuring that treatments are as personal as we are individual. Massive-scale data analytics will enable real-time tracking of disease and targeted responses to potential pandemics. Our virtual "macroscope" can now be used on ourselves, as well as on our planet. And all of these advances will help medicine scale to meet the needs of the more than 4 billion people who today lack even basic care.

As computing becomes exponentially more powerful, it will also enable more natural interactions with scientists. Systems that are able to "understand" and have far greater contextual awareness will provide a level of proactive assistance that was previously available only from human helpers. For scientists, this will mean deeper scientific insight, richer discovery, and faster breakthroughs. Another major advance is the emergence of megascale services that are hosted in the cloud and that operate in conjunction with client computers of every kind. Such an infrastructure will enable wholly new data delivery systems for scientists—offering them new ways to visualize, analyze, and interact with their data, which will in turn enable easier collaboration and communication with others.

This enhanced computing infrastructure will make possible the truly global digital library, where the entire lifecycle of academic research—from inception to publication—will take place in an electronic environment and be openly available to all. During the development of scientific ideas and subsequent publishing, scientists will be able to interact virtually with one another—sharing data sources, workflows, and research. Readers, in turn, will be able to navigate the text of a publication and easily view related presentations, supporting images, video, audio, data, and analytics—all online. Scientific publication will become a 24/7, worldwide, real-time, interactive experience.

I am encouraged to see scientists and computer scientists working together to address the great challenges of our age. Their combined efforts will profoundly and positively affect our future.

The well-formed.eigenfactor project visualizes information flow in science. It came about as a collaboration between the Eigenfactor project (data analysis) and Moritz Stefaner (visualization). This diagram shows the citation links of the journal Nature. *More information and visualizations can be found at http://well-formed.eigenfactor.org.*

Conclusions

TONY HEY, STEWART TANSLEY, AND KRISTIN TOLLE | Microsoft Research

B Y THE MID-1990S, JIM GRAY HAD RECOGNIZED that the next "big data" challenges for database technology would come from science and not from commerce. He also identified the technical challenges that such data-intensive science would pose for scientists and the key role that IT and computer science could play in enabling future scientific discoveries. The term "eScience" was coined in the year 2000 by John Taylor, when he was director general of the UK Research Councils. Taylor had recognized the increasingly important role that IT must play in the collaborative, multidisciplinary, and data-intensive scientific research of the 21st century and used the term eScience to encompass the collection of tools and technologies needed to support such research. In recognition of the UK eScience initiative, Jim Gray called his research group at Microsoft Research the eScience Group, and he set about working with scientists to understand their problems and learn what tools they needed.

In his talk to the Computer Science and Telecommunications Board of the U.S. National Research Council in 2007, Jim expanded on his vision of data-intensive science and enumerated seven key areas for action by the funding agencies:

1. Foster both the development of software tools and support for these tools.
2. Invest in tools at all levels of the funding pyramid.
3. Foster the development of generic Laboratory Information Management Systems (LIMS).
4. Foster research into scientific data management, data analysis, data visualization, and new algorithms and tools.

5. Establish digital libraries that support other sciences in the same way the National Library of Medicine supports the bio-sciences.
6. Foster the development of new document authoring tools and publication models.
7. Foster the development of digital data libraries that contain scientific data (not just the metadata) and support integration with published literature.

We believe that these challenges to the funding agencies are just as important today. This is why we have introduced this collection of essays, along with a version of Jim's talk to the NRC-CSTB constructed from the transcript of his lecture and his presentation slides. It is also educational to see the continuing momentum and progress of the eScience community since the report "Towards 2020 Science" published by our colleagues at Microsoft Research, Cambridge, UK.[1] That was based on a workshop in July 2005, attended by some of the authors in this new book, and subsequently inspired *Nature's* "2020 Computing" special issue in March 2006.[2]

At the heart of scientific computing in this age of the Fourth Paradigm is a need for scientists and computer scientists to work collaboratively—not in a superior/subordinate relationship, but as equals—with both communities fueling, enabling, and enriching our ability to make discoveries that can bring about productive and positive changes in our world. In this book, we have highlighted healthcare and the environment, just two areas in which humanity faces some of its biggest challenges. To make significant progress, the research community must be supported by an adequate cyberinfrastructure comprising not only the hardware of computing resources, datacenters, and high-speed networks but also software tools and middleware. Jim also envisaged the emergence of a global digital research library containing both the research literature and the research data. Not only are we seeing the maturing of data-intensive science, but we are also in the midst of a revolution in scholarly communication. This is driven not only by technologies such as the Internet, Web 2.0, and semantic annotations but also by the worldwide movement toward open access and open science.

This book is really a labor of love. It started with Jim's desire to enable scientific research through the technologies of computer science—cutting across the disciplines highlighted herein and beyond. We see this book as a continuation of Jim's work with the science community. We deliberately asked our scientific contributors

[1] http://research.microsoft.com/en-us/um/cambridge/projects/towards2020science/background_overview.htm
[2] *Nature*, vol. 440, no. 7083, Mar. 23, 2006, pp. 383–580.

to move out of their professional comfort zones and share their visions for the future of their research fields on a 5-to-10-year horizon. We asked them to write their contributions not only in essay form, which is often a greater challenge than writing a purely technical research article, but often in collaboration with a computer scientist. We are grateful to all of our contributors for rising to this challenge, and we hope that they (and you!) will be pleased with the result.

Several decades ago, science was very discipline-centric. Today, as evidenced by the articles in this book, significant advances are being made as a result of multi-disciplinary collaboration—and will continue to be made into the future. The essays in this book present a current snapshot of some of the leading thinking about the exciting partnership between science and computer science—a data revolution—which makes this information timely and potentially fleeting. However, it is our fervent hope and belief that the underlying message presented by the totality of these articles will be durable for many years.

Finally, we offer this book as a call to action for the entire research community, governments, funding agencies, and the public. We urge collaboration toward a common goal of a better life for all humanity. We find ourselves in a phase in which we need to use our scientific understanding to achieve specific goals for the sake of humanity's survival. It is clear that to achieve this aim, we very much need experts with deep scientific knowledge to work closely with those who have deep experience with technology.

This situation is somewhat analogous to the 1940s, when U.S. and European physicists answered an urgent call from governments to collaborate on the Manhattan Project. Today, scientists must collaborate globally to solve the major environmental and health problems facing humanity in a race that is perhaps even more urgent. And ironically, the nuclear physics developed in the Manhattan Project is likely to provide part of the answer in supplying the world with zero-carbon energy.

Tony Hey, Kristin Tolle, and Stewart Tansley

Microsoft External Research, http://research.microsoft.com/ collaboration

NEXT STEPS

WE HOPE THIS BOOK WILL INSPIRE YOU to take action as well as embark on further study. We are "walking the talk" ourselves at Microsoft Research. For example, we have reformulated our academic partnership organization, External Research, to focus on the themes presented in this book.

These themes incorporate active research in dynamic fields, so it is hard to track and predict the future evolution of the ideas presented in this book. But here are some suggested ways to remain engaged and to join in the dialogue:

- If you're a scientist, talk to a computer scientist about your challenges, and vice versa.

- If you're a student, take classes in both science and computer science.

- If you're a teacher, mentor, or parent, encourage those in your care toward interdisciplinary study in addition to giving them the option to specialize.

- Engage with the editors and authors of this book through the normal scholarly channels.

- Keep up to date with our eScience research collaborations through our Web site: http://research.microsoft.com.

- Be active in the eScience community—at the Fourth Paradigm Web site below, we suggest helpful resources.

www.fourthparadigm.org

ACKNOWLEDGMENTS

THE EDITORS EXPRESS THEIR HEARTFELT THANKS to all the contributors to this book for sharing their visions within the Fourth Paradigm. We also thank our families and colleagues for their support during the intensive editorial process. The exceptional efforts of the project team, including Ina Chang, Marian Wachter, Celeste Ericsson, and Dean Katz, are also gratefully acknowledged. And, of course, we thank Jim Gray, for inspiring us.

CONTRIBUTORS

Mark R. Abbott
Oregon State University

Dennis D. Baldocchi
University of California, Berkeley

Roger S. Barga
Microsoft Research

Mathias Bavay
WSL Institute for Snow and Avalanche Research SLF

Gordon Bell
Microsoft Research

Chris Bishop
Microsoft Research

José A. Blakeley
Microsoft

Iain Buchan
University of Manchester

Graham Cameron
EMBL-European Bioinformatics Institute

Luca Cardelli
Microsoft Research

Michael F. Cohen
Microsoft Research

Nicholas Dawes
WSL Institute for Snow and Avalanche Research SLF

Del DeHart
Robertson Research Institute

John R. Delaney
University of Washington

David De Roure
University of Southampton

John Dickason
Private practice

Lee Dirks
Microsoft Research

Jeff Dozier
University of California, Santa Barbara

Dan Fay
Microsoft Research

Craig Feied
Microsoft

Anne Fitzgerald
Queensland University of Technology

Brian Fitzgerald
Queensland University of Technology

Peter Fox
Rensselaer Polytechnic Institute

William B. Gail
Microsoft

Dennis Gannon
Microsoft Research

Michael Gillam
Microsoft

Paul Ginsparg
Cornell University

Carole Goble
University of Manchester

Alyssa A. Goodman
Harvard University

Daron Green
Microsoft Research

Jonathan Handler
Microsoft

Timo Hannay
Nature Publishing Group

Charles Hansen
University of Utah

David Heckerman
Microsoft Research

James Hendler
Rensselaer Polytechnic Institute

Eric Horvitz
Microsoft Research

James R. Hunt
University of California, Berkeley, and the Berkeley Water Center

Chris R. Johnson
University of Utah

William Kristan
University of California, San Diego

Carl Lagoze
Cornell University

James Larus
Microsoft Research

Michael Lehning
WSL Institute for Snow and Avalanche Research SLF

Jeff W. Lichtman
Harvard University

Clifford Lynch
Coalition for Networked Information

Simon Mercer
Microsoft Research

Eliza Moody
Microsoft

Craig Mundie
Microsoft

Suman Nath
Microsoft Research

Kylie Pappalardo
Queensland University of Technology

Savas Parastatidis
Microsoft Research

Marc Parlange
École Polytechnique Fédérale de Lausanne

Valerio Pascucci
University of Utah

Hanspeter Pfister
Harvard University

Catherine Plaisant
University of Maryland

Corrado Priami
Microsoft Research - University of Trento Centre for Computational and Systems Biology and University of Trento

Dan Reed
Microsoft Research

R. Clay Reid
Harvard University

Joel Robertson
Robertson Research Institute

Ben Shneiderman
University of Maryland

Claudio T. Silva
University of Utah

Mark Smith
University of Maryland

Christopher Southan
EMBL-European Bioinformatics Institute

Alexander S. Szalay
The Johns Hopkins University

Kristin Tolle
Microsoft Research

Herbert Van de Sompel
Los Alamos National Laboratory

Catharine van Ingen
Microsoft Research

John Wilbanks
Creative Commons

John Winn
Microsoft Research

Curtis G. Wong
Microsoft Research

Feng Zhao
Microsoft Research

A Few Words About Jim...

TURING AWARD WINNER AND AMERICAN COMPUTER SCIENTIST Dr. James Nicholas "Jim" Gray (born 1944, missing at sea on January 28, 2007) was esteemed for his groundbreaking work as a programmer, database expert, engineer, and researcher. He earned his Ph.D. from the University of California, Berkeley, in 1969—becoming the first person to earn a doctorate in computer science at that institution. He worked at several major high-tech companies, including Bell Labs, IBM Research, Tandem, Digital Equipment Corporation, and finally Microsoft Research in Silicon Valley.

Jim joined Microsoft in 1995 as a Senior Researcher, ultimately becoming a Technical Fellow and managing the Bay Area Research Center (BARC). His primary research interests were large databases and transaction processing systems. He had a longstanding interest in scalable computing—building super-servers and work group systems from commodity software and hardware. His work after 2002 focused on eScience: applying computers to solve data-intensive scientific problems. This culminated in his vision (with Alex Szalay) of a "fourth paradigm" of science, a logical progression of earlier, historical phases dominated by experimentation, theory, and simulation.

Jim pioneered database technology and was among the first to develop the technology used in computerized transactions. His work helped develop e-commerce, online ticketing, automated teller machines, and deep databases that enable the success of today's high-quality modern Internet search engines.

In 1998, he received the ACM A.M. Turing Award, the most prestigious honor in computer science, for "seminal contributions to database and transaction processing research and technical leadership in system implementation." He was appointed an IEEE Fellow in 1982 and also received the IEEE Charles Babbage Award.

His later work in database technology has been used by oceanographers, geologists, and astronomers. Among his accomplishments at Microsoft were the TerraServer Web site in collaboration with the U.S. Geological Survey, which paved the way for modern Internet mapping services, and his work on the Sloan Digital Sky Survey in conjunction with the Astrophysical Research Consortium (ARC) and others. Microsoft's WorldWide Telescope software, based on the latter, is dedicated to Jim.

"Jim always reached out in two ways—technically and personally," says David Vaskevitch, Microsoft's senior corporate vice president and chief technical officer in the Platform Technology & Strategy division. "Technically, he was always there first, pointing out how different the future would be than the present."

"Many people in our industry, including me, are deeply indebted to Jim for his intellect, his vision, and his unselfish willingness to be a teacher and a mentor," says Mike Olson, vice president of Embedded Technologies at Oracle Corporation. Adds Shankar Sastry, dean of the College of Engineering at UC Berkeley, "Jim was a true visionary and leader in this field."

"Jim's impact is measured not just in his technical accomplishments, but also in the numbers of people around the world whose work he inspired," says Rick Rashid, senior corporate vice president at Microsoft Research.

Microsoft Chairman Bill Gates sums up Jim's legacy in this way: "The impact of his thinking is continuing to get people to think in a new way about how data and software are redefining what it means to do science."

Such sentiments are frequently heard from the myriad researchers, friends, and colleagues who interacted with Jim over the years, irrespective of their own prominence and reputation. Known, loved, and respected by so many, Jim Gray needs no introduction, so instead we dedicate this book to him and the amazing work that continues in his absence.

—The Editors

GLOSSARY

POWERS OF TEN

exa-	E	1,000,000,000,000,000,000	10^{18}	quintillion
peta-	P	1,000,000,000,000,000	10^{15}	quadrillion
tera-	T	1,000,000,000,000	10^{12}	trillion
giga-	G	1,000,000,000	10^{9}	billion
mega-	M	1,000,000	10^{6}	million
kilo-	k	1,000	10^{3}	thousand
hecto-	h	100	10^{2}	hundred
deca-	da	10	10^{1}	ten
-	-	1	10^{0}	one
deci-	d	0.1	10^{-1}	tenth
centi-	c	0.01	10^{-2}	hundredth
milli-	m	0.001	10^{-3}	thousandth
micro-	μ	0.000001	10^{-6}	millionth
nano-	n	0.000000001	10^{-9}	billionth
pico-	p	0.000000000001	10^{-12}	trillionth

Adapted from http://en.wikipedia.org/wiki/Order_of_magnitude

COMMON ABBREVIATIONS

ASKAP	Australian Square Kilometre Array Pathfinder
ATLUM	Automatic Tape-Collecting Lathe Ultramicrotome
AUV	autonomous underwater vehicle
BPEL	Business Process Execution Language
CCD	charge-coupled device
CEV	Center for Environmental Visualization
CLADDIER	Citation, Location, And Deposition in Discipline and Institutional Repositories
CML	Chemistry Markup Language
CPU	central processing unit
CSTB	Computer Science and Telecommunications Board
DAG	directed acyclic graph
DDBJ	DNA Data Bank of Japan

DOE	Department of Energy
EBI	European Bioinformatics Institute
ECHO	Earth Observing System Clearinghouse
EHR	electronic health record
EMBL	European Molecular Biology Laboratory
EMBL-Bank	European Molecular Biology Laboratory Nucleotide Sequence Database
EOSDIS	Earth Observing System Data and Information System
ET	evapotranspiration
FDA	Food and Drug Administration
FFT	Fast Fourier Transform
FLUXNET	A global network of micrometeorological tower sites
fMRI	functional magnetic resonance imaging
FTP	File Transfer Protocol
GCMD	NASA's Global Change Master Directory
GEOSS	Global Earth Observation System of Systems
GOLD	Genomes OnLine Database
GPU	graphics processing unit
GPGPU	general-purpose graphics processing unit
GUI	graphical user interface
H1N1	swine flu
INSDC	International Nucleotide Sequence Database Collaboration
IT	information technology
KEGG	Kyoto Encyclopedia of Genes and Genomes
KLAS	Keystone Library Automation System
LEAD	Linked Environments for Atmospheric Discovery
LHC	Large Hadron Collider
LIDAR	Light Detection and Ranging
LLNL	Lawrence Livermore National Laboratory
LONI	Laboratory of Neuro Imaging
MESUR	Metrics from Scholarly Usage of Resources
MMI	Marine Metadata Interoperability
NASA	National Aeronautics and Space Administration
NHS	National Health Service (UK)
NIH	National Institutes of Health
NLM	National Library of Medicine

NLM DTD	National Library of Medicine Document Type Definition
NOAA	National Oceanic and Atmospheric Administration
NRC	National Research Council
NSF	National Science Foundation
OAI	Open Archives Initiative
OAI-ORE	Open Archives Initiative Object Reuse and Exchange protocol
OAI-PMH	Open Archives Initiative Protocol for Metadata Harvesting
OBO	Open Biomedical Ontologies
OO	object-oriented
OOI	Ocean Observatories Initiative
OWL	Web Ontology Language
Pan-STARRS	Panoramic Survey Telescope And Rapid Response System
PHR	personal health record
PubMed	Free National Library of Medicine online database of biomedical journal articles
RDF	Resource Description Framework
RDFS	RDF Schema
ROV	remotely operated vehicle
RSS	Really Simple Syndication
SCEC	Southern California Earthquake Center
SOA	service-oriented architecture
SWORD	Simple Web-service Offering Repository Deposit
TCP/IP	Transmission Control Protocol/Internet Protocol (the Internet Protocol Suite)
TM	transactional memory
UNICEF	United Nations Children's Fund
UniProt	Universal Protein Resource
URI	Uniform Resource Identifier
USGS	U.S. Geological Survey
VT 100	A Digital Equipment Corporation (DEC) video terminal
WATERS Network	WATer and Environmental Research Systems Network
WHO	World Health Organization
XML	eXtensible Markup Language

INDEX

IEEE floating-point standard, 180
imaging techniques. *See also* visualization
  in developing computational microscope for
    neurobiologists, 84, 85, 86–88
  role in ocean research, 31–32
  for tracking neuronal circuits in the brain,
    75–82
immunization, in developing countries, 65
information overload, in medicine, 58, 92–93.
    See also data, exponential increases in
    volume
information technology (IT) infrastructure.
    See also cyberinfrastructure; data-intensive
    science; scientific computing
  and eScience, xx, 227
  impact on science community, 114–115
  new tools for data-intensive era, 115–116
  present day, 113–114
  recent history, 112
InnoCentive, 218
INSDC (International Nucleotide Sequence
    Database Collaboration), 117
INSPIRE Directive, 205
intellectual property, xxviii. *See also* copyright
interdisciplinary research, 25–26, 44, 170
International Human Genome Sequencing
    Consortium, 203
Internet. *See also* World Wide Web
  and astronomical investigation, 40–43
  interconnectedness of computers, 215
  public nature, 211–212
  and rapid dissemination of environmental
    information, 18–19, 48
  role in cabled ocean observatories, 30, 31,
    34, 36
  role in ecological synthesis studies, 23
  unifying data with literature, xxvii–xxix
INTERNIST-1 expert system, 67
invertebrate nervous systems, 85–87
Isenberg, David, 211
IT. *See* information technology (IT)
    infrastructure

J
JISC (Joint Information Systems Committee),
    xvii
journal articles. *See* scientific papers
Juan de Fuca Plate, 33

K
Kapoor, Ashish, 86, 87
Karman dataset, 161
KEGG (Kyoto Encyclopedia of Genes and
    Genomes), 138
Kepler, Johannes, xiii
Kepler Conjecture, 180
Kepler workflow system, 140
Kepler's Laws, xx
Kuhn, Thomas, 209
Kurzweil, Ray, 59

L
Laboratory Information Management Systems
    (LIMS), xxiv, 227
LabVIEW, xxvi
Lancaster, James, 57
Language Integrated Query (LINQ), 133
Large Hadron Collider (LHC), xv, xxii, xxiii,
    147
Large Synoptic Survey Telescope (LSST), 40
Lawrence Livermore National Laboratory
    (LLNL), 154
LEAD workflows, 141
libraries, serials crisis, 193. *See also* digital data
    libraries; scientific papers
licensing, open, 212
life sciences. *See also* Earth and environmen-
    tal science; ecology; medical knowledge;
    ocean science
  application of semantic enhancement that
    integrates data with text, 148, 189, 190
  computational vs. bioinformatics, xxi
  creating machine-actionable representations
    of knowledge in scholarly literature, 194
  developing data infrastructure, 117–123
  Entrez search engine, xxxi–xxxii
  exponential increases in volume of data, 77,
    117–120, 218
  growth and complexity of available data
    sources, 92–93, 121–122, 137
  visualization in process algebra models,
    99–105
Life Under Your Feet program, 23, 47
Lind, James, 57
LINQ (Language Integrated Query), 133
Linux, xxvi
LONI Pipeline workflow system, 140

M

machine learning, 56, 83, 84, 85, 86, 94–95
"macroscope," 224
mapping. *See also* SensorMap; visualization
  brain circuitry, 76–77
  and Ocean Observatory Initiative, 33
  terrestrial laser scan for snow distribution in
    Swiss Alps, 47
MapReduce, 7, 8, 133, 166, 171
Marine Metadata Interoperability (MMI)
  project, 148
markup, 150, 170, 182, 183, 186, 188
mashups, xxxii, 22, 170–171
MATLAB, xxiii, xxvi, 25
Maxwell's equations, xx
Mayo Clinic Health Advisory, 62–63
medical knowledge. *See also* healthcare
  accuracy and efficiency of diagnoses, 67–68
  data integrity issue, 71
  exponential rate increase, 58–59, 92
  information overload, 58, 92–93
  NxOpinion platform, 66, 67
  and patient data clouds, 62–63
  translation to medical practice, 57–64, 92,
    93, 224
medical records
  in data-intensive healthcare systems, 92–93
  electronic, 91–92, 93
  issues in developing countries, 65–69, 71–72
  need for scalable systems, 66–67
  paradigms of healthcare information, 96
  patient de-identification, 65, 67, 71, 72
  patient identification, 71
medications. *See* drugs
Medicity, 62
MEDSEEK, 62
MESUR project, 196
meteorology. *See* weather science
microscopes, computational, 84, 87–89. *See
  also* electron microscopy, "macroscope"
Microsoft
  and aggregation of data, 166
  Amalga system, 62, 63
  Azure platform, 133
  Bing, xxviii
  Conference Management Tool (CMT), xxx,
    xxxi

Dryad, 133, 166, 171
DryadLINQ, 133
HealthVault, 62, 63
and MapReduce tool, 133
SenseWeb project, 48, 49
SQL Server, 25, 48
Trident Scientific Workflow Workbench, 141
Word, article authoring add-in, 188
WorldWide Telescope, 41–43, 44
Millennium Development Goals, U.N., 66
MMI (Marine Metadata Interoperability)
  project, 148
mobile phones. *See* cell phones
modeling
  language-based approaches for biological
    systems, 99–105
  for prediction of phenomena-based
    environmental data, 48
  unified approach to data-intensive
    healthcare, 91–97
Moderate Resolution Imaging Spectro-
  radiometer (MODIS), 18
Moglen, Eben, 212–213
Moore's Law, 59, 126
mountains, surface variability, 45, 46–47
MSR Computational Microscope, 87, 88
multicore processors, 126–127, 128, 129
Murray, Christopher, 65
Murray-Rust, Peter, 194
myExperiment project, 142–143, 168, 197
myGrid project, 168

N

NASA (National Aeronautics and Space
  Administration)
  and coming flood of ecological data, 23
  Earth Observing System Data and Informa-
    tion System, 112, 113, 115
  Global Change Master Directory, 150
  Moderate Resolution Imaging Spectro-
    radiometer, 18
National Center for Atmospheric Research
  (NCAR), xiv, xvi
National Center for Biotechnology
  Information, xxxii, 118
National Climatic Data Center, 22
National Ecological Observatory Network, 23

National Human Genome Research Institute, 120–121
National Institutes of Health (NIH), xxvii
National Library of Medicine (NLM), xxvii, xxix, xxx, xxxii
National Science Foundation (NSF), xiv, xvii, xxii, xxiii, 32, 111, 198
natural language processing, 167, 169, 170, 189
Nature Network, 217
NCAR (National Center for Atmospheric Research), xiv, xvi
NEPTUNE program, xxiii, 29, 32, 34
nervous system, 83–89. *See also* brain
NetCDF (Network Common Data Form), xxv
network effects, 212, 216
networks, and data deluge, 210–215. *See also* Internet
neurobiologists, new tools for, 83–89
neurons, brain, 78–81. *See also* nervous system
NeuroTrace, 81
Newton's Laws of Motion, xx
NIH (National Institutes of Health), xxvii
Nijmegen Medical Centre, The Netherlands, 141
NLM (National Library of Medicine), xxvii, xxix, xxx, xxxii
North American Carbon Program, 25
nowcasting, 48–49
Noyes, Henry, 58
NSF (National Science Foundation), xiv, xvii, xxii, xxiii, 32, 111, 198
nucleotide sequencing, 117–120
Nurse, Paul, 99
NxOpinion Knowledge Manager (NxKM), 66, 67, 68, 70, 71

O

OAI (Open Archives Initiative), 194, 198
observatories. *See* telescopes; virtual observatory efforts
Ocean Observatory Initiative (OOI), 32–34
ocean science, 27–38, 148
OECD (Organisation for Economic Co-operation and Development), 206–207
OMB (U.S. Office of Management and Budget), 204–205
ontologies, defined, 148. *See also* semantics
OOI (Ocean Observatory Initiative), 32–34

Open Archives Initiative (OAI), 194, 198
Open Geospatial Consortium, 24
open source software, 133, 140, 156, 212
OpenCyc, 167
OpenURL, 194
OpenWetWare, 217
oreChem project, 170–171
Oregon State University, 32
O'Reilly, Tim, 216
out-of-core computing, 154
overlay journals, xxix–xxx
OWL (Web Ontology Language), 167, 169, 197

P

PageRank, Google algorithm, 116, 218
Pan-STARRS project, xv, 9, 40, 141
papers. *See* scientific papers
paradigm shifts, 209–210. *See also* science paradigms
parallel computing
  background, 125–126
  exploiting at individual node level, 134
  exploiting in cloud computing, 132–133
  and multicore computers, 126–127
  programming challenges, 126–129
ParaView, 158–159
PDF files, 188, 193
peer-review process
  compared with wikis, xxx–xxxi
  future, xxx–xxxi, 115
  Jim Gray's view, xix, xxviii–xxxi
  pros and cons, xxx, 111, 179, 193
Pegasus workflow system, 140
petascale databases, 8–9, 119, 161
physical sciences, need for coordinated semantic enhancement effort, 148, 189, 190–191
Pipeline Pilot workflow system, 140
plate tectonics. *See* Juan de Fuca Plate
pneumonia, in developing countries, 66
policies, for accessing and sharing data within and among nations, 201–208
powers of ten, 237
Powerset service, 167
probabilistic graphical models, 87, 94
probabilistic similarity networks, 67, 68
process calculi, 99
professional societies, xxx, 151
Project NEPTUNE, xxiii, 29, 32, 34

provenance, xiv, xxxi, 156, 157, 158, 197.
    See also citation data in scholarly
    communication
PubChem, xxxii, 217
public. *See* citizen science
public health, 66, 69, 71. *See also* healthcare
publications. *See* scientific papers
PubMed Central, xxvii, xxviii, xxix, xxx, xxxii,
    185, 186

R
RDF (Resource Description Framework), 167, 197
reference data collections, 181–182
Reflect tool, EMBL Germany, 186
registration, as core function in scholarly
    communication, 195
remote sensing. *See* sensors
research, reexamining structures, 111–116
rewarding, as core function in scholarly
    communication, 195
Robertson Research Institute, 66
robotics, role in ocean research, 31, 32
rofecoxib (Vioxx), 61
Royal Society of Chemistry, 186
RSS format, 197, 198

S
San Diego Supercomputer Center (SDSC), xvi
Sanger Institute, 118, 120–121
satellites
    role in astronomical investigations, 42
    role in ecological synthesis studies, 23, 24
    role in environmental applications, 13, 17, 18,
        46, 148–149
    role in ocean science, 28, 31, 32
scaling
    in medical records systems, 66, 67
    as network capability, 211, 213
    processing vs. data considerations, 143, 154
scanning electron microscope (SEM), 79.
    See also electron microscopy
SCEC (Southern California Earthquake
    Center) CyberShake project, 140, 143
schema, xv, xxv, xxxi
scholarly communication. *See also* digital data
    libraries; scientific papers
    availability of Web for furthering scientific
        collaboration, 216–217

citation data, 25, 151, 178, 186, 187, 195–196,
    226
core functions, 195
creating machine-actionable representations
    of knowledge in scientific literature,
    194–195
ever-growing scale of scientific record,
    179–180, 182
impact of data-intensive science on scientific
    record, 177–183
Jim Gray's view of coming revolution,
    xxvii–xxix, 198
linking documents to data, xxx–xxxi, 181,
    182, 186–188, 190, 219, 224–226
long-term trends in scientific research,
    217–219
machine-friendly, 193–199
need for collaboration and peer relationships
    between domain scientists and computer
    scientists, 7–8, 35, 45–51, 150, 228
origin of division between experimental data
    and creation of theories, xiii
tracking evolution and dynamics of scholarly
    assets, 195–197
School Health Annual Report Programme
    (SHARP), 69
science. *See* astronomy; data-intensive science;
    Earth and environmental science; ocean
    science
science of environmental applications, 13–19
science paradigms. *See also* fourth paradigm
    first, empirical, xx, 96, 223
    second, theoretical, xx, 96, 223
    third, computational, xx–xxi, 96, 177, 180,
        223
    fourth, eScience, xx, xxi, 96, 223
    in healthcare information, 96
    Jim Gray's view, xx–xxi
scientific communication. *See* scholarly
    communication
scientific computing. *See also* cloud computing;
    data-intensive science
    communication between computer
        scientists and domain scientists, 7–8, 35,
        45–51, 150, 228
    new tools for neurobiologists, 83–89
    and parallel processing, 125–129
    and plethora of data, 5–6, 8, 9, 131–135

scientific computing, *continued*
    process algebra models of biological systems, 99–105
scientific papers. *See also* archiving; digital data libraries
    changes in publishing practices, xxx, 183
    creating machine-actionable representations, 194–195
    digital model vs. electronic model, 181
    exponential growth in number, 58, 92
    instantaneous translation, 61
    linking to data, xxx–xxxi, 181, 182, 186–188, 190, 219, 224–226
    semantic enhancement, 186–190
    serials crisis in libraries, 193
    as tip of data iceberg, xix
    vs. scientific data, xiv, xxix–xxxii, 185
scientific record, 177–183
scientists. *See* citizen science; domain scientists; scientific computing
SciScope, 24
Scripps Institution of Oceanography, 32
scurvy, 57–58
second paradigm, xx, 96, 223
Sedna workflow system, 140
SEEK (Science Environment for Ecological Knowledge), 148
Semantic Computing, 169
Semantic Web, 151, 167, 170, 171, 198
semantics
    applying tools to eScience, 147–152
    enhancing text to include data links, 186–190
    and interoperability, 150–151, 167, 168, 188, 197
SenseWeb project, 48, 49
SensorMap, 49
sensors
    role in ecological synthesis studies, 23–25
    role in environmental science, 45–51, 148, 224
    role in ocean research, 31–33
SensorScope, 49
SETI@Home project, xxvi
sharing data, 65, 69–71, 128, 202, 203–204.
    See also collaboration
Shirky, Clay, 215
Short Read Archive, 118, 119

Shotton, D., 186
simulation
    comparison to fourth paradigm, 177, 180, 210
    need for new data analysis techniques, 161–162
    process algebra models of biological systems, 99–105
singularity, medical, 55–64
sky browsers, 41
Sloan Digital Sky Survey (SDSS), xxii, 40–41
sneakernet, 166
snowmelt runoff, as example of relationships between basic science and applications, 14–18
software tools, need for more in science disciplines, xxii, xxiii, xxvi–xxvii. *See also* data-intensive science; scientific computing; workflows
solar-terrestrial physics, 148, 149
SourceForge, 188
Southern California Earthquake Center (SCEC) CyberShake project, 140, 143
SQL Server, 25, 48
stationarity, 14, 16
Stefaner, Moritz, 226
Stoermer, Mark, 29, 36
Suber, Peter, xxvii
surface parameterization, 159–160
Sustainable Digital Data Preservation and Access Network Partners (DataNet) program, 198
Swiss Alps, terrestrial laser scan for snow distribution, 46, 47
Swiss Experiment, 47, 48–49
synthesis studies, ecology, 21–26
Szalay, Alex, 235

T
Taverna workflows, 138, 139, 140, 141
Taylor, John, 227
telescopes, 39, 40, 41. *See also* WorldWide Telescope (WWT)
Teradata, 7
text. *See also* scientific papers
    role as type of data, 185–191
    semantic enhancement, 186–190
    tools for mining, 141, 182, 186, 189, 219
third paradigm, xx–xxi, 96, 177, 180, 223

PHOTO | IMAGE CREDITS

FRONT COVER: Luis Alonso Ocaña/age fotostock. Rights reserved.

PAGE XII: *Galileo calculates the magnification of his telescope.* Mary Evans/Photo Researchers, Inc. Rights reserved.

PAGE XVIII: *Jim Gray speaking at the Computing in the 21st Century conference in Beijing, October 2006.* Microsoft Research.

PAGE 2: *USGS/NASA image of the Bogda Mountains, China.* U.S. Geological Survey. Public domain.

PAGE 54: *Colored magnetic resonance imaging (MRI) scan of a woman.* Simon Fraser/Photo Researchers, Inc. Rights reserved.

PAGE 108: *A wafer containing the Intel Teraflops Research Chip.* © Intel Corporation. Rights reserved.

PAGE 174: *Central Library, Seattle (Rem Koolhaas, principal architect).* Vetala Hawkins/Filmateria Digital. Rights reserved.

PAGE 222: *Two stars orbit one another in the core of the large emission nebula NGC 6357 in Scorpius, about 8,000 light-years from Earth.* NASA, ESA, and Jesús Maíz Apellániz (Instituto de Astrofísica de Andalucía, Spain). Public domain.

PAGE 226: *Visualization showing the citation links of the journal* Nature. Image courtesy of Moritz Stefaner and Carl Bergstrom, http://well-formed.eigenfactor.org.

PAGE 229: *Tony Hey, Kristin Tolle, and Stewart Tansley of Microsoft External Research.* Vetala Hawkins/Microsoft Corporation.

PAGE 234: *Jim Gray on* Tenacious, *January 2006.* Photo by Tony Hey.

BACK COVER: Microsoft Tag from www.microsoft.com/tag. Get the free app for your phone at http://gettag.mobi and "snap it!"

NOTE: URLs can go offline for various reasons, either temporarily or permanently. Not all of the URLs in this book were still live at the time of publication, but we have successfully accessed such pages using various services such as Internet Archive's Wayback Machine, www.archive.org/web/web.php.

Book design, editing, and production by Katz Communications Group, www.katzcommunications.com

Made in the USA
Lexington, KY
19 August 2012